General Henry Atkinson
A Western Military Career

GENERAL HENRY ATKINSON

A Western Military Career

By Roger L. Nichols

UNIVERSITY OF OKLAHOMA PRESS
NORMAN

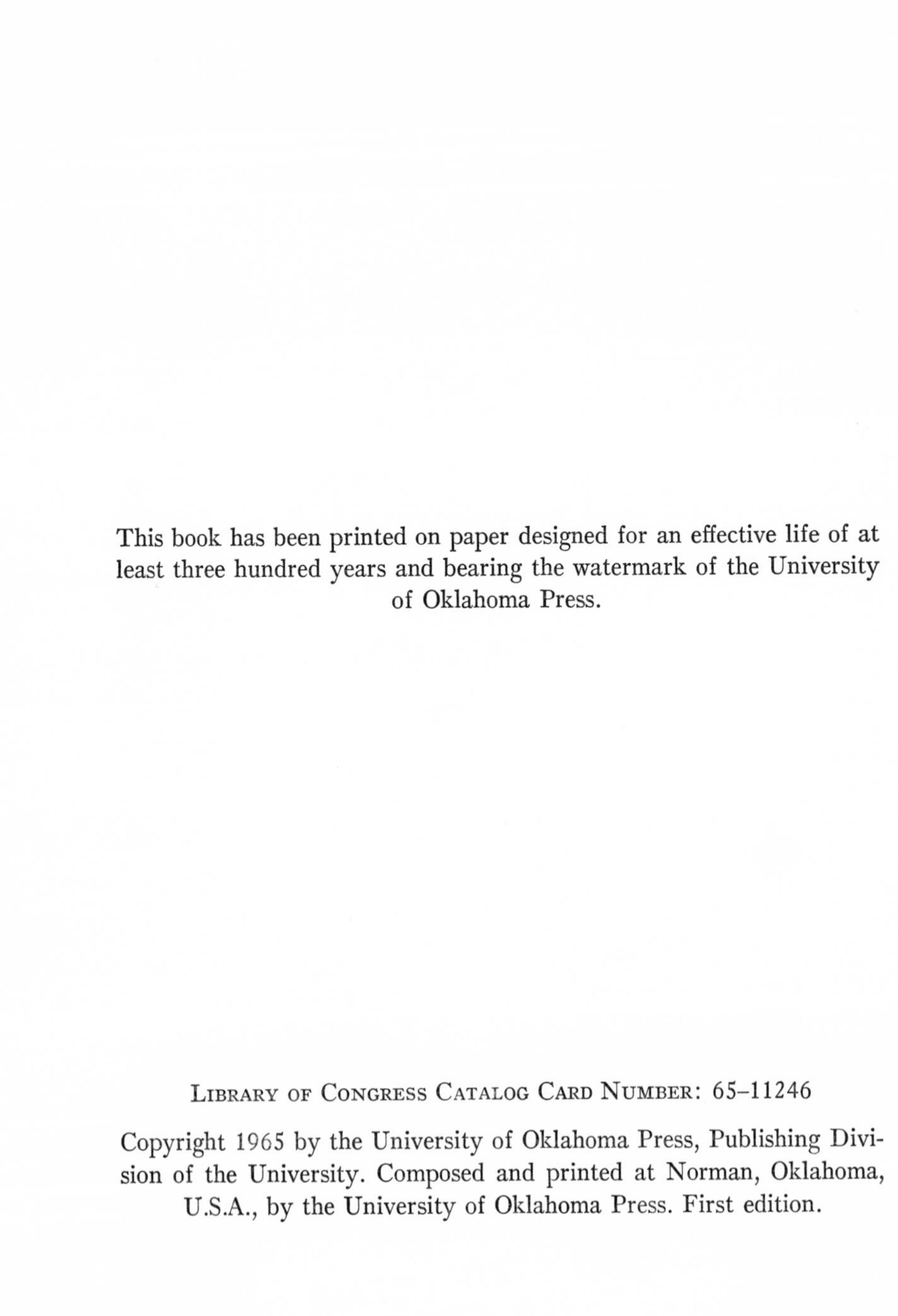

This book has been printed on paper designed for an effective life of at least three hundred years and bearing the watermark of the University of Oklahoma Press.

Library of Congress Catalog Card Number: 65–11246

 Composed and printed at Norman, Oklahoma, U.S.A., by the University of Oklahoma Press. First edition.

To George and Antoinette

Preface

Although General Henry Atkinson became involved in nearly every type of army activity in the Mississippi and Missouri river valleys between 1819 and 1842, the study of his life has been difficult. No large collection of Atkinson papers exists, a fact which has, perhaps, discouraged scholars. Because of the lack of personal material this study cannot be a biography, but must, rather, discuss Atkinson's military career almost to the exclusion of his family and business activities. In spite of this limitation, however, Atkinson's story is interesting and helpful in reaching an understanding of American expansion and "growing pains" as the Republic reached and crossed the Mississippi River during the first half of the nineteenth century.

Various individuals and institutions have lent their support and co-operation in making this study possible. Professor Thomas Clark of the University of Kentucky offered suggestions concerning the location of source material at the beginning of the study. Professor Vernon Carstensen of the University of Wisconsin has offered advice and assistance at all stages of the project. The History Department of the University of Wisconsin provided funds, through a President Adams Fellowship in 1962–63, which enabled me to travel in search of material. The Wisconsin State College Board of Regents provided funds for clerical assistance and preparation of the manuscript during 1963–64.

Many libraries and historical societies and their staffs have been of assistance by answering inquiries, by arranging for photocopy work, and by making their collections available for research. Among those who provided the material for this study the following gave invaluable assistance: Mrs. Ellen Whitney and the staff of the Illinois Historical Library; Mrs. E. A. Stadler, archivist at the Missouri Historical Society in St. Louis; Mrs. Sara Jackson and Mr. Milton Chamberlain of the Army and Air Corps Branch of the National Archives; Mrs. Mary Rogers at the North Carolina State Department of History and Archives; Miss Josephine Harper, manuscript librarian at the State Historical Society of Wisconsin; and Mr. Benton Wilcox and the staff of the State Historical Society of Wisconsin Library.

Special thanks are due Brigadier General B. W. Atkinson, USMC (Ret.), of San Diego, California, a great-grandson of Henry Atkinson, for his co-operation in furnishing family genealogical information, letters, and a picture of Mary Atkinson.

Among my friends and associates, Miss Nancy Jo Tice, Mr. Richard M. Clokey, and Mr. Edwin D. Karn, all of the University of Wisconsin, furnished valuable leads to material and offered innumerable suggestions for the organization, content, and style of the manuscript.

My wife Marilyn has cheerfully helped in every phase of my work for the past three years and has done her best to make this project enjoyable.

Roger L. Nichols

Oshkosh, Wisconsin
June, 1965

Contents

Illustrations and Maps

MAPS

Abbreviations

The following is a list of abbreviations used in the footnotes.

AGO: Records of the Adjutant General's Office, Record Group 94, National Archives, Washington, D.C.

ASP:MA: *American State Papers: Military Affairs.*

B. W. A.: Private collection of Gen. B. W. Atkinson, Jr., San Diego, California.

HQA: Records of the Headquarters of the Army, Record Group 108, National Archives.

HSP: Historical Society of Pennsylvania, Philadelphia.

ISA: Illinois State Archives, Springfield.

ISHL: Illinois State Historical Library, Springfield.

LC: Library of Congress, Washington, D.C.

MHS: Missouri Historical Society, St. Louis.

NCSD: North Carolina State Department of History and Archives, Raleigh.

NCU: University of North Carolina Library, Chapel Hill.

OIA: Records of the Office of Indian Affairs, Record Group 75, National Archives.

QMG: Records of the Office of the Quartermaster General, Record Group 92, National Archives.

SHSM: State Historical Society of Missouri, Columbia.

SHSW: State Historical Society of Wisconsin, Madison.

SW: Records of the Office of the Secretary of War, Record Group 107, National Archives.

USAC: Records of the United States Army Commands, Record Group 98, National Archives.

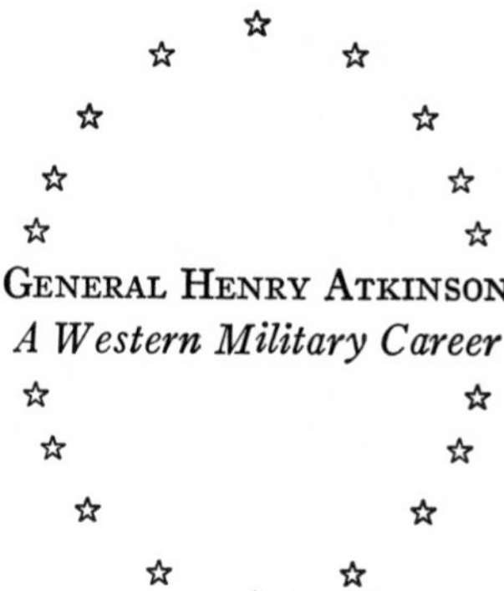

GENERAL HENRY ATKINSON

A Western Military Career

Introduction

THE PERIOD BETWEEN THE WAR FOR AMERICAN INDEPENDENCE and the Mexican War was one of nearly continuous geographical expansion for the United States. The spread of population, from the seaboard states into the trans-Appalachian region and then into the Ohio, Mississippi, and Missouri river valleys, occupies an important place in early nineteenth-century American history. Although the United States Army did play a part in this expansion, during the past ten or fifteen years the pendulum of historical thought seems to have swung to a position which gives the army more credit than it deserves. While military units provided some protection for settlers from the Indians and for the Indians from intruders, explored and surveyed many parts of the West, built countless "military roads" and forts, and occasionally escorted groups of traders on the trails and rivers, the army often hindered American expansion and settlement. By examining the career of an important but little-known army officer who directed the work of the army in the trans-Mississippi West for nearly twenty-five years, this study will try to place the role of the army in the proper perspective as a part of the American westward movement.

General Henry Atkinson was the son of a North Carolina squire, who was a large landholder and a local politician. Henry grew to manhood among the leading families of his home county and took a place among them as the owner of a large plantation when he was only eighteen years old. He adopted the code of a southern gentleman and acted as a leader in local affairs. Family tradition and personal interest led him to join the army, a career that occupied nearly all of his adult life. Except for two short campaigns in New York State and Canada during the winter of 1813–14 and in the summer of 1832 when he commanded an army of regulars and volunteers in the Black Hawk War, most of his career was spent at the routine tasks of army administration and training. Because most of his training was in noncombat situations, when he faced the Sac and Fox Indians in the Black Hawk War, he had little experience upon which he could draw.

Because he did not win fame in battle and because he matter-of-factly handled his assignments, Atkinson left no record of great military victories, of exciting or colorful statements, or of heated personal quarrels with his associates. He was overshadowed by his more famous contemporaries such as Andrew Jackson, Winfield Scott, and Zachary Taylor. Henry Atkinson would have driven a press agent to despair. He was well known to his contemporaries, but seemed to shun or ignore the publicity which is necessary to attract the attention or interest of historians. He failed to leave any inspiring statements or interesting records of his exploits. As a result, except for two towns named in his honor and an inscription on the façade of a chipped, yellow mess hall with broken windows and rust stains at Jefferson Barracks, Missouri, his career seems to be forgotten. In his native North Carolina he was forgotten as long ago as 1900, and a recent inquiry at the National Cemetery at Jefferson Barracks, just outside St. Louis, showed that the records there had no file for the man who had located, built, and commanded the post and who had been buried there. Except in articles on local midwestern history or in army records in the National Archives, one rarely encounters the name of General Henry Atkinson.

Atkinson, a pleasant, sociable man of medium build, wavy brown hair, blue eyes, and an easy smile, held an army commission for thirty-four years. He entered the army in 1808 as an infantry captain and served in and around New Orleans during the invasion scare of 1808–1809. After five years in the South, he joined General Wade Hampton on the New York–Upper Canada border in 1813 as an inspector general. There he served under Hampton and later under General James Wilkinson in two brief campaigns against the British and Canadians. He was promoted to the rank of colonel in 1814, and received command of the Thirty-seventh Infantry at New London, Connecticut. After the Treaty of Ghent and the subsequent reduction of the army, he retained his commission and organized the Sixth Infantry Regiment which he commanded for most of the next twenty years. In 1819 he led his regiment from Plattsburg, New York, to St. Louis, where he assumed command of the Missouri Expedition. This assignment took him to Council Bluffs on the Missouri River where he built a military post that came to be named Fort Atkinson. In 1819 he received command of the Ninth Military Department that included the states of Kentucky, Tennessee, and Illinois, and the area west of the Mississippi River from Missouri Territory to Canada. At times the official name of this command was changed, but it included this general area. In 1820, Atkinson was promoted to the rank of brigadier general. Five years later he led a successful expedition up the Missouri to the Yellowstone River. On this project he and Benjamin O'Fallon signed treaties of peace and friendship with fifteen Indian tribes. In 1826 he chose the site for and supervised the building of Jefferson Barracks, the first infantry school of the army. He led troops from that post north into Wisconsin in 1827 and probably prevented an Indian war with the Winnebagos. He commanded the army during the Black Hawk War in the summer of 1832, and after that campaign he continued to command Jefferson Barracks and subsidiary posts in the North and West. In 1837 he directed the removal of the Potawatomi Indians from northwestern Missouri to western Iowa, and in 1840 moved the Winnebago Indians from Wisconsin into northern Iowa. Atkinson, as the highest-ranking subordinate officer in the West, often commanded the Western Department of the army for short periods of time between 1823 and 1842 when his immediate superior temporarily left his position.

During his twenty-three years on the frontier, Atkinson dealt with over forty Indian tribes, who knew him as the White Beaver. Unlike some of his contemporaries, such as Andrew Jackson and Edmund P. Gaines, he was suspicious of reported Indian depredations and tried to have each incident investigated rather than rush troops to the frontier before he knew the circumstances. He viewed white and Indian depredations with equal abhorrence, railed against whisky vendors and illegal traders who entered the Indian country, and attempted to keep white squatters off Indian lands. He also distrusted frontier whites and accused them of breaking the national laws in their relations with the army and the Indians. At the same time, he attempted to prevent Indian wars and investigated reports of Indian attacks on and robberies of frontier whites. In opposition to stated Indian Office policy, he maintained that the Indians should be permitted to settle their quarrels without interference from the whites. Like most Regular Army officers, Atkinson distrusted the American militiaman, particularly after the difficulties he experienced with the Illinois troops during the Black Hawk War.

He served in both administrative and field positions and possessed a thorough knowledge of army responsibilities, particularly in the West. Although an infantry officer, he frequently asked for mounted troops to use against the Indians. Because of his life on a North Carolina tobacco plantation, he remained interested in agriculture and mechanics. He experimented with various seeds at the frontier posts under his command and developed a manually powered paddle wheel for keelboats on the Missouri River.

Henry Atkinson's skill as a general is difficult to assess. As a leader of fighting men he had little training or experience. He commanded troops in only one battle, that of Bad Axe during the Black Hawk War. In that instance he proved himself brave and able. In the campaign leading to that battle Atkinson was hesitant and did not appear to know how to finish the war. This, however, was the only time he failed to demonstrate a high degree of competence, organizational skill, and strong leadership. From the time he assumed his duties as leader of the Missouri Expedition in 1819 until he supervised the removal of the Winnebago Indians from Wisconsin Territory in 1840, he carried out every assignment with a minimum of fuss or delay. Compared to his contemporaries he was certainly among the most competent and conscientious officers.

Throughout his career, he consistently demonstrated a desire to maintain peace, an abhorrence of disorder, and humane treatment of subordinates. He viewed the army as an instrument for keeping peace rather than for making war. In meeting threats of Indian uprisings, he investigated carefully before bringing any troops into the field and often dismissed the reports as rumor started by frontier settlers anxious to force Indian removal.

In concluding his discussion of Atkinson in the *Dictionary of American Biography*, William J. Ghent declared: "His name is inseparably connected with the earlier period of the conquest of the frontier, and the part he bore is equaled in importance by that of no contemporary with the possible exception of William Clark." Henry Atkinson's name is interwoven into the history of Missouri, Illinois, Wisconsin, Minnesota, Iowa, Kansas, Nebraska, and the Dakotas, where he directed American military operations for more than twenty years. Therefore, a study of Atkinson and of his career as the highest ranking military officer actually stationed in the West should be of help in understanding the part the army took in the movement of the American people into the Mississippi and Missouri river valleys.

I. The Young Squire—1782–1808

HENRY ATKINSON, the sixth child of John Atkinson, Esq., and his wife, was born in 1782 on the family plantation in Person County, North Carolina. Few families living on the North Carolina piedmont at this time left complete records, and the Atkinsons were no exception. Therefore, neither the day nor the month of Henry's birth is known.[1] His mother died soon after his birth. Almost nothing about her has survived, but there is a small plain headstone bearing the epitaph "Mrs. John Atkinson, first consort of John Atkinson"[2] in a rural cemetery in North Carolina. Henry's father married again, probably within a year after his first wife's death, this time to Frances Dickens, daughter of a close friend.[3]

John Atkinson, Henry's father, probably arrived on the piedmont during the late 1740's. In 1748 he and several others petitioned the governor and council of North Carolina for land grants, and twice that year he received grants of one hundred acres each in what was then Johnston County. Two years later he obtained another grant of seventy-nine acres.[4]

1 Gravestone of Henry Atkinson, Cave Hill Cemetery, Louisville, Kentucky; Atkinson Genealogy, furnished by Gen. B. W. Atkinson, San Diego, California.

2 North Carolina Gravestone Index, State Department of History and Archives, Raleigh (hereafter NCSD).

3 Will of John Atkinson, Apr. 5, 1792, Person County Records, NCSD.

4 "Council Journals," Oct. 6, 1748, Oct. 14, 1748, and Apr. 6, 1750, in Walter

The existing records provide only a dim outline of John Atkinson's rise to a position of successful plantation ownership. He may have been allied with the local courthouse ring in Orange County, but its activities became so notorious that his participation would have been publicly noticed. More likely he remained neutral when his friends and neighbors split during the tumultuous days of the Regulator movement, and he may have purchased the lands of the disappointed and defeated farmers when they moved farther west beyond the power of Governor Tryon and his supporters.

It is clear that John Atkinson took an active interest in politics and early identified himself with the Revolutionary movement in North Carolina. In August, 1775, he represented his county at the General Congress meeting at Hillsboro and, a few months later, became a member of the Hillsboro District Committee of Safety. The next spring he was appointed a member of a committee to "receive, procure and purchase fire arms for the use of the troops" against the British.[5] On November 12, 1776, he was elected to the House of Commons, the lower house of the new state legislature, even though rioters at the polling places forced election officials to halt voting four times that day. Only one fourth of the voters, it was claimed, had cast their ballots. This brought an immediate protest from the defeated candidates, which the legislature initially sought to ignore. Near the end of the session, however, a new election was called and Atkinson lost.[6] Subsequently he was appointed a major in the Second Battalion of North Carolina Militia, then being raised to help defend South Carolina. In December, 1776, he became a justice of the peace for Orange County.[7]

In 1777, John Atkinson served as House of Commons representative from Caswell County, recently formed from Orange County. The next year he was named entry taker for his home county, a position analogous to the later receiver and register at a federal land office. In 1781 he became a tobacco purchasing agent

Clark and William L. Saunders (eds.), *The Colonial and State Records of North Carolina*, IV, 894; IV, 897; IV, 1038.

5 *Ibid.*, X, 215; X, 524–26. 6 *Ibid.*, X, 914. 7 *Ibid.*, X, 931–32; XXIII, 995.

for the state. As such he was ordered to borrow, buy, or impress tobacco, which was then sold to pay the state war debts. Although the position tended to make him unpopular and subjected him to the displeasure of some of his neighbors, it produced "a liberal reward out of the Commodity itself in proportion to the Quantity" he collected.[8] Three years later John Atkinson again served as a county representative in the House of Commons. After a one-year term, he returned to his farm, and in 1788 he resigned as justice of the peace.[9]

During these years of political activity, John Atkinson continued to increase his land holdings until, by 1785, he owned more than 6,100 acres of land scattered along the banks of eleven creeks and rivers in what had become Caswell and Person counties, an area of rolling, pine-covered hills, with thin, light-grey loam over red clay subsoil. Atkinson cultivated part of his land, aided by his sons, slaves, and hired men. He raised tobacco as a cash crop and corn, wheat, oats, garden vegetables, and livestock for family consumption. Because of inadequate transportation facilities, the Atkinsons tried to make their plantation as self-sufficient as possible. At John Atkinson's death the livestock included six horses, thirty-four cattle, thirty-two hogs, thirteen sheep, twenty-six geese, nine ducks, and three turkeys. The property inventory also showed that Atkinson had owned such implements as hoes, mattocks, plows, axes, augers, chisels, hammers, wedges, pails, iron nails, and one wagon.[10]

No description of the plantation home exists, but it seems clear that the Atkinsons had few of the comforts often associated with southern plantations, in spite of the fact that theirs was the third largest estate in an area of predominantly small landholders and independent farmers.[11] The meager household possessions listed in

[8] *Ibid.*, XII, 265; XII, 860; XV, 582–84.

[9] *Ibid.*, XXI, 513; XX, 508–509; will of John Atkinson, NCSD.

[10] Inventory of the estate of John Atkinson, Aug. 1792, Person County Records, NCSD; will of John Atkinson, NCSD.

[11] Caswell County List of Taxables, St. Lawrence District, 1785, NCSD.

1792 included five feather beds, two walnut tables, one desk, one trunk, one large chest, nine chairs, one loom, spinning wheels for cotton and flax, copper kettles, pewter plates, brass candlesticks, a few silver spoons, a dozen books, and one shotgun.[12]

In 1792, John Atkinson, Esq., died at his plantation home. He was survived by his wife Frances, six sons, and two married daughters. His estate included 3,655 acres of land and seventeen Negro slaves. John, Jr., by this time a property owner in his own right, appears to have received the largest single portion of the inheritance. He got two slaves and two large tracts of land and several smaller ones totaling nearly 1,000 acres. Edward, the second son, inherited two slaves, and the daughters, one slave each. Frances and her two young sons, Carter and Thomas, received the home and some of the livestock, land, and slaves. After the executor sold enough of the property to pay claims against the estate, the remaining land, equipment, and slaves were held in trust to be equally divided between Richard and Henry when they became twenty-one. Edward Atkinson, the oldest of the sons living at home, then took charge of family affairs.[13]

Edward entered local politics soon after his father's death, serving first as Caswell County sheriff in 1794 and then as one of two county representatives in the House of Commons in 1795 and 1796. In late summer, 1797, death cut short his career, and Richard, his younger brother, took charge as head of the family. In 1806 he was elected to the House of Commons. After serving two terms in that body, he advanced to the state senate, where he served almost continuously until his death in 1821.[14]

During these years young Henry Atkinson lived on the family plantation with his stepmother and brothers. No family records exist for this period, and, perhaps significantly, as an adult Henry never wrote about his youth to friends or correspondents. It seems

[12] Inventory of the estate of John Atkinson; will of John Atkinson, NCSD.

[13] Will of John Atkinson, NCSD.

[14] John H. Wheeler, *Reminiscences of North Carolina*, II, 343–44; will of Edward Atkinson, Aug. 22, 1797, Person County Records, NCSD.

clear the Atkinson boys enjoyed some educational opportunities not available to many of their contemporaries. Henry's later penmanship, vocabulary, grammar, and, in particular, his spelling, which was unusually consistent at a time of few standards, point to a fairly extensive formal education. Perhaps after some private tutoring, he attended one of the small private academies in the area. In addition to this academic training, Henry and his brothers learned to hunt, shoot, ride, and dance. As sons of one of the leading planters and politicians in the county, they became members of the emerging polite society. Thus, Henry Atkinson enjoyed membership in a large and active family, one prominent in local affairs. From this position of inherited leadership, he came to know leading citizens in Person and nearby counties.

In 1800, Henry, now a young man of eighteen, received his inheritance from his older brother Richard. This consisted of slightly over one thousand acres of land in Caswell County, just west of the family home in Person County. Henry's stepmother planned to remarry the next year, and this may have prompted Richard to release his brother's land three years before the time stipulated in their father's will. In any case, at age eighteen Henry Atkinson became an independent landowner. Now ranking among the ten largest landholders in Caswell County, young Atkinson soon came to know many county leaders.[15]

In 1802, Henry, then only twenty, and nine other prominent men of the county obtained a legislative charter to establish and operate Caswell Academy, an institution "for the promotion of learning," to be located near the county seat. The Academy, opened on January 1, 1803, offered courses in "Literature, Reading, Writing, Arithmetic, Latin, Greek, Geography, Natural and Moral Philosophy, Astronomy, &c.," and charged its students between seven and fourteen dollars a year. Henry Atkinson first served as clerk of the board of trustees, and in December, 1804, he advanced to the post of treasurer.[16] Apparently his associates accepted him

15 U.S. Census, 1800, Caswell County, North Carolina, National Archives; Person County Marriage Records, 1801; Caswell County List of Taxables, 1800, NCSD.

as a man of maturity and trustworthiness. In 1804 he opened a small store, probably near the county courthouse. Either his business failed to make money or the novice storekeeper lost interest and turned to other ventures, because the store had collapsed or changed hands by 1805.[17]

While living in Caswell County, Henry Atkinson made friends with several men who later helped his career. One of his fellow trustees, Marmaduke Williams, served in the House of Representatives from Atkinson's home district. During the summer of 1808, Williams probably nominated his friend for a commission as a captain in the United States Army. The young planter also became acquainted with Bartlett Yancy, a man his own age, who joined the Academy staff in 1804. Yancy served in Congress during and after the War of 1812, when Atkinson needed all the Congressional support he could muster. Finally, Romulus M. Saunders, a young lawyer from Caswell County, became one of his friends, and while serving in the House of Representatives from 1821–27, supported Atkinson when some Congressional leaders wanted him removed from the army.

During these years Henry Atkinson developed interests in farming and mechanics and acquired considerable knowledge about both. By 1808, Atkinson's efforts as a farmer may have met disaster or perhaps his interest waned. More likely, however, he accepted the interest in military life then common among social leaders in the South. Both his father and older brother had served in the Revolution, so the family already had some military tradition. Whatever the case, when President Thomas Jefferson received power to enlarge the army in the spring of 1808, Henry Atkinson's name was submitted for a commission, and later that summer the War Department offered him a commission as an infantry captain.

[16] Chapter XXXVII, *North Carolina Laws*, 1802, quoted in Charles L. Coon (ed.), *North Carolina Schools and Academies*, 1790–1840, 18; *Raleigh Register,* Nov. 22, 1802, Aug. 1, 1803, and Jan. 28, 1805, quoted *ibid.*, 18–19.

[17] Caswell County List of Taxables, 1804–1805, NCSD.

II. *Novitiate in the Old Southwest—1808–13*

In August, 1808, Henry Atkinson, now a mature man of twenty-six, received a commission as a captain in the Third Infantry Regiment of the United States Army. He had not served in the militia companies in his home county, and probably he had had no prior military experience other than watching a few annual militia musters. His ideas of army life stemmed, perhaps, from stories told by his father and elder brother about their experiences during the Revolution. From 1808 to 1813, Henry Atkinson served at several army posts along the lower Mississipi River and on the Gulf Coast. At these he faced sickness and death, acted as a member of several courts-martial, handled the petty details for which a company commander was then responsible, became an acting staff officer, and made friends among career officers. He acquired a knowledge of army routines and of the responsibilities of an officer. Upon the experience and knowledge gained during these years of his novitiate, Henry Atkinson went on to build a career in the United States Army.

Atkinson's military career began with Thomas Jefferson's call for a stronger army. War between France and Great Britain caused trouble for American shippers. When they traded with France, the British navy harassed them and confiscated their ships; if they stopped in Britain, the French seized their ships. Although American merchants and shippers protested, they continued to trade. National leaders and chauvinists, however, refused to accept continuing European violations of American rights. After the *Chesapeake-Leopard* affair in June, 1807, President Jefferson asked for and got Congressional authority to proclaim an embargo on December 22, 1807. He also asked Congress to consider an immediate "augmentation of our military force, as well regular as of volunteer militia." He urged Congress to provide for eight new regiments—an additional six thousand men—divided into five regiments of infantry, one of riflemen, one of dragoons or cavalry, and one of light artillery. Each regiment would include ten companies, except the dragoons which would have only eight.[1] Some Congressmen opposed what they considered budding militarism, but on April 12, 1808, Congress adopted legislation authorizing the President to make additions to the army.[2]

Congress empowered the President to name "all or any of the officers, proper to be appointed under this act" to command these new units, but reserved confirmation for the Senate. The legislation provided no method of obtaining nominations, so either the secretary of war asked the Congressmen for their suggestions or they simply presented them. In any case, each of the North Carolina senators and representatives submitted a short list of nominees, nearly all of whom received appointments in the summer of 1808. Representative Marmaduke Williams, Atkinson's friend and fellow trustee at Caswell Academy, was then serving in the House of Representatives. Although his list of nominees is the only one from the North Carolina Congressional delegation which failed to survive, it probably contained Atkinson's name since none of the others did.

Early in August, 1808, Henry Atkinson received a letter from

1 "Report of Secretary of War," Dec. 2, 1807, *American State Papers*: *Military Affairs*, I, 227–28 (Hereafter ASP:MA).

2 10 Cong., 1 sess., *Annals of Congress* (1807–1809), 1902–74; 1978–2063; *The Public Statutes at Large of the United States of America, 1789–1845*, II, 481–83.

the War Department telling of the President's "special trust and confidence in [his] valor and patriotism" and offering him a commission as a captain in the Third Infantry. He promptly accepted. Atkinson, like other new captains, was to recruit his own company.[3] In already established units, low-ranking officers took turns as recruiters, but new units had to be raised entirely by their commanding officer.

The legislation approving the army increase had established the size of each new infantry company at four sergeants, four corporals, four musicians, and sixty-eight privates. Atkinson, under his orders, was directed to recruit these men. Each recruit received a bounty of twelve dollars for enlisting, six when he first signed the enlistment papers and six when he was formally mustered into his particular unit.[4] To obtain his quota, Henry Atkinson had handbills printed and posted, and then toured the northern piedmont counties of North Carolina. He ordered his men to report to Hillsboro, the Orange County seat, on October 25. Apparently his recruiting efforts were successful, because by late September he wrote to Secretary of War Dearborn, "there is hardly a doubt, that I shall compleat my levies . . ." by the end of October. He was so confident that he asked the Secretary of War to send the promised arms and clothing for his men "as soon as practicable." Atkinson had hoped his subordinate officers would report and relieve him of some of the recruiting duty, but by late September they had not yet arrived.[5]

During a lull in his recruiting activities, the new captain visited a tailor and, after sessions of fittings and alterations, donned his first military uniform. A square-shouldered man, he stood five feet nine or ten inches tall and weighed about one hundred and fifty pounds. His round face had a ruddy complexion, deep-blue eyes, a

[3] Henry Atkinson to Henry Dearborn, Aug. 9, 1808, Register of Letters Received, Record Group 107, Records of the Office of the Secretary of War, National Archives (hereafter SW). No copy of Dearborn's letter to Atkinson exists, but letters to fellow captains show them to be form letters with only minor variations, depending on the recipient's rank and branch of service.

[4] *U.S. Statutes at Large*, XX, 135.

[5] Atkinson to Dearborn, Sept. 22, 1808, Letters Received SW.

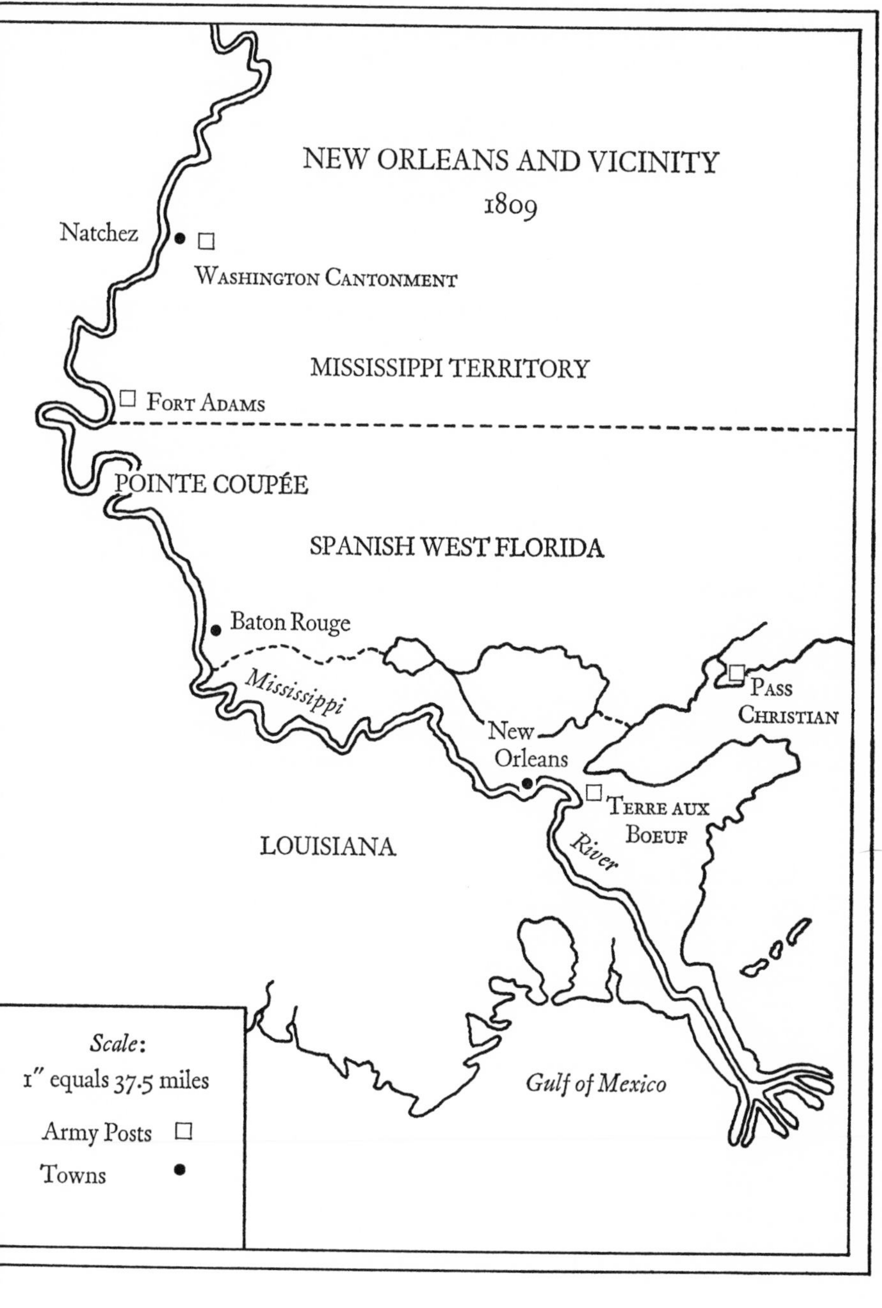
NEW ORLEANS AND VICINITY
1809
Natchez
Washington Cantonment
MISSISSIPPI TERRITORY
Fort Adams
POINTE COUPÉE
SPANISH WEST FLORIDA
Baton Rouge
Mississippi
River
New
Orleans
Pass
Christian
Terre aux
Boeuf
LOUISIANA
Gulf of Mexico
Scale:
1″ equals 37.5 miles
Army Posts
Towns

straight nose, a pleasant smile, and a cleft chin. He had thick, wavy, dark-brown hair.[6]

While Atkinson and his fellow officers completed their recruiting duties, President Jefferson decided that most of the new units should be used to defend New Orleans and the Gulf Coast from possible British attack. Therefore, in December, 1808, the War Department ordered Brigadier General James Wilkinson, a proud career officer of some skill but with a dubious reputation because of his part in the Burr conspiracy, to command that area.[7]

That same month, Wilkinson ordered the scattered units of the newly organized Third Infantry, to which Atkinson belonged, and the Fifth and Seventh Infantry Regiments to proceed to the nearest seaport from which they would be transported to New Orleans. The orders for Atkinson's company have not survived, but they directed him to lead his company either to Norfolk, Virginia, or to Charleston, South Carolina. Since Norfolk is nearly one hundred miles closer to Hillsboro than Charleston, Atkinson probably traveled overland to that place.[8] If Captain Atkinson and his men boarded a transport at Norfolk, they probably embarked during the first week of February, 1809; if they left from Charleston, their departure was at least two weeks later. Nevertheless, by April 10 they had arrived at New Orleans. Many of the soldiers were tired from the voyage, and some of them suffered from stomach disorders which may have been caused by poor food and dirty water, as well as by the crowded conditions aboard the troop transports.[9]

General Wilkinson stationed the inexperienced troops in and around New Orleans where he tried to organize and train the new

[6] Based on a description of a full-length color portrait owned by Gen. B. W. Atkinson, and a study of other Atkinson pictures.

[7] Henry Dearborn to James Wilkinson, Dec. 2, 1808, quoted in James Wilkinson, *Memoirs of My Own Times*, II, 342–43.

[8] *Ibid.*, II, 343.

[9] Garrison and General Orders, New Orleans, Apr. 10, 1809, Post Revolutionary Commands, Record Group 94, Records of the Adjutant General's Office, National Archives (hereafter AGO), Vol. 83; Third Infantry, Provision Returns, May–June, 1809, Post Revolutionary Commands, Vol. 360, AGO.

units. Many companies arrived with a minimum of military clothing and equipment, and several weeks passed before they received all their equipment and finished placing identifying marks on their tents and other possessions. By June, Wilkinson's army had increased to such an extent that barracks, hospitals, and other facilities at New Orleans became hopelessly overcrowded. This overcrowding, combined with poor sanitation and the rigors of a New Orleans summer, brought renewed sickness to the army. Captain Atkinson, like most of his fellow officers, contracted a fever by mid-May and spent several days in the hospital. He recovered, but two months later became sick again, this time for several weeks.[10]

During the spring of 1809, Henry Atkinson and the other company commanders soon learned their duties. Atkinson had to inspect the food, equipment, and medicine his men received. Frequently he served as officer of the day, of the guard, for general police, and for general fatigue. He also had to serve on company, regimental, and general court-martial boards, each of which met at least once a week.[11] During these weeks General Wilkinson examined the surrounding country seeking a place to build a permanent camp. Secretary of War William Eustis directed him to move the army to Fort Adams, on the Mississippi River five miles north of the Louisiana-Mississippi border, or to Natchez even farther north. Before these orders arrived, however, Wilkinson had decided to move the troops south to Terre aux Boeuf, a swampy area along the east bank of the Mississippi nearly thirteen miles south of New Orleans.[12]

On June 3, Wilkinson dispatched an advance party to prepare the campgrounds, and on June 10 he led the rest of his force out of the city. By late afternoon the army, including Henry Atkinson and his men, arrived at Terre aux Boeuf. New Orleans had not been a healthful location, but the new camp proved worse. The

[10] Orders, May 13, 1809, Post Revolutionary Commands, Vol. 84, AGO.

[11] Orders, May–June, 1809, Post Revolutionary Commands, Vol. 84, AGO.

[12] Eustis to Wilkinson, Apr. 30, 1809, ASP:MA, I, 273; Wilkinson to Eustis, May 29, 1809, *ibid.*

camp site was on low, swampy ground near the levee and three feet below the summer water level of the Mississippi River. Beset by malarial mosquitoes and lacking clean water and good food, many men contracted malaria, yellow fever, dysentery, and scurvy. Almost daily rain and oppressive heat created more discomfort for the troops. Within a month after the camp was established, a combination of sickness and wretchedness enveloped the army. There were many deaths.[13]

In spite of his years of army experience and a personal familiarity with climate and health problems near New Orleans, General Wilkinson remained strangely inactive. On July 12, Captain John Bently, the camp police officer, filed a report on existing conditions. He noted the "very unpleasant smell" encountered when walking down the levee and complained, "It is no uncommon thing to see four or five men and women easing themselves at the same time, on the farthermost side of the levee." He could not choose "the company having the greatest quantity of filth about it." In the cemetery "the lids of many of the coffins [were] but very little, if any, below the surface, and covered with but a few inches of earth." Rotting corpses polluted both air and water.[14] Under these conditions, Henry Atkinson learned the relationship of sanitation and cleanliness to army efficiency.

When Secretary of War Eustis learned that Wilkinson had ignored his earlier order, he commanded him "immediately to embark all the troops . . . and proceed with them to the high ground in the rear of Fort Adams, and to the high ground in the rear of Natchez, and form encampments."[15] Wilkinson promised to move quickly, and during the following weeks he arranged to have several condemned barges at Fort Adams repaired and brought south. While he made ready to move, sickness and death among the troops

[13] Statement of Captain John Darrington, Apr. 11, 1810, ASP:MA, I, 282–84; Captain William E. Williams, Apr. 17, 1810, *ibid.*, I, 286–88.

[14] Statement of John Bently, July 12, 1809, quoted in Wilkinson, *Memoirs*, II, Appendix CVII, 4–5.

[15] Eustis to Wilkinson, June 22, 1809, ASP:MA, I, 274.

continued. In Captain Atkinson's company, for example, the toll climbed, and between July 15 and September 12, the company shrank from sixty-nine to fifty-four men.[16]

On September 23, 1809, after leaving the sickest men in hospitals at New Orleans, the army began moving north to Natchez. The able-bodied men loaded their weakened comrades on four naval barges and thirteen keelboats and then marched along the riverbank, taking turns pulling the boats upstream. For the next five weeks the army struggled northward, making, according to their estimates, between eight and fifteen miles a day and losing hundreds of men to sickness, desertion, and death. En route most of the troops became so sick that the officers established two hospitals with their own money and left the weakest men there. During the 250- to 300-mile march along the bank of the Mississippi, nearly three hundred men died or deserted, including seventeen men in Captain Atkinson's company. On October 31 the convoy of transports and column of marching men arrived at Natchez.[17]

From there, the troops moved seven miles east to Washington Cantonment, near the village of Washington, then capital of Mississippi Territory. Since midsummer Captain Atkinson's company had dwindled from sixty-seven to thirty-seven sickly, worn-out men.[18] A tally of the army as a whole showed that more than 1,000 of a force of 2,036 had either died or deserted that year.[19] With nearly half of his army gone and much of the rest out of action, General Wilkinson consolidated his men and officers to keep the remaining units at or near full strength. Twice in December, 1809, Atkinson's company received men from units that were being disbanded. In spite of these additions, continuing sickness again re-

16 Third Infantry, Provision Returns, July–September, 1809, Post Revolutionary Commands, Vol. 360, AGO.

17 Third Infantry, Provision Returns, September–October, 1809, Vol. 360, AGO; William D. Beall, Mar. 21, 1810, ASP:MA, I, 279.

18 Third Infantry, Provision Returns, June–October, 1809, Post Revolutionary Commands, Vol. 360, AGO.

19 Wilkinson, *Memoirs*, II, 373; Esaias Preble, Mar. 16, 1810, ASP:MA, I, 278; Darrington, Apr. 11, 1810, *ibid.*, I, 283; *ibid.*, 270.

duced his particular company to only thirty-eight men fit for active duty.[20]

In December, 1809, Wilkinson's management of the troops brought a Congressional investigation and later a court-martial. Secretary of War Eustis ordered him to Washington to face his critics. There Wilkinson successfully defended himself and later was returned to duty. Eustis, meanwhile, appointed Brigadier General Wade Hampton, a wealthy South Carolina planter and Revolutionary War veteran, to replace "His Serene Highness."[21] The new general allowed his force time to recover both its health and morale before he tried to rebuild the still weakened units.

At Washington Cantonment the soldiers moved back into the routine of military life. The officers spent much of their free time visiting the nearby village of Washington, which, although it had only thirty houses, a few stores, and a tavern, provided parties, dances, banquets, and even hot or cold mineral baths.[22] During duty hours courts-martial met, and Captain Atkinson often presided over trials of enlisted men indicted for petty offenses. In one such case the court tried Private Moses Hubbard, accused of signing his commanding officer's name to a two-dollar order at the post sutler's store. After examining the evidence and listening to Hubbard's testimony, Atkinson and his fellow officers sentenced the Private "to be confined two weeks on bread & water & one month hard labor & to ware his coat wrong side out, also to ware a fools cap both for the said term of one month." The court may have been trying to brighten their usually dull existence, but the commanding officer disapproved of the sentence and ordered the prisoner back to his regular duties.[23]

Gambling and drinking, both prohibited in the enlisted men's

20 Third Infantry, Provision Returns, Dec., 1809, Post Revolutionary Commands, Vol. 360, AGO.

21 James R. Jacobs, *Tarnished Warrior: Major General James Wilkinson*, 250.

22 Fortescue Cuming, *Sketches of a Tour to the Western Country*, 1807–1809, (Vol. IV of *Early Western Travels*, ed. by R. G. Thwaites), 318–319.

23 Washington Cantonment, Orders, Dec. 28, 1809, Post Revolutionary Commands, Vol. 156, AGO.

quarters, were the most frequent offenses for which soldiers were tried. In one case the court, under Atkinson's jurisdiction, convicted a sergeant of gambling in his quarters and reduced him to the rank of private. Army courts, however, often sided with soldiers accused of disorderly conduct off the post. The same court that had reduced the sergeant for gambling, exonerated another charged with "rioting & offering violence to D. Henry a sitison of the town of Washington."[24]

In addition to disciplinary problems, matters of health and sanitation needed constant attention. Many officers and enlisted men had apparently failed to learn much from their experience at Terre aux Boeuf. Sanitary conditions at Washington Cantonment soon resembled those at the former encampment. Poor enforcement of regulations led to carelessness with garbage and human waste and raised fears of a recurrence of sickness. The commanding officer at the cantonment ordered a guard be stationed along one flank of the camp to prevent the men from using the nearby creek rather than the sinks to relieve themselves. He also commanded that "the old sinks should be filled up and new ones dug below the Mill and that all the ground within the chain [of guards] should be cleared of filth and rubage of every kind."[25] This order suggests the laxity of both officers and men.

Spring slipped away, and during the hot Mississippi summer, guard duty, fatigue details, and inspections filled the days. Fatigue parties worked to build barracks, officers' quarters, storehouses, and magazines. While these buildings were being built, piles of scrap lumber, shavings, and tools littered the camp. This caused the new post commandant, Lieutenant Colonel Zebulon M. Pike to order that the troops clean the camp. The great quantity of timber or planks in the vicinity of the houses, he noted, was unnecessary. He ordered "that no timber or plank shall be left in front of any

[24] Washington Cantonment, Orders, Apr. 14, 1810, Post Revolutionary Commands, Vol. 156, AGO.

[25] Washington Cantonment, Orders, Apr. 25, 1810, Post Revolutionary Commands, Vol. 156, AGO.

officers quarters in the street between them and the mens huts after retreat." At least twice each week shavings were to be piled and burned at the rear of camp, and every company supplied two men to remove stumps from the company streets and from in front of the officers' quarters.[26]

Leaving the problems of health and local discipline to his subordinate officers, General Hampton tried to rebuild his weakened army. In February, 1810, he decided that the soldiers had recovered enough to begin regular training and drill. He ordered the company officers "to superintend the drill of the soldiers and . . . to be themselves acquainted with what is taught." Daily drills took place between 7:00 and 9:00 A.M. and again from 3:00 to 5:00 P.M. Henry Atkinson and his fellow officers now had to observe their men drilling, so they might be able to assist when necessary, and had to assume personal responsibility "for the discipline of their respective corps."[27] General Hampton preferred that his men receive their training from the "Modern System of exercise and manouvores compiled by Colonel Smythe from the French school," but if copies of this were unavailable, he directed the officers to use "the ancient one of the Baron Von Steuben."[28] Thus, even within the same command, a simple lack of training manuals might lead to two methods of drill.

During the summer of 1810, the pace of training had slackened, but when autumn weather brought cool breezes, the troops renewed their concentration on drill. Bugle notes and rolling drums marked time throughout the day. After reveille and breakfast, the bugle and drum called the men to their first drill at 9:00 A.M. During the early afternoons, the troops had fatigue details, and late each afternoon they stood roll-call formation, ate their evening

26 Washington Cantonment, Orders, July 27, 1810, Post Revolutionary Commands, Vol. 156, AGO.

27 Washington Cantonment, Orders, Feb. 21, 1810, Post Revolutionary Commands, Vol. 156, AGO.

28 Washington Cantonment, Orders, Sept. 24, 1810, Post Revolutionary Commands, Vol. 155, AGO.

meal, and, lacking anything else to do, retired to their huts where they were required to remain after the bugler sounded tattoo at 8:00 P.M. To ensure that the men remained in camp, the commandant ordered guards to patrol the perimeter of the camp.[29]

Because there were practically no recreational facilities for officers or enlisted men, desertion increased. This had always been a problem, but here in the wild back country of southwestern Mississippi Territory, the army had few inducements to offer its sickly and underpaid troops. Spanish West Florida was less than forty-five miles south of Washington Cantonment, and in spite of a policy of severe punishment—usually fifty lashes administered before the assembled troops after the evening roll call—desertion continued.

Life for the officers was also dull, although they did participate in parties in the town of Washington and also made occasional trips to nearby Natchez. Despite these diversions, the officers spent much of their time drinking, telling stories, and playing cards. Henry Atkinson joined his associates in these activities, but he also spent some of his time reading about past military leaders and studying military organization and tactics.[30] He participated in the social activities at the post, but tried to remain aloof from the petty quarrels that arose. He also avoided taking a stand in the bickering between the partisans of Generals Wilkinson and Hampton. Atkinson became skillful at avoiding personal clashes with his fellow officers even when he was in the midst of controversy, and he often used this skill during his military career.

Unlike many of his contemporaries, he refused to push for promotion. He claimed that if his personal industry and ability failed to attract his superiors' attention, he would resign rather than ask for promotion. Yet he complained when his associates,

29 *Ibid.*

30 Winfield Scott, *Memoirs of Lieut.-General Scott*, I, 24–25; Atkinson to Bartlett Yancy, Mar. 10, 1814, Yancy Papers, in Southern Historical Collection, University of North Carolina Library (hereafter NCU).

who wrote the secretary of war for personal advancement, received promotions. His discontent, however, did not overcome his scruples, and he refused to beg for rank.[31]

While Henry Atkinson continued to learn his duties as an army officer, American frontiersmen had been moving into Spanish West Florida. In September, 1810, they revolted, formed an army, and captured the fort at Baton Rouge. Then they applied for annexation by the United States. On October 27, President Madison issued a proclamation of annexation.[32] This move brought a flurry of activity to the army posts in the area. Some troops left Natchez and Fort Adams for New Orleans. Atkinson and his company stayed at Washington Cantonment until March, 1811, when Colonel Pike led a detachment south to Baton Rouge where they occupied the old fort. For the next fifteen months this square, log structure, with a small tower at each corner and surrounded by an earthen rampart topped with a picket stockade, served as their home. Here the cycle of training and garrison duties continued.

When Anglo-American tensions increased during the winter of 1811–12, some Congressional leaders demanded the annexation of Canada and war with Great Britain. Congressmen wrote the War Department asking for promotion or appointment of their local favorites. In this scramble for rank and promotion, Henry Atkinson was not overlooked. Representative James Cockran, from Caswell County, North Carolina, submitted his name for promotion to lieutenant colonel in one of the regiments sure to be formed once the expected war began. Secretary of War William Eustis refused. Cockran wrote Atkinson that the Secretary had said that any expansion of the army would have to be accomplished by giving others, not then among the ranks of officers, command of the new units. Once the war ended and army strength dropped to pre-war levels, officers remaining in the regular force would be retained,

31 Atkinson to Yancy, Mar. 10, 1814, Yancy Papers, NCU.

32 For a more complete discussion see Isaac J. Cox, *The West Florida Controversy, 1798–1813*, 388–436, 487–529.

while those holding more recent appointments would be retired. This disappointed Atkinson, but he remained stoic until 1814, when several officers then his juniors received promotions to the new regiments, regardless of what Eustis had said.[33]

In April, 1812, President Madison asked Congress for a commercial embargo, hoping to use this weapon in negotiations with Great Britain. He received power to proclaim the embargo, but the ensuing negotiations failed. On June 1, Madison asked Congress to declare war on Great Britain, but opposition delayed the declaration of war until June 18.

During April, 1812, General Wilkinson was ordered back to New Orleans as commander of all troops in the Old Southwest. When he arrived at New Orleans in July, 1812, he found the fortifications in disrepair, troop morale low, supplies scarce, and the units scattered. He regrouped his three regiments to defend New Orleans and the Gulf Coast and decided to build fortifications at English Turn, fifteen miles south of the city. In September, Wilkinson dispatched several companies, Atkinson's among them, to Pass Christian on the Gulf Coast, east of New Orleans.[34]

After Atkinson arrived at his new post, he was given the additional task of serving as assistant deputy inspector general for the detachment. As an inspector, he mustered and inspected the detachment at least once each month. Before he learned his new duties, however, he suffered an attack of fever, from which he took four weeks to recover. When he did return to active duty, he complained that he was still too weak "to pay that strict attention to some of the returns" that he thought necessary. Atkinson was bewildered by the procedures and paper work of his new position. Because of this and his desire to perform his new duties correctly, he enclosed a request for directions with his first official returns to Washington. "I shall feel thankful," he wrote, "if you will inform

33 James Cockran to Secretary of War, Jan. 9, 1812, Letters Received, SW; Atkinson to Yancy, Mar. 10, 1814, Yancy Papers, NCU.

34 Louisiana, Orders, Oct. 7, 1812, Post Revolutionary Commands, Vol. 86, AGO.

me whether I shall in future forward the individual returns or consolidate them."[35] Adjutant General Thomas Cushing wrote in reply that Atkinson should submit monthly post, cantonment, and corps returns, along with an inspection return for each company and a semiannual muster roll.[36] As an inspector, Captain Henry Atkinson had responsibilities beyond those of a company commander. Now he began to learn the details and procedures that governed the movement and operation of larger army units.

The stay at Pass Christian was short. On January 3, 1813, Major Matthew Arbuckle led the detachment of five companies back to New Orleans, where Wilkinson put the soldiers to work rebuilding the fortifications at English Turn. Apparently at this time Atkinson attracted Wilkinson's attention. "I have looked at him for a month or two," Wilkinson wrote, "and I find he has taste & talent also, for details, and is qualified to rise to prominance in the General staff." Wilkinson recommended him for the position of deputy inspector general which he received later that spring.[37] From then on, Henry Atkinson devoted more time to his staff duties, often being forced to relinquish his company command functions to a subordinate. Here, at last, was recognition and a chance to advance to the rank of major—a step he had waited five years to take.

During the winter of 1812–13, the British blockade closed the port of New Orleans, bringing depression, uncertainty, and fear to the inhabitants. In April, 1813, the local banks suspended *specie* payments, and interest rates climbed to 3 and 4 per cent a month.[38] Several weeks earlier, on March 14, General Wilkinson had received orders from the Secretary of War to lead a part of the army against Mobile and West Florida.[39] The American government claimed West Florida east to the Perdido River. The Spanish held this area, but, to protect New Orleans, Wilkinson thought it neces-

[35] Atkinson to Thomas Cushing, Nov. 20, 1812, Letters Received, AGO.

[36] Cushing to Atkinson, Jan. 28, 1813, Letters Sent, Vol. 3, AGO.

[37] Wilkinson to Cushing, Feb. 9, 1813, Letters Received, AGO.

[38] John S. Kendall, *History of New Orleans*, I, 95.

[39] John Armstrong to Wilkinson, Feb. 16, 1813, quoted in Wilkinson, *Memoirs*, III, 339–40.

sary to capture Mobile. On March 16 he ordered a detachment from English Turn east to Pass Christian. As Wilkinson's deputy inspector general, Atkinson accompanied him and the expedition. On April 3 they arrived at Pass Christian. Here Atkinson became acting deputy adjutant general in addition to his duties as inspector for the expedition. In this capacity he often acted as a personal messenger for General Wilkinson. In fact, he worked so closely with the General that Wilkinson directed that "all orders from him [Atkinson] written or verbal are to be received as if from the General himself."[40]

On April 7, accompanied by several naval gunboats, Wilkinson embarked a six hundred-man army for Mobile. His gunboats seized a Spanish transport laden with supplies for the garrison at Fort Charlotte in Mobile. Next they captured the small Spanish detachment on Dauphin Island at the mouth of Mobile Bay, and cut all communication between Mobile and Pensacola by water. At the same time Colonel John Bowyer led a force down the Tensaw River from Fort Stoddart and camped just north of the city. Then Wilkinson landed his infantry south of Mobile. Cayetano Pérez, the Spanish commander, his garrison at Fort Charlotte reduced to less than sixty starving and poorly equipped men, held a council of war with his officers and agreed to negotiate.[41]

Wilkinson notified Pérez that the American troops had come at the orders of the President of the United States to "relieve the garrison which you command, from the occupancy of a post within the legitimate limits of those states." He asked Pérez to retire peacefully and demanded that he surrender the fort and ordnance to the Americans.[42]

The Spanish commander accepted Wilkinson's terms and surrendered the fort the next day. While the Americans waited, the small Spanish garrison collected its property and, at 5:00 P.M.,

[40] Wilkinson, Orders, Apr. 3, 1813, Letters Received, AGO.

[41] Wilkinson, Orders, Apr. 7, 1813, Letters Received, AGO; Wilkinson, *Memoirs*, I, 507–508; Peter J. Hamilton, *Colonial Mobile*, 359–60.

[42] Wilkinson to Fort Charlotte commandant, Apr. 12, 1813, quoted in Wilkinson, *Memoirs*, I, 508.

April 14, filed out of the fort to the waiting American transports. When the Spanish marched to the harbor, a detachment of American artillerists entered the fort, fired a twenty-four-gun salute and raised the American flag, signaling Wilkinson to move his remaining force into the city.[43]

General Wilkinson stationed some of his troops in Fort Charlotte and, on April 20, moved another portion of them to Mobile Point, where he established a defensive position using a battery of nine of the heaviest Spanish artillery pieces. On May 5 he marched east, taking possession of the right bank of the Perdido River "about five leagues from Pensacola," where he began construction of a "strong stockade work with blockhouses."[44] From the Perdido, Wilkinson and Atkinson returned overland to Mobile and then sailed back to New Orleans.

There on May 24, 1813, Henry Atkinson received an order from the War Department appointing him temporary lieutenant colonel and assistant inspector general for General Thomas Flournoy, new commander of the Seventh Military District, with headquarters at New Orleans. The next day Atkinson accepted his appointment.[45] Before he could assume his duties as Flournoy's assistant inspector general, however, Atkinson received an order to proceed to Washington. Traveling overland he arrived in Washington on August 1. The next day he received notice of another appointment which superseded the previous one. The second appointment was to the temporary position of inspector general for the Ninth Military District commanded by General Wade Hampton who was then training an army at Burlington, Vermont. His new appointment carried the rank and pay of colonel, certainly an advancement from his position as a captain.[46]

Atkinson's trip to Washington ended his tour of duty and his army apprenticeship in the Old Southwest. Except for a possible

43 *Ibid.*, 508–509; Hamilton, *Colonial Mobile*, 361.

44 Wilkinson, *Memoirs*, I, 522–23; Hamilton, *Colonial Mobile*, 356.

45 Atkinson to Armstrong, May 26, 1813, Letters Received, AGO.

46 Atkinson to Armstrong, Aug. 2, 1813, Letters Received, AGO.

attendance at a court-martial in New Orleans, he never again served in that theater. His first five years as an army officer had been both routine and eventful. He gained valuable experience at Terre aux Boeuf and later by participating in the movement against Mobile. As a company commander he faced specific problems; and as inspector general and adjutant general on General Wilkinson's staff, he learned much about army administration. He probably learned that his success would depend on commanding competently trained, well-equipped, and healthy troops, but that promotion in rank depended at least as much on one's friends as on one's own abilities. He had made friends and acquaintances who continued as his close associates for the next thirty years and seems to have remained relatively free from army factions.

Although the United States had been at war with Great Britain for over a year, Henry Atkinson had not yet been in battle. His five years' duty in the South had taught him many things. Perhaps his new post would provide an opportunity for him to employ his knowledge and skill.

III. War in the North—1813-14

THE WAR OF 1812 was a period of frustration for Henry Atkinson. When he served at New Orleans, all was quiet and the capture of Mobile was simply an exercise in moving men and supplies to that city. While he remained in the South, battles were fought and lost in the North; when he went north, except for two minor and unsuccessful campaigns into Canada, the commands to which he was attached saw no combat. After he left the South, the Creek War and the later Battle of New Orleans took place there. During his stay at Plattsburg, New York, that post was merely a training center and recovery area for the American Army. Only a few months after he moved to New London, Connecticut, to command the harbor defenses of that city, Plattsburg became the focal point for a large British and Canadian counteroffensive. Thus Henry Atkinson had little chance to build a reputation or to practice his leadership and abilities in battle. When the war ended, he had a record as a capable and conscientious officer; one who was willing to attend to army paper work, but who was without experience as a combat officer.

In 1812 during Atkinson's tour of duty at New Orleans, a three-pronged thrust into Canada had failed completely. At Detroit, General William Hull surrendered his army without firing a shot. General Stephen Van Rensselaer's push into Canada failed at the

Battle of Queenston Heights when the New York Militia refused to cross into Canada to sustain the regular troops. General Henry Dearborn was stopped north of Plattsburg, New York.

During the winter of 1812–13, the British increased their blockading squadrons and closed many American ports. General William Henry Harrison met defeat at the Battle of Frenchtown, and his forces retreated to a defensive line based on the Maumee and Wabash rivers in Indiana Territory. Meanwhile, General Dearborn led a force across Lake Ontario to York (Toronto), which he captured in April, 1813. The victory proved costly, however, because General Zebulon M. Pike was killed and 320 of his men were killed or wounded when a powder magazine exploded. Dearborn returned to Sackets Harbor, New York, without gaining control of the lake. Thus except for two minor victories, the American offensive campaigns had been frustrated.

In January, 1813, President Madison replaced Secretary of War William Eustis with General John Armstrong. Madison and Armstrong decided to mount a new offensive against Canada, and the President replaced the aging General Dearborn with Generals James Wilkinson and Wade Hampton. These men, bitter personal enemies, would command the two wings of an army in what was supposed to be a co-operative push from New York State into Canada.

Captain Henry Atkinson, after missing the earlier American offensives, traveled north to take part in the new campaign. Now thirty-one-years old and serving as an inspector general with the temporary rank of colonel, he arrived at Albany, New York, on August 16, 1813. From there he went to Burlington, Vermont, to join General Wade Hampton, who was gathering and training an army. Hampton, although a veteran of the Revolutionary War and the second-ranking brigadier general in 1812, was proud, obstinate, and overcautious.

As inspector general for Hampton's army of four thousand men, Atkinson's duties differed from his earlier experience because he now dealt with thousands rather than hundreds of men. The duties of an inspector general were similar to those of that position today, but included several which have since been delegated to other officers. Atkinson had to muster and inspect all regular and militia troops within the territorial command of his division, select camp sites at the direction of his commanding officer, post guards and oversee local security measures, superintend the police of all camps and marching units, inspect parades, and make semiannual confidential reports to the War Department.[1] This position broadened Atkinson's military experience and allowed him to observe the organization and operation of a large army. At the same time, however, it prevented him from gaining a personal command and limited his experience to paper shuffling and acting as a messenger for General Hampton.

While Atkinson served with General Hampton at Burlington, Vermont, Secretary of War Armstrong traveled to Sackets Harbor, New York, to discuss the coming campaign with General Wilkinson. Armstrong and Wilkinson quarreled about whether to attack Montreal or Kingston, but finally decided on Montreal. Wilkinson was to move down the St. Lawrence from his camp at Sackets Harbor, while Hampton traveled overland north from Burlington. They hoped to combine forces south of Montreal.

On September 10, 1813, General Hampton moved his army from Burlington across Lake Champlain to Cumberland Head, a finger-shaped projection of land jutting into the lake just north of Plattsburg, New York. Atkinson accompanied Hampton and the army. On September 19, Lieutenant Thomas MacDonough arrived with a naval escort. Hampton immediately loaded his force of four thousand men on the boats and at 6:00 P.M. headed north for Canada. At midnight he landed at Champlain, two miles south of the Canadian border. From there, an hour later, he sent two advance parties against the British at Odletown. Both got lost in the darkness and accomplished nothing more than to alert the

[1] ASP:MA, I, 427.

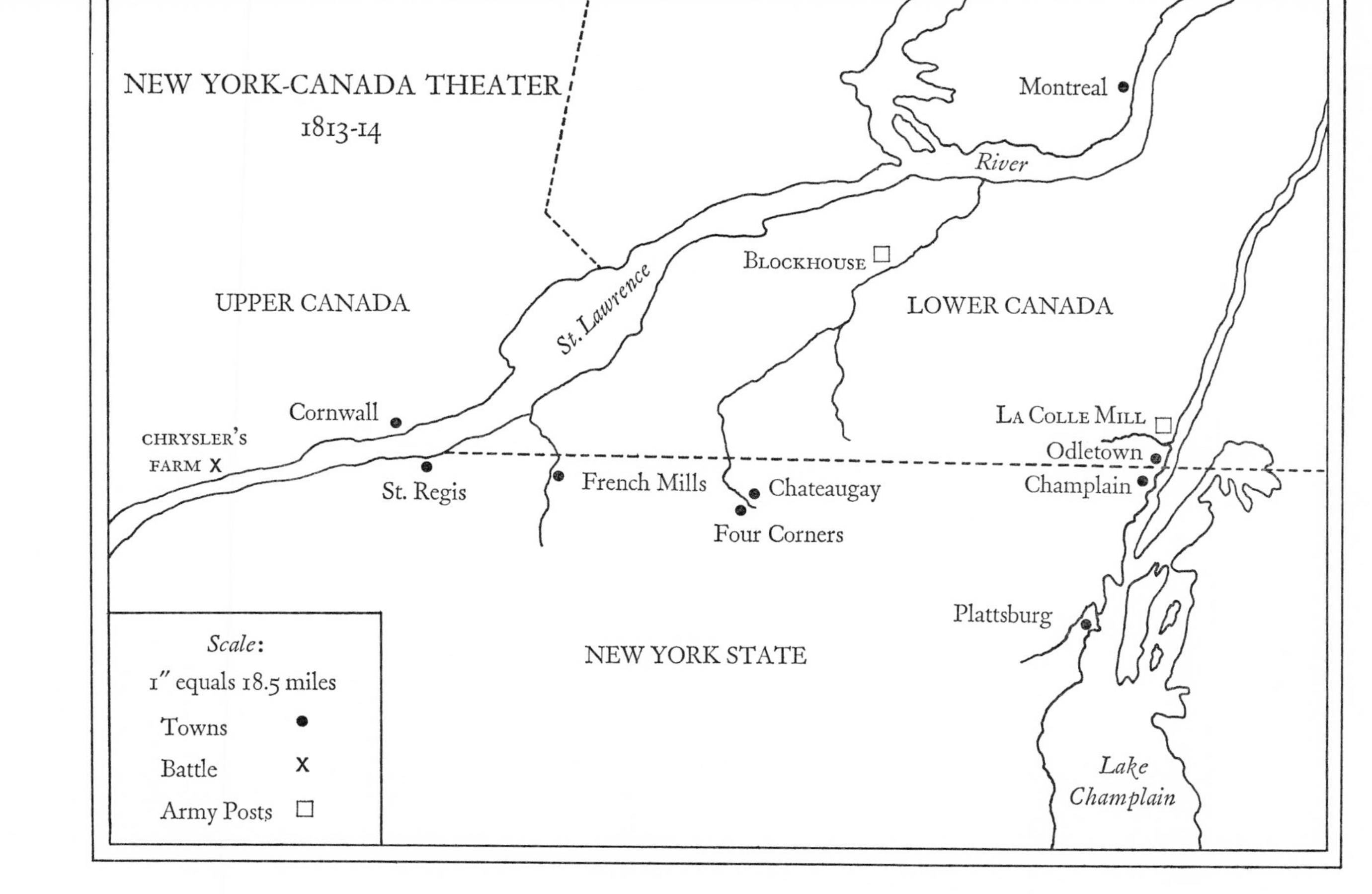
NEW YORK-CANADA THEATER
1813-14
Montreal
River
St. Lawrence
BLOCKHOUSE
UPPER CANADA
LOWER CANADA
LA COLLE MILL
Odletown
Champlain
Cornwall
CHRYSLER'S FARM
St. Regis
French Mills
Chateaugay
Four Corners
Plattsburg
NEW YORK STATE
Lake Champlain
Scale:
1″ equals 18.5 miles
Towns
Battle
Army Posts

enemy. By nine o'clock the next morning the rest of Hampton's command joined his advance force at Odletown.[2]

There the officers reported that the men were suffering from a water shortage because a summer drought had dried most creeks and wells in the area. Here was an unexpected problem. General Hampton consulted his staff and unit commanders and decided to shift his invasion route farther west to the Chateaugay River, because it would provide sufficient water. On September 21, Hampton's men headed south to Champlain. The next day they moved to Chazy and, on the morning of September 23, began the march to Chateaugay, about fifty miles farther west.[3]

Hampton regrouped his troops and dispatched Henry Atkinson to Sackets Harbor with messages for the Secretary of War and General Wilkinson. As inspector general with Hampton's forces, Atkinson had been present during the abortive move into Canada. He knew the strengths and weaknesses of the command and could describe the capabilities of that force. In fact, Hampton had such confidence in him that he wrote, "Of every matter and thing relating to mine, Col. Atkinson will give you as full an idea, as if you had been with me for the last 5 days."[4] The 150-mile trip from Chateaugay to Sackets Harbor took about thirty-five hours by horse, and during the following weeks Henry Atkinson often traveled this route as liaison officer between Generals Hampton and Wilkinson and the Secretary of War.

On October 16, Armstrong ordered Hampton to begin the invasion of Canada. Atkinson was at Hampton's headquarters when the order arrived, and on October 21 he accompanied the General and the army north. After turning back light British resistance, they advanced twenty-four miles in the next two days, when they halted to "complete the road and [bring] up the artillery and stores." Another short advance brought Hampton's force face-to-

[2] Benson J. Lossing, *The Pictorial Field Book of the War of 1812*, 632; *The War*, Sept. 21, 1813; Hampton to Armstrong, Sept. 22, 1813, ASP:MA, I, 459.

[3] Hampton to Armstrong, Sept. 22, 1813, ASP:MA, I, 459.

[4] *Ibid.*

face with British troops, defending a stone blockhouse. Once more the American commander resorted to a night maneuver to turn the enemy flank. Hindered by an all-night rain, the attacking battalion got lost in the tangled forest and, not only failed to surprise the British, but were themselves surprised and repulsed with losses. Hampton, meanwhile, after waiting in vain for news from the advance column, sent the rest of his army against the enemy the next afternoon. The Americans drove forward, pushing the defenders behind log breastworks. But news of the defeat of the advance party, coupled with a British feint against his left flank, frightened the cautious Hampton into sounding retreat. His army withdrew three miles to the south, where they established a new camp.[5]

Hampton's position was not strong. His army of four thousand men had no water transportation and lacked supplies for an extended campaign. At Montreal, only twenty-five miles to the northeast, Sir George Prevost had an army reputed to contain fifteen thousand men. In these circumstances, Hampton called a council of war with his officers. After some discussion they decided the army should return south to Chateaugay, and on October 28 the American army withdrew to its former base of supply.[6]

While Hampton's force marched overland, General Wilkinson moved another army down the St. Lawrence by boat. Bad weather and his failure to keep boats and men together hampered Wilkinson's operations. When he learned of Hampton's retreat from Canada, Wilkinson ordered his fellow general to march his command west from Chateaugay to St. Regis on the St. Lawrence and there join him. This order arrived on November 8, and Hampton sent Colonel Atkinson west with his refusal. Leaving Chateaugay that same evening, Atkinson reached French Mills by midnight. There he halted because British troops lined the river banks and he could not cross to join Wilkinson.[7]

[5] Hampton to Armstrong, Nov. 1, 1813, ASP:MA, I, 461.

[6] *Ibid.*

[7] Hampton to Wilkinson, Nov. 8, 1813, ASP:MA, I, 462; Atkinson to Hampton, Nov. 9, 1813, Letters Received, unregistered series, SW.

On November 12, Atkinson finally reached Wilkinson and presented Hampton's refusal. Instead of moving west to join Wilkinson at St. Regis, Hampton was then marching east to Plattsburg. This, Wilkinson complained, defeated "the grand object of the campaign" and would force him to go into winter quarters.[8] After receiving Wilkinson's reply, Atkinson set out for Hampton's new headquarters at Plattsburg, rejoining his commander on November 14. With the campaign over, General Hampton left Plattsburg for Washington and furloughed most of the officers under his command, leaving Colonel Atkinson as the only staff officer at the post.

After the two-pronged campaign into Canada failed in November, 1813, the bickering between Generals Wilkinson and Hampton gradually became a bitter quarrel. The two came to hate each other. Each seized every opportunity to damage the military reputation of the other. Henry Atkinson found that this was one quarrel he could not avoid. He had served under both of the quarreling generals, and probably owed his position as an inspector general to General Wilkinson's earlier recommendation. By late 1813, however, he had become a close associate of General Hampton. Throughout the winter months Atkinson remained loyal to Hampton and kept him informed of any news of Wilkinson.[9] At the same time, he kept his personal feelings hidden and continued to work with officers in both factions. As a result of the dismal failure of the campaign, General Hampton resigned and returned to his plantation in South Carolina, and General Wilkinson took command of both armies.

Atkinson remained at Plattsburg where he experienced difficulty preparing returns and muster rolls. He denounced many of the remaining officers as ignorant and incompetent; in fact, he considered their company records in such deplorable condition that it was "utterly impossible to obtain correct returns." Several times he refused to sign company returns and forwarded them to Wash-

[8] Wilkinson to Hampton, Nov. 12, 1813, ASP:MA, I, 463.

[9] Atkinson to Hampton, Nov. 28, 1813, Letters of Officers of the War of 1812, in Dreer Collection, Historical Society of Pennsylvania (hereafter HSP).

ington "in their pristine state" rather than "bestowing a month's labour to correct them."[10] The difficulties he encountered in trying to overcome the incompetence or laziness of some of his subordinates, and in trying to retain a working relationship between the Wilkinson and Hampton factions, probably kept Atkinson tired and nervous.

In late January, 1814, the War Department ordered General Wilkinson to abandon his winter quarters at French Mills, send two thousand men southwest to Sackets Harbor, and then lead the remaining troops east to Plattsburg. "Even the very order & manner of march is pointed out," Atkinson noted. "From this positive command and not leaving W. a semblance of exercise of judgement, we should not be surprised if another is sent to command us."[11] This was not the case although Wilkinson was replaced in the spring.

Throughout the long winter months Henry Atkinson labored at his administrative tasks. On February 23, 1814, General Wilkinson assigned him the entire force then at Plattsburg. His duties included inspecting "the quarters & police of every company once a week" and preparing reports of their condition for the General. Recent British raids into the area led Wilkinson to order nightly mounted patrols on the roads from Plattsburg north to Champlain and west to Chateaugay. Atkinson had to dispatch these each evening. Thus the leaden-sky winter days passed.[12]

When the list of spring promotions arrived early in March, 1814, Henry Atkinson was disappointed and angry at again being passed over. Many of his friends and associates had now left him behind in the race for advancement. Much to his disgust, Josiah Snelling, William King, William S. Hamilton, and James Gibson, all received promotions to lieutenant colonel or colonel while he remained an infantry captain serving as a temporary inspector

[10] Atkinson to Adjutant and Inspector General, Jan. 15, 1814, Letters Received, AGO.

[11] Atkinson to Charles Gardner, Jan. 30, 1814, Gardner Papers, New York State Library.

[12] Ninth Military Dept., General Orders, Plattsburg, Feb. 23, 1814, Post Revolutionary Command, Vol. 114, AGO.

general with the rank of colonel. He did not begrudge his fellow officers the honor and pay increase they received, but their promotions bore no relation to the reasoning used two years before when the Secretary of War had denied him a promotion. The Secretary had claimed that he wanted the regular officers to remain with their own units, thus avoiding the danger of being dropped after the war when a reduction of the army was certain. Atkinson had said little at the time, and because of pride and his personal code of honor he had refused to push openly for his promotion. Unlike some of his contemporaries, he did not write the Secretary of War begging for new assignments or promotion. Now, however, after a disheartening winter, during which several of his acquaintances received promotions and appointments to command newly formed regiments, he wrote to his friend Congressman Bartlett Yancy. Yancy replied that promotions came slowly and urged that he wait for his with patience. The usually laconic Atkinson responded with a seven-page letter bristling with accusations. "To an officer who cares but little about anything else, but a mere occupation, these things to Him may pass well enough—But to the soldier & man of honor, it is killingly mortifying." He complained that excellence in office was not the criteria used for advancement. "It would seem from your expression to me," he wrote, "that even when I may be entitled to promotion I might require proposing to get it—God forbid! For if my own merit will not ensure it I may be struck from the roles of this army." He decided, however, that because of his temporary appointment as inspector general, which carried with it the rank and pay of a colonel, he would remain in the army and "be governed by the circumstances."[13]

Whether this correspondence with Yancy had an effect or whether Atkinson was already under consideration for a promotion is unknown. In either case, Atkinson did receive a promotion late in April. On April 11 the Secretary of War recommended to the President that Henry Atkinson be appointed a colonel and be given command of the Forty-fifth Infantry Regiment. President Madison

[13] Atkinson to Yancy, Mar. 10, 1814, Yancy Papers, NCU.

relayed the recommendation to the Senate, which confirmed the appointment on April 15, 1814.[14] When he received news of Atkinson's appointment, Secretary Armstrong apparently shifted his assignment and included an endorsement that changed the command to that of the Thirty-seventh Regiment. On April 27, Henry Atkinson received the order which included his promotion and new appointment. Impressed that he advanced from captain to colonel, by-passing the ranks of major and lieutenant colonel, he was happy to accept that same day.[15]

Eager to proceed to New London, Connecticut, where the Thirty-seventh Regiment was then being recruited and organized, Atkinson immediately applied to General Alexander Macomb, his commanding officer at Plattsburg, for permission to resign as inspector general. When he got no reply the next day, he wrote a second letter to Macomb. When this, too, brought no immediate response, he wrote to General George Izard, who had assumed command of the forces at Plattsburg on May 1. Izard, like Macomb, was too busy to reply immediately, and the frustrated Atkinson remained at Plattsburg as an inspector general.[16]

Here was a problem he had not anticipated. After nearly six years he had received his first promotion, and now he could not get permission to assume his new command. Perhaps Atkinson made some unfavorable comments about General Izard or complained unduly about the delay, because while awaiting permission to leave for New London, Atkinson became involved in a dispute with Captain Gabriel H. Manigault, an aide-de-camp to General Izard. Since both principals later refused to testify when ordered to do so, the cause of their quarrel remains obscure. But it is clear that the two officers became involved in a quarrel which reached such intensity that they risked both their careers and lives rather than back down.

[14] *Journal of the Executive Proceedings of the Senate . . .*, II, 525, 527.

[15] Armstrong to Atkinson, Apr. 18, 1814, Letters Sent, Vol. 3, AGO; Atkinson to Armstrong, Apr. 27, 1814, Letters Received, AGO.

[16] Atkinson to Macomb, Apr. 27, 1814, Letters Received, AGO; Atkinson to Macomb, Apr. 29, 1814, *ibid.*; Atkinson to Izard, May 3, 1814, *ibid.*

After a heated argument, Manigault challenged Atkinson to a duel. Whatever the reason for their quarrel, Atkinson's pride would not allow him to refuse Manigault's challenge. Early Monday morning, May 9, before the sun rose over mist-shrouded Lake Champlain, two small groups of officers rode from the cantonment toward their rendezvous at Odletown just over the Canadian border. Arriving in the chill dawn, the participants waited while their seconds conferred and measured the ground. Then everything was ready. The duelists stood facing each other at a distance of twenty-four feet, their pistols primed and pointed down, their seconds stationed where they could ensure adherence to the rules. The count began. Atkinson and Manigault fired and missed simultaneously. As the acrid smoke dissipated, the seconds conferred; there would be another exchange. Again they carefully loaded the weapons. On the command "fire," Manigault fired slightly faster than Atkinson. His shot was low, but it smashed into Atkinson's right leg "slightly below the knee . . . severely fracturing the bone." Atkinson's second shot went wild, and the accompanying surgeon hurried to examine his wound. The doctor placed him in a carriage, and the group returned to the army hospital at Plattsburg.[17]

For the first time in his military career, Henry Atkinson had done something to distinguish himself from the host of practically nameless junior officers in the American army. The duel, however, further blocked his attempt to join his new unit. On May 11 he reported his plight, assuring the Secretary of War that he would be "up in four weeks" and then hoped to travel to his new post. Atkinson refused to discuss his duel except to blame Major John E. Wool, who having "raised so much strife in the army, although not immediately concerned, was at the bottom of this unfortunate affair."[18]

No sooner was Atkinson's duel reported than the Adjutant General of the Army issued an order reaffirming an old and usually

[17] *Plattsburg* (New York) *Republican*, May 14, 1814, quoted in *Buffalo* (New York) *Gazette*, May 31, 1814.

[18] Atkinson to Armstrong, May 11, 1814, Letters Received, AGO.

overlooked army policy which made dueling punishable by dismissal.[19] Two weeks later General Izard relayed an order from the War Department directing that the principals and seconds in the Atkinson duel be arrested and ordered to Greenbush, New York, for trial as soon as Atkinson recovered.[20]

On June 6, Atkinson learned that he was under military arrest; but since he was still in the hospital at Plattsburg, this proved little imposition. In late June after he recovered, Atkinson wrote to the War Department, asking to be released from his arrest and, if possible, from the necessity of standing trial. He acknowledged his action as a violation of military law, but pleaded for release on the grounds that his act was similar to that taken by many officers without prosecution. "Indeed," he claimed, "in some of the divisions of the army in which I have served, this practice of settling private disputes has been indirectly recommended (& here sanctioned) in preference to preparing military tribunals [for] them." Finally, he acknowledged the "alarming extent" to which dueling had spread in the army, but countered that prior to the general order of May 20 "there existed no grounds for an honorable excuse for deviating from a custom so long established." His thinking reflected early training in North Carolina. There he had adopted the social code of his contemporaries under which a man of leadership and pride had to accept a challenge—thus the duel.[21] His plea for clemency must have fallen on receptive ears since no record of a court-martial or board of inquiry dealing with the incident exists.

Once recovered from his wound, he set out for New London and his duties as commander of the Thirty-seventh Infantry. Moving from Plattsburg, Henry Atkinson once again left an area which had remained peaceful. In late August, after Atkinson left, Sir George Prevost led a British and Canadian army south from Montreal to Lake Champlain. There on August 31 he met the force commanded by General Alexander Macomb and drove the Americans south to

[19] *New York Herald*, June 1, 1814.

[20] Izard to Ninian Pinkney, June 3, 1814, Letters Received, AGO.

[21] Atkinson to Armstrong, June 24, 1814, Letters Received, SW.

Plattsburg by September 6. Prevost waited for his naval squadron to take command of the lake, but on September 11 the American forces under Commodore Thomas MacDonough defeated the British fleet, and Prevost retreated to Canada.

Atkinson arrived at Fort Trumbull, his new post, on July 19. After a brief inspection he introduced several modifications that brought the regiment closer to his ideal. He found the recruiting service in a state of confusion, and to correct this he "formed the detachments that were in [the] garrison into companies, selected a proper proportion of officers for their command, & designated the supernumeraries for the recruiting service." These extra officers he planned to send recruiting as soon as more funds arrived from the paymaster. In spite of his actions, he felt the garrison was "in wretched order." He was not discouraged, however, for he commented, "the materials of the Regiment is . . . of good stuff."[22]

At New London, Atkinson came within the Second Military District commanded by General Thomas H. Cushing. The two officers had served together before, and although Cushing was a Wilkinson supporter, they managed to co-operate. While Atkinson supervised the organization of his new regiment, the American Army began a summer offensive into Canada. By mid-September, when they withdrew from Fort Erie, the last American offensive of the war had ended. The British, however, began a major counter-offensive which continued until the Battle of New Orleans in January, 1815. These battles had little effect on Henry Atkinson in his out-of-the-way post at New London. His task was to build a strong regiment.

With his orders of appointment as commander of the Thirty-seventh Regiment, Atkinson received instructions "to take charge of the recruiting service" of his regiment. Although he had been responsible for raising his own company when he first entered the army in 1808, the pressure of wartime needs had altered recruiting

[22] New London, *Connecticut Gazette*, July 20, 1814; Atkinson to Armstrong, July 19, 1814, Letters Received, AGO; Atkinson to Armstrong, July 26, 1814, *ibid.*

procedures. Now, one officer, not usually the regimental commander, acted as the recruiting superintendent for each regiment. Only two weeks after reaching New London, he received a communication from Major John R. Bell, then acting adjutant general, in which Bell noted that Atkinson was violating War Department regulations which prohibited his acting as both regimental commander and chief recruiting officer.[23]

Bell's letter angered Atkinson. "I am not a little astonished to observe that I am charged with a violation of the recruiting regulations," he replied. Noting his earlier orders from the War Department, he commented, "I presume you were not aware of the orders . . . or you would not have charged me with so high a military offence." His retort quickly brought an apology from Bell and a plaintive remark that the Adjutant General's Office faced much confusion when the recruiting officers "are changed without authority or knowledge of this Department."[24]

In September, 1814, increasing British offenses caused the departmental commander to order that defenses be improved and that forts be immediately placed in the best possible condition. The New London townspeople co-operated with the troops in rebuilding both Fort Trumbull and Fort Griswold across the river at Groton. In addition, they built two new batteries, one on each side of the harbor and "a line of handsome and efficient breast works" near the southern end of the town.[25]

During the last months of the war, Colonel Henry Atkinson remained at Fort Trumbull, supervising recruiting for his regiment and preparing the fort for defense. Compared to the New York–Canadian border, his duty at New London was certainly less exciting. His year at Plattsburg under Generals Hampton and Wilkinson had given him experience in planning large troop movements and

[23] John R. Bell to Atkinson, Aug. 2, 1814, Letters Sent, AGO, Vol. 3½.

[24] Atkinson to Bell, Aug. 8, 1814, Letters Received, AGO; Bell to Atkinson, Aug. 15, 1814, Letters Sent, AGO, Vol. 3½.

[25] Second Military Dept., Orders, Sept. 12, 1814, Post Revolutionary Commands, Vol. 46, AGO; *Connecticut Gazette*, Oct. 26, 1814.

an opportunity to participate in the discussions and operations of the campaigns. Now his military outlook was limited by the bounds of one fort.

When the war ended in 1815, Atkinson, along with hundreds of other officers, faced the prospect of being released from the army in a few months. His original appointment in 1808 was for five years, but had been extended because of the war. Now, thirty-three-years old and with a war record that could not compare with that of innumerable contemporaries, he had ample reason to worry about his army career.

During the War of 1812, those officers who usually received the fastest promotions were those who had been in the battle areas. In this, Henry Atkinson was unfortunate. He had been in at least three areas where major battles were fought, but always at the wrong time. He left New Orleans in 1813, but the battle there was not until January, 1815. In 1813 he visited Sackets Harbor, but the battle there took place the following year. He left Plattsburg only two months before the battle there. Thus, throughout the war Atkinson missed the battles. He spent most of his time as an administrative officer. When he did have a personal command, he was simply in the wrong areas to have made any reputation for himself.

IV. Peace and the Move West—1815-19

BETWEEN 1815 AND 1818, except for the "invasion" of Florida, no war or major emergency interrupted the routine duties of the army. This period was also one of quiet for Henry Atkinson. During it he unknowingly prepared himself and his regiment for participation in the Yellowstone Expedition of 1818–19. That venture took him and the Sixth Infantry west to Council Bluffs and resulted in new duties, new associates, and increased responsibilities. His move west, to an important command, changed the course of his military career. At Plattsburg he was a practically unknown army colonel, but his work at Council Bluffs and, subsequently, at St. Louis placed him in a position in which he played a prominent role in the history of the West.

The Yellowstone Expedition was organized, in part, because of the Indian depredations in the Mississippi and Missouri river valleys. Western newspaper editors claimed that British traders and officials were responsible for these attacks, and cried, "End British domination of the American West." To accomplish this, in 1815, Secretary of War James Monroe proposed locating military posts on the upper Mississippi near the Canadian border. A year later William Clark, governor of Missouri Territory, suggested establishing a post on the Platte River. Both were ignored.[1]

[1] Edgar B. Wesley, "A Still Larger View of the So-Called Yellowstone Expedition," *North Dakota Historical Quarterly*, Vol. V (July, 1931), 219–20.

On March 16, 1818, Secretary of War John C. Calhoun, then an ardent nationalist, took the first step in what became a broad plan for the employment of the military in the West. He wanted an army post at the mouth of the Yellowstone River and ordered preparations to establish one. The resulting project came to be called the Yellowstone Expedition. After the troops and supplies had been collected, he changed his plans. It was then too late in the season for the men to reach the Yellowstone, so on August 22 he suggested to General Andrew Jackson that an intermediate post be built at the Mandan Indian villages in central North Dakota. By October, Calhoun decided that a second post, located at the junction of the St. Peters and Mississippi rivers, would also be useful. He then proposed a third post on the St. Croix River. This would complete a cordon of military forts stretching from central North Dakota to the Great Lakes.[2]

During the winter of 1818–19, Calhoun suggested that a temporary post be built either at Council Bluffs or on the Great Bend of the Missouri.[3] Thus by the end of winter, Calhoun's idea of a single post at the mouth of the Yellowstone had grown into a plan for a number of forts so located as to wrest the northwest from the influence of British traders. What was originally to be the Yellowstone Expedition proliferated into three separate expeditions: the Missouri Expedition, the Mississippi Expedition, and a scientific expedition under Major Stephen H. Long.

One newspaper proclaimed "there is no measure, which has been adopted by the present administration, that has received such universal commendation." A St. Louis editor remarked, "The future historian of America will delight to trace" the improvement in literature and science, the advancement of prosperity, and the end of the Indian menace which would result from the Yellowstone

[2] John C. Calhoun to Andrew Jackson, Aug. 22, 1818, in *The Correspondence of John C. Calhoun* (ed. by J. F. Jameson), II, 138; Calhoun to Jacob Brown, Oct. 17, 1818, *ibid.*, 147–49.

[3] Calhoun to Jackson, Mar. 6, 1819, *ibid.*, 152–53; Calhoun to Brown, Mar. 6, 1819, Jacob Brown Letter Books, Library of Congress (hereafter LC).

Expedition. It would, he continued, advance geographic knowledge of the Missouri River Valley, increase western emigration, protect the fur trade, and open communications between the Mississippi and the Pacific. Other papers, although not so ecstatic, joined the chorus.[4] These newspaper accounts tended to confuse the public. By continuing to refer to all three projects collectively as the Yellowstone Expedition, they obscured the fact that three related, but separate, western expeditions were launched in 1818 and 1819.

During the spring and summer of 1818, President Monroe, Secretary of War John C. Calhoun, and Generals Andrew Jackson and Jacob Brown, then commanding the two divisions of the army, exchanged ideas on the management of the expeditions. At first they decided that Colonel Thomas A. Smith, commanding the Rifle Regiment on the Mississippi, should lead the expedition up the Missouri River. Smith gathered his troops at Bellefontaine, a post four miles up the Missouri from the Mississippi and nearly twenty miles north of St. Louis. There he reorganized the men into three companies of one hundred men each, but wrote that he "almost dispair[ed] of the Commanding officer being enabled to reach his point of destination, without suffering a very material dimunition of the effective strength of the command . . ." Another officer echoed these sentiments. He believed that because of their "slow and arduous march" the troops would not reach the mouth of the Yellowstone that season. Nearly one third of the men would have to be released when partly up the Missouri because their enlistments would have expired; the remainder were mere recruits and "of such a description as will never answer the purpose."[5]

Nevertheless, on August 30, 1818, the First Battalion of the Rifle Regiment, consisting of 347 men and ten officers, boarded a fleet of ten keelboats and pushed away from Bellefontaine to begin

[4] St. Louis, *Missouri Gazette and Public Advertizer*, Apr. 21, 1819; *Daily National Intelligencer*, June 30, 1819; *Niles Register*, Sept. 4, 1818; *Ibid.*, Apr. 23, 1819.

[5] Thomas A. Smith to Calhoun, July 29, 1818, Thomas A. Smith Papers, State Historical Society of Missouri, Columbia (hereafter SHSM).

the journey.[6] Colonel Talbot Chambers, given immediate command of the expedition by Colonel Smith, left the flotilla shortly after it began moving up the Missouri and placed Captain Wyly Martin, the senior captain, in command. With some difficulty Martin and his inexperienced boatmen traveled up the river to Isle des Vaches or Cow Island where the troops disembarked and built temporary winter quarters. The journey, described as "a very fatiguing and arduous march of nearly 60 days," brought the men to the island located about twenty miles north of Leavenworth, Kansas.

Back in Washington, Calhoun worried about possible conflict with the Indians, and the experiences of the riflemen at Cow Island showed this concern to have a real basis. Bands of Indians robbed the soldiers of horses, guns, boats, and food and also attacked white traders and messengers along the river.[7] For these offenses, Captain Martin ordered several Pawnee chiefs and braves held in chains until they agreed to refrain from their molestations. Late in December, Calhoun wrote Jackson, "You, no doubt, are aware of the great importance I attach to the [Missouri] expedition. As much of its Success will depend upon the Commander, I have to request that the ablest and most experienced officer of the rifle regiment, be selected for that Command."[8]

In January, 1819, Calhoun reiterated that "the command requires great prudence and skill" for success. Early in February he decided to appoint a more experienced officer than Captain Martin to lead the expedition. The choice fell upon Colonel Henry Atkinson. On February 8, 1819, the Adjutant General ordered Atkinson to prepare his regiment for the journey to St. Louis. Shortly after this, Quartermaster General Thomas S. Jesup told Atkinson that Calhoun had selected the Sixth Regiment, the new designation of

[6] Thomas Kavanaugh, "Journal of the Advance Corps of the Military Branch of the Yellowstone Expedition," entry, Aug. 30, 1818, Coe Collection, Yale University Library (hereafter Kavanaugh Journal, YUL).

[7] Kavanaugh Journal, entries, Oct. 28, Nov. 1, and Nov. 8–9, 1818, YUL.

[8] Calhoun to Jackson, Dec. 28, 1818, in *Correspondence*, II, 150–51.

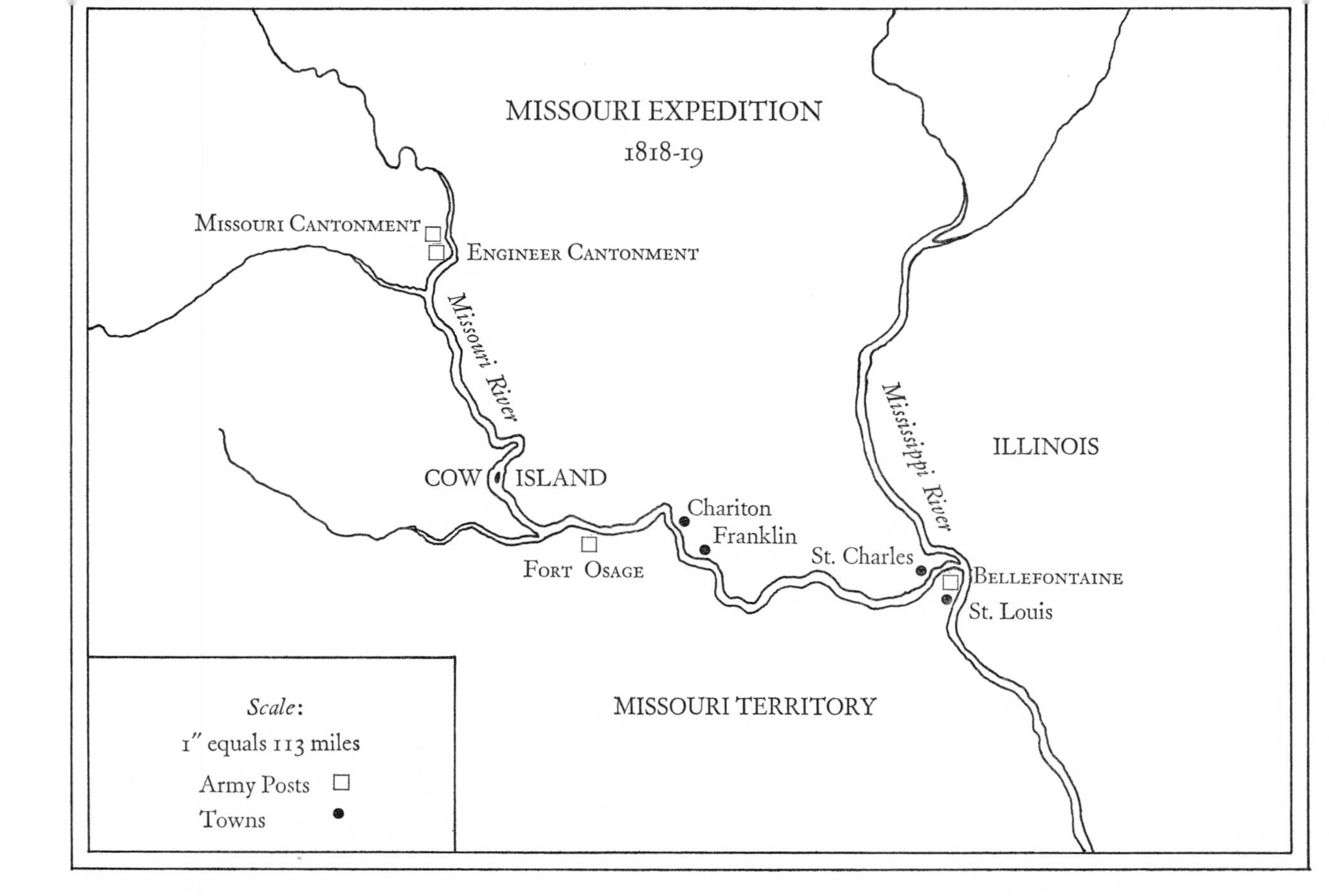
MISSOURI EXPEDITION
1818-19
Missouri Cantonment
Engineer Cantonment
Missouri River
COW ISLAND
Fort Osage
Chariton
Franklin
St. Charles
Bellefontaine
St. Louis
Mississippi River
ILLINOIS
MISSOURI TERRITORY
Scale:
1″ equals 113 miles
Army Posts
Towns

Atkinson's command, because he thought "it was one of the best in service, [and because of] his entire confidence in yourself and his wish to place you in an important command."[9] Thus, Henry Atkinson, a bachelor of thirty-seven, received command of the Missouri Expedition, a command that took him west, provided him with experience in leading and co-ordinating large numbers of men, and resulted in his promotion to brigadier general the next year.

Between 1815 and 1819, Henry Atkinson had served as a regimental commander. He had survived the army reduction after the War of 1812, retaining both his rank and the command of an infantry regiment. In 1815, Congress had passed a bill that authorized a regular army of ten thousand men.[10] The new reduction meant that of the forty-seven infantry regiments then in service, only eight remained. The reduced army also included an Engineer Corps, an Ordnance Corps, one regiment of light artillery, and one rifle regiment. The reorganization law established two major administrative units, the Northern and the Southern Divisions. These in turn were subdivided into nine military departments, five in the North and four in the South.[11]

On April 8, 1815, President Madison appointed a board of generals, consisting of Andrew Jackson, Jacob Brown, Winfield Scott, Edmund P. Gaines, Alexander Macomb, and Eleazar Ripley, to manage the reduction of the army. They appointed themselves to the six generalships and then turned to the task of deciding which officers should be retained.[12]

Atkinson had served with Winfield Scott since first entering the army in 1808, and they were friends of long standing. In addition, he had served with General Gaines in Louisiana and New

[9] Thomas S. Jesup to Atkinson, Feb. 11, 1819, Letters Sent, Vol. I, Record Group 92, Records of the Office of the Quartermaster General, National Archives (hereafter QMG).

[10] *U.S. Statutes at Large*, III, 224–25.

[11] Raphael B. Thian, *Some Notes Illustrating the Military Geography of the United States*, 7.

[12] James W. Silver, *Edmund Pendleton Gaines, Frontier General*, 52–53; Charles W. Elliott, *Winfield Scott: The Soldier and the Man*, 192–93.

York, and as inspector general during 1813 and 1814 he had met Generals Macomb and Brown. Because most of the board knew him, Atkinson was in a favorable position to remain in the army. In addition, as inspector general his strict attention to details, accounts, and proper record-keeping may have impressed his superiors, particularly at a time when competence and a willingness to face stacks of paper work were not common. Certainly neither his rank as forty-sixth in a list of forty-nine colonels nor his mediocre record during the war particularly recommended him.

Apparently he received special consideration, for on May 17, 1815, when the Board of Generals completed its list of officers to be retained in the army, Atkinson's name was ninth among the eleven remaining colonels. He was given command of the Sixth Infantry Regiment, to be reorganized by merging units and men of the Eleventh, Twenty-fifth, Twenty-seventh, Twenty-ninth, and Thirty-seventh Regiments. These units were all in New England or New York State, and the new Sixth was assigned to the forts in the New York City harbor.[13]

When the army reorganization was completed, the War Department shifted the Sixth Infantry from New York City to Plattsburg, New York. Atkinson's regiment, along with the Second Infantry stationed at Sackets Harbor, provided the defensive force along the New York State–Canadian border.[14] There, for the next three years, Atkinson drilled the regiment, supervised the work on several military roads and on the fortifications at Rouse's Point on Lake Champlain just south of the Canadian border, and carried on the routine activities of peacetime army life. He worked to make life pleasant for the enlisted men and officers in his command. He started a regimental library, enlarged the band, and proposed various changes in the uniform to make it more colorful and yet more serviceable. Atkinson also tried to help individual soldiers in his regiment. For example, one of his men, Private Thomas Clayton, upon his discharge, after serving for years as a "faithful soldier,"

[13] Jacob Brown, Orders, June 1, 1815, quoted in *Buffalo Gazette*, June 13, 1815.
[14] Atkinson to Adjutant General, Jan. 5, 1816, Letters Received, AGO.

was entitled to a land warrant for his enlistments and service. Now an old man, he could not travel to Washington nor afford to pay an agent to obtain the warrant for him. Therefore, Atkinson sent Clayton's discharge and application for a warrant to Adjutant General Daniel Parker, a personal friend. He asked Parker to "have the kindness to let one of [his] young men apply at the proper office and obtain upon the discharge the necessary certificates and warrant." Then he asked Parker to return the papers to him so that he might be sure that Clayton got them.[15] In spite of Atkinson's efforts, however, peacetime army life offered few inducements for the enlisted men, and desertion and drunkenness remained difficulties.

Atkinson's regiment drilled enough to pass the periodic inspections with high ratings and worked on road construction. In October, 1818, Major General Jacob Brown, commander of the Northern Division of the army, found the road work excellent and complimented the regiment that "although [it had been] devoted exclusively to labor for the previous three months, its appearance conformed to the high reputation it has always sustained."[16] Two months later, he again praised Atkinson's command in a letter to John C. Calhoun, the new secretary of war. The Sixth Infantry had won a reputation for outstanding work. Perhaps it is not surprising that Calhoun chose it to take part in the Yellowstone Expedition of 1819.

In February, 1819, Atkinson received orders directing him and his troops to St. Louis. He assumed the trip would lead him up the Missouri. "It is necessary for me to premise the probability of our destination being high up the Missouri," he wrote to Jesup. If this were the case, he asked, would it not be "all together best" to use steamboats for the trip? These boats would be more economical, faster, and they would "save all that fatigue & indisposition incedential to troops who have to be on the water in Barges for several months; well exemplified in our ascending the Mississippi in 1809."

15 Atkinson to Parker, Jan. 24, 1817, Dreer Collection, HSP.

16 Fifth Military Dept., Orders, Oct. 8, 1818, Post Revolutionary Commands, Vol. 75, AGO.

By the time he suggested using steamboats, however, the contracts for transportation had been let to transport the troops to St. Louis.[17]

On March 29, Atkinson led his regiment of nearly 500 men and a detachment of recruits for the Fifth Infantry from Plattsburg. They marched south and passed through Burlington, Vermont, two days later. They continued south toward Albany, where they arrived on March 27. There the officers met with General Jacob Brown to complete plans for the move to Pittsburgh, and Atkinson himself prepared for his trip to Washington. General Brown ordered Atkinson to send the Sixth Regiment overland from Albany, southwest to Olean on the Allegheny River in southwestern New York State. There they would board transports and drop downstream to Pittsburgh.[18] But a combination of bad weather and poor roads forced the troops to continue south by water to New York City, where they boarded transports and sailed to Philadelphia. From there they marched across Pennsylvania to Pittsburgh.[19]

In the meantime, Colonel Atkinson traveled to Washington. Calhoun was not there but had left explicit instructions. He assigned Atkinson to command the Ninth Military Department which included the states of Kentucky, Tennessee, and Illinois and Missouri Territory.[20] Calhoun directed him to "extend kindness and protection" to all Americans lawfully residing or trading within the area of his command. Finally, he ordered Atkinson to build a strong military post before moving against any foreigners illegally trading in American territory. Calhoun stressed that Atkinson's most important single task involved providing for the "permanent security of our frontier."[21]

Atkinson rejoined his regiment at Philadelphia on April 10, but then continued west ahead of the troops to make sure that the supplies and transportation would be ready when they arrived at

17 Atkinson to Jesup, Feb. 23, 1819, Consolidated File, Atkinson, QMG.

18 Brown to Calhoun, Mar. 24, 1819, Brown Letter Books, LC.

19 Atkinson to Jackson, Apr. 17, 1819, Andrew Jackson Papers, 1st series, Vol. 51–52.

20 Thian, *Military Geography*, 48.

21 Calhoun to Atkinson, Mar. 27, 1819, *Correspondence*, II, 159–60.

Pittsburgh. He arrived there five days later, and found that the contractor had failed to assemble either boats or supplies. Disappointed because of the contractor's failure, yet relieved to have learned of it before his troops arrived, Atkinson assigned the task of getting both supplies and transportation to the Quartermaster General's agents at Pittsburgh. In spite of this delay, he still hoped to get the troops to St. Louis by the end of May.

It was not until May 8 that keelboats were ready and loaded for the troops. These shallow draft craft were about one hundred feet long and twenty feet wide. A low, box-like structure covered most of the deck and acted as the cargo hold. The boats could be propelled by oars, poles, and sails. Late that afternoon the soldiers boarded the flotilla of nine keelboats and pushed away from shore at Pittsburgh. The expedition sailed and poled downstream to Cincinnati in a week. Strong headwinds impeded their progress, and Atkinson now hoped to get the troops to St. Louis sometime during the first week of June.[22]

When the flotilla reached the mouth of the Ohio River, Atkinson boarded a passing steamboat for St. Louis. On June 1 he arrived there and relieved Brigadier General Daniel Bissell of the command of the Ninth Military Department. The flotilla arrived at St. Louis on June 7 and moved north to Bellefontaine on the Missouri River the following day.[23] The camp, built in 1810, consisted of a hollow square of log buildings resting on masonry foundations and perched on top of a steep bluff about seventy-five feet above the river. After the men disembarked, unloaded their possessions, and climbed the steep bank, Atkinson held a post formation. Expressing "his entire satisfaction, of the conduct of the 6th Regt. during its long & fatiguing march," he continued, "altho so much has been done, there still remains, further duty, to close the march." Their destination that year was Council Bluffs, near

22 Atkinson to Calhoun, May 8, 1819, Letters Received, AGO; Atkinson to Jackson, May 15, 1819, Jackson Papers, 1st series, Vol. 53–54.

23 Orders, June 1, 1819, Ninth Military Department, Orders and Letters, Vol. 93, Record Group 98, Records of United States Army Commands (hereafter USAC); Atkinson to Jackson, June 7, 1819, Jackson Papers, 1st series, Vol. 53–54.

present Fort Calhoun, Nebraska, a journey of another three months up the Missouri.[24]

In St. Louis, Atkinson encountered countless delays, which eventually frustrated this attempt to reach the Yellowstone in 1819. One continuing difficulty faced by army commanders was that of obtaining supplies on time and in usable condition. Henry Atkinson found this, one obstacle he could not overcome. "Colonel" James Johnson of Kentucky held contracts with the government to transport the ordnance, clothing, and medical supplies from Pittsburgh to St. Louis, to furnish food for the troops, and to transport men and supplies up the Missouri River.[25] Johnson, however, lacked capital, depended upon faulty steamboats, and was in debt to the Bank of Missouri.

His contract called for the food to be delivered at St. Louis between March 1 and 21, 1819, and for the steamboats to be there by March 1. He was two months late with both. Once he reached St. Louis, the directors of the Bank of Missouri tried to seize the boats and supplies for his debts. The bankers claimed Johnson owed them nearly $50,000. He landed his boats on the Illinois side of the Mississippi about fifteen miles north of St. Louis to prevent the sheriff from taking possession of his property.[26] Johnson unloaded the food on the Illinois side of the river, and the military storekeeper, Thomas Hempstead, inspected it. The inspection caused considerable delay because Hempstead and his assistants made daily trips from St. Louis, and temporary shelters had to be erected for the supplies. Hempstead refused to accept any of the meat until it was inspected, resalted and repacked. Johnson protested both the inspection and forced repacking, but to no avail.[27]

[24] Atkinson, Orders, June 8, 1819, Stephen W. Kearny Papers, Missouri Historical Society, St. Louis (hereafter MHS).

[25] 16 Cong., 1 sess., *House Exec. Doc. No. 110*, 246; ASP:MA, II, 324–25.

[26] James Johnson to Richard M. Johnson, May 23, 1819, in "The Life and Letters of James Johnson of Kentucky" (ed. by James A. Padgett), *Register of Kentucky State Historical Society*, Vol. XXXV (Oct., 1937), 320–22.

[27] 16 Cong., 1 sess., *House Exec. Doc. No. 110*, 293; Thomas Hempstead Letter Book, May–September, 1819, YUL.

While waiting for Colonel Johnson to repack the food and get the steamboats loaded, Atkinson spent some time examining the paddle wheels on the steamboats. He had some of his troops construct paddle wheels for the keelboats. On June 27 he loaded a boat equipped with a paddle wheel and made a trial run from Bellefontaine a few miles up the Missouri and back. The paddle wheels were successful, at least according to one of the local editors who claimed, "this improvement which he [Atkinson] has put on these barges will prove of vast importance to the government, both in expedition and saving of expense." Final preparations for the expedition stopped these experiments at that time, but Atkinson resumed them during the winter of 1823–24 when he modified the paddle wheels and used them during the Yellowstone Expedition of 1825.[28]

In his capacity as commander of the Ninth Military Department, Henry Atkinson also supervised preparations to send men and supplies to the Fifth Infantry, then moving up the Mississippi to Fort Crawford and St. Peters. By June 19, Colonel Johnson had not furnished all the food or steamboats that he had promised. Atkinson chafed at the continued delay; he wanted to reach Council Bluffs in time to get his command settled before winter. Irritated by Johnson's inaction, Atkinson threatened to "have six month's supply [of food] completed by the commissary" officer and decided to "proceed with the three Steam Boats already [there] & four of our Keels, in six or seven days."[29]

Johnson reacted to this decision and bought enough provisions for five months. This, Atkinson claimed, was the minimum amount of food necessary before he could safely lead his force west from Bellefontaine. Once the provisions arrived, he was ready to move. On July 4 and 5, Atkinson had the equipment and men loaded on three steamboats and several keelboats, and at noon on July 5 the flotilla left Bellefontaine and began moving up the Missouri River.

[28] *Missouri Gazette and Public Advertizer*, June 30, 1819.

[29] Atkinson to Jackson, June 19, 1819, Jackson Papers, 1st series, Vol. 53–54; *St. Louis Enquirer*, June 23, 1819.

After a "very slow" start the steamboats all ran aground, hardly out of sight from their point of embarkation. When Atkinson saw that the men were unable to free the steamers, he decided the flotilla could not be kept together without great difficulty. He ordered each boat to fend for itself, at least as far as Cantonment Martin at Cow Island some 420 miles farther up the river. He remained with the steamboats another day and then returned to St. Louis, persuaded that "these Boats in the present state of the water cannot navigate the Missouri." Disgusted, Atkinson decided to substitute the slower but more dependable keelboats.[30]

When, only three days after the expedition left Bellefontaine, the steamboats had proved unable to navigate the Missouri, Atkinson complained that only the Rifle Regiment, sent ahead in keelboats two weeks earlier, would be able to reach Council Bluffs in 1819. The infantry would probably have to remain at Cantonment Martin on Cow Island for the winter.[31]

On July 12, Atkinson and Quartermaster General Thomas Jesup, who had come to St. Louis to help Atkinson with the final preparations for the expedition, left St. Louis and started west along the Missouri River on horseback, so that they could "more readily . . . supply any deficiency that may occur in transportation by the failure of the steamboats."[32]

By mid-July the expedition presented a sorry spectacle. Half of the Rifle Regiment already stationed at Cantonment Martin was spread from Fort Osage to Council Bluffs hunting for food. The three steamboats broke down, ran aground, were relaunched, and moved upriver at a snail's pace. The troops with supplies in the keelboats pushed along laboriously toward Cantonment Martin. If

[30] William D. Hubbell, "The First Steamboats on the Missouri" (ed. by Vivian K. McLarty), *Missouri Historical Review*, Vol. LI (July, 1957), 377; John O'Fallon to T. A. Smith, July 7, 1819, Smith Papers, SHSM; Atkinson to Calhoun, July 11, 1819, in 16 Cong., 1 sess., *House Exec. Doc. No. 110*, 161–62.

[31] O'Fallon to Smith, July 7, 1819, Smith Papers, SHSM.

[32] Atkinson to Calhoun, July 11, 1819, in 16 Cong., 1 sess., *House Exec. Doc. No. 110*, 161–62; O'Fallon to Dennis Fitzhugh, July 11, 1819, John O'Fallon Papers, MHS.

Atkinson was discouraged by the slow progress up the Missouri, he kept his feelings hidden. Richard M. Johnson wrote to Calhoun: "My brother [James Johnson] thinks that Col. Atkinson's presence was most fortunate. He never desponded, and his uniform confidence in my brother alone has sustained him."[33] Atkinson arrived at Franklin, nearly 180 river miles from St. Louis, on July 26. The next morning an early messenger brought welcome news. Lieutenant John Clark, Jr., the commissary officer at St. Louis, reported that Colonel Johnson had "nearly met the demands" made upon him for supplying Atkinson's force. In fact, by the time Atkinson read the message, the food had already been inspected, repacked, and loaded, and was on the way up the river. "I feel greatly relieved by the consumation of this event," he wrote, "& hope we shall yet get along pretty well."[34]

Atkinson decided to make Franklin his temporary base of operations and remained there until August 13, when he rode to Fort Osage. From there he traveled to Cantonment Martin, arriving on August 31. The next day he assumed command of all troops of the expedition. After Paymaster Thomas Biddle inspected, mustered, and paid the troops, they unloaded and repaired the transports and then repacked them in preparation for their move to Council Bluffs, which was another 230 miles away.[35]

On September 2, Henry Atkinson met with his subordinate officers to plan the final move to Council Bluffs. His manner and leadership gave confidence to some of them. Lieutenant Colonel Willoughby Morgan wrote that if the expedition were "permitted to proceed next year, his [Atkinson's] views of the course we should pursue appears to me to be very correct; and will meet with the approbation of all the officers who have acquired any experience on this river."[36]

[33] Johnson to Calhoun, July 26, 1819, in 16 Cong., 1 sess., *House Exec. Doc. No. 110*, 232–33.

[34] Atkinson to Jesup, July 27, 1819, Consolidated File, Atkinson, QMG.

[35] Kavanaugh Journal, entries, Aug. 31 to Sept. 4, 1819, YUL; Atkinson, Ninth Military Dept., Orders, Sept. 3, 1819, Vol. 93, USAC.

[36] Morgan to Smith, Sept. 3, 1819, Smith Papers, SHSM.

After the meeting Atkinson and his aides prepared specific instructions for the brigade that was to continue upriver. The flotilla was to include sixteen keelboats, six for the Rifle Regiment, one as Atkinson's flagship, six for the Sixth Infantry, one for the sutler, and two supply boats. Atkinson gave the commanding officer of each boat a list of drum-beat, rocket, and swivel-gun signals to be used throughout each day. At 12:30 P.M. on September 5, the troops assembled and boarded their respective boats, and Atkinson ordered the flotilla into the mainstream of the Missouri.[37]

From Cantonment Martin the expedition moved farther into Indian country. Each morning at sunrise the troops awakened to reveille beaten by the Sixth Infantry Band drum and fife unit; half an hour later, a rocket fired from Atkinson's keelboat signaled the time to sail. The boat crews maintained one hundred yard intervals, closing to within fifty yards of each other only at mealtimes or in case of accident. To avoid surprise attack, Atkinson used squads of riflemen as flank guards along the river banks. The first halt each morning came at eight o'clock for breakfast. An hour later at the bugler's signal the boats again pulled away from shore. They traveled until noon when a signal from the swivel gun on Atkinson's flagship announced a halt for dinner. Again the bugler signaled the next move, and an hour before sundown the swivel on the flagship sounded a halt for the day. In the evening the troops moved their boats close to each other and drew them up to the riverbank. They pitched their tents parallel to the river, facing away from the water. The end units faced to right and left to protect the flanks. A few guards patrolled the shore, while details of guards stood their posts eighty paces beyond the line of tents. Atkinson also ordered that men be stationed on each of the boats, and he held a nightly inspection of soldiers' weapons. Thus the little army moved up the Missouri.[38]

When dense morning fogs obscured the vision of the men pull-

[37] Kavanaugh Journal, entry, Sept. 5, 1819, YUL; Atkinson, Ninth Military Dept., Orders, Sept. 5, 1819, Vol. 93, USAC.

[38] Atkinson, Ninth Military Dept., Orders, Sept. 4, 1819, Vol. 93, USAC.

ing the tow ropes or cordelles, Atkinson ordered a squad of eight men to act as trail-blazers, removing brush and helping clear a path along the riverbank for the towers. On September 15, Atkinson halted the expedition for a day to allow the men time to rest, do their laundry, and bring in fresh game. During the following weeks, as they continued up the river, the hunters furnished wild goose, deer, bear, honey, hazelnuts, and fruit to supplement the regular army diet.[39]

The expedition proceeded without any major accidents, but minor incidents occurred. On September 18, Lieutenant Daniel Keith fainted, fell overboard, and was nearly drowned before his companions rescued him. Three days later, Captain James S. Gray steered a boat under some overhanging tree branches and broke the yardarm from the mast. Another boat rammed a sunken log and had to stop for repairs. After one of the privates accidentally shot and killed himself, Atkinson banned any "discharging of Fire arms either in camp or within four hundred yards of the lines or from the Flotilla, except by special permission . . ." He commanded his officers not only to enforce this order, but also to "implicitly obey it" themselves.[40]

Early on the morning of September 29, the expedition reached Council Bluffs. Major Long's men had already built their winter quarters, called Engineer Cantonment, about one mile north of Manuel Lisa's trading post. As soon as the keelboats arrived, Atkinson appointed a board of officers to "examine the adjacent country and report the most eligible spot for Cantoning." The boats were to remain loaded until his officers had selected a suitable site. On October 2, Atkinson received the report of the board. He ordered his men back into the boats, and the flotilla again moved upstream to the site selected for the camp. Twelve miles north of

[39] T. F. Smith, Ninth Military Dept., Orders, Sept. 9, 1819, Vol. 93, USAC; Kavanaugh Journal, entries, Sept. 15–30, 1819, YUL.

[40] Smith, Ninth Military Dept., Orders, Sept. 9, 1819, Vol. 93, USAC; Kavanaugh Journal, entries, Sept. 18, 21, and 24, 1819, YUL.

Long's camp, at a cottonwood grove on "an extensive riverbottom" along the Nebraska side of the river, about three miles above Council Bluffs, the keelboats pulled to shore. The first part of the journey was over.[41]

After reveille the next morning, the troops cleared a space for their tents near the river, unloaded the keelboats, and erected a temporary camp. On October 4 they started work on barracks for winter quarters. Some officers organized work parties to fell, trim, and saw the cottonwoods along the river bottom. Another group found limestone that they began to quarry for foundations. Others organized hunting parties that crossed the nearby prairies, although grass fires drove away all the game but a few ducks and geese.[42]

The troops constructed officers quarters, barracks, munitions magazines, a hospital, and storage buildings. During the construction, Atkinson directed the squads to preserve "the Elms within the lines marked for the Cantonment & those on the outside within two hundred yards . . . with the exception of such as may interfere with the line of Barracks."[43] Within two weeks the buildings were ready to be roofed, and a large supply of timbers and boards for siding and roofing already lay in piles about the camp. Situated on a level, low stretch of river-bottom land, the walls of the fort arose sixteen feet above the surrounding terrain and formed a square 520 feet on each side. This palisade, made of heavy logs and pierced with loopholes for musketry and cannon, served also as the outside wall of the barracks. At the center of each side stood a twenty-foot tower with a second story and a platform for three cannons to cover all angles for that side of the fort. Beneath these, the soldiers constructed heavy ten-foot doors. The barracks rooms themselves were twenty feet square with a fireplace in each room. There were loopholes for musketry and small arms in the outer walls, and,

41 *Ibid.*, Sept. 29 to Oct. 2, 1819, YUL; Atkinson to Calhoun, Oct. 3, 1819, in 16 Cong., 1 sess., *House Exec. Doc. No. 110*, 168.

42 Atkinson to Jackson, Oct. 3, 1819, Jackson Papers, 1st series, Vol. 54; Kavanaugh Journal, entries, Oct. 4–20, 1819, YUL.

43 Smith, Ninth Military Dept., Orders, Oct. 7, 1819, Vol. 93, USAC.

according to Atkinson, "when completed, no force will be able to carry the work without the aid of cannon."[44]

Atkinson had sent runners to the Pawnee bands, asking them to meet him in council at Engineer Cantonment. During the trip upriver from Cow Island to Council Bluffs, a band of Pawnees had stolen horses and guns from Major Thomas Biddle and his escort. On October 5 the delegates from the Grand Pawnee, Republican Pawnee, and Pawnee Loup bands arrived at Council Bluffs to meet with Atkinson and Indian Agent Benjamin O'Fallon. After some haggling, the Indians promised to punish the braves who were responsible for the attack on Major Biddle and his party and to return the stolen goods and horses. When the negotiations ended, Atkinson gave each of the chiefs a saber and, with O'Fallon, joined them for a ceremonial feast, after which the Indians returned to their camps.[45]

In this meeting, his first attempt at Indian negotiations, Atkinson tried to follow Calhoun's orders. He wanted to show the Indians that the whites wanted peace and friendship, but still demonstrate the strength of the American government and army.[46] Atkinson's well-meaning gifts and his act of providing a ceremonial feast for the Pawnees were criticized by other Indians and frontier whites. For example, at another council several days later, Big Elk, an Omaha chief, asked if it were true that the white men had given presents to and eaten with the Pawnees. The chief said that it was unusual for the whites to have treated their enemies in such a manner. This action, he concluded, "is what I cannot understand." When Big Elk finished, Agent Benjamin O'Fallon sprang to his

[44] Atkinson to Calhoun, Oct. 9, 1819, in 16 Cong., 1 sess., *House Exec. Doc. No. 110*, 170.

[45] Kavanaugh Journal, entry, Oct. 9, 1819, YUL; O'Fallon to Smith, Oct. 5, 1819, Smith Papers, SHSM; Edwin James, *Account of an Expedition from Pittsburgh to the Rocky Mountains . . .*, (Vol. XIV in *Early Western Travels*, ed. by R. G. Thwaites), 240–41, 244, 258–59, 261.

[46] Atkinson to Calhoun, Oct. 19, 1819, in 16 Cong., 1 sess., *House Exec. Doc. No. 110*, 169–70.

feet. "I did not smoke the pipe of peace with them," he shouted. "Neither will I, until our differences are settled."[47]

Atkinson, however, seems not to have understood this exchange. His hospitality and his efforts to conciliate the Pawnees had damaged his reputation as a war chief among the Indians near the post and, perhaps, created a gulf between him and O'Fallon. Unfortunately, the Agent never explained the niceties of Indian diplomacy which might have helped Atkinson as the highest ranking military commander on the Mississippi-Missouri frontier.

Meanwhile, Atkinson's fellow officers hurried the men to complete the camp buildings before the first snowfall, and, despite the loss of one keelboat of limestone, Atkinson seemed satisfied with the pace of construction. On the evening of October 27 he gave a dinner for his brigade officers, complimenting them on their achievements and exchanging toasts. On November 1 the officers reciprocated with a dinner honoring their commander. The next morning Atkinson officially named the new post Cantonment Missouri, then boarded a small keelboat with several other officers, and set out for St. Louis, so that he could maintain communications with the War Department through the winter. The trip down-river took twenty days, and, after a brief stop at Franklin, Atkinson arrived at St. Louis on November 22.[48]

With the Missouri Expedition at Council Bluffs for the winter, Atkinson and his staff prepared to continue the movement the following spring. Atkinson reported the progress of the expedition to General Jackson and Secretary Calhoun. Calhoun replied, commending him for his "caution, prudence, and industry," but warned that the coming move would take longer than the War Department had planned. "It is not intended to extend the expedition, at least 'til we are fully established there, beyond the Mandane Villages," he wrote. If the troops encountered any un-

[47] James, *Expedition*, 258–59, 261.

[48] Kavanaugh Journal, entries, Oct. 27, 1819, and Nov. 1, 1819, YUL; Atkinson, Ninth Military Dept., Orders, Nov. 2, 1819, Vol. 93, USAC.

expected hazards or delays, an "intermediate post about the great bend will probably be necessary . . ."[49]

The difficulties with Colonel Johnson and his steamboats the previous summer led Atkinson to ask that the Quartermaster General's Corps be allowed to transport the supplies and provisions in the spring. To his dismay, he learned that the War Department had already let contracts to Johnson again. When Atkinson complained, Calhoun assured him that Johnson had promised to deliver the goods before mid-April. If he failed to do so, the Quartermaster General promised to have his officers furnish transportation and procure food for the troops.[50] In spite of Colonel Johnson's failure to meet his contracts for transportation the previous year, Calhoun still hoped that the expedition could use steamboats in 1820. He wrote to Atkinson, "If there is a reasonable prospect of their success, [their use] would give much more interest and eclat to the expedition . . ." Although earlier convinced that steamboats were indeed the best mode of transportation, Atkinson was now persuaded to the contrary.[51]

The Panic of 1819 and the depression that followed provided the impetus for economy-minded Congressmen to begin a general attack on government spending. They criticized military spending in particular and demanded that Calhoun provide an estimate of expenses for the next three years. He, in turn, directed that costs throughout the army be cut to an absolute minimum and ordered that all food and supplies for posts on the Mississippi and Missouri rivers be transported in boats manned by soldiers. He asked Atkinson if the establishment of posts on the Missouri River above Council Bluffs could not be arranged by using only military keelboats. "Retrenchment is the order of the day," complained a subordinate, "and unless our expenses be diminished, the army will be disbanded."[52]

49 Calhoun to Atkinson, Feb. 7, 1820, *Correspondence*, II, 168–69.

50 *Ibid.*; Jesup to Atkinson, Feb. 22, 1820, Letters Sent, Vol. II, QMG.

51 Calhoun to Atkinson, Feb. 7, 1820, *Correspondence*, II, 170.

52 Trueman Cross to James McGunnegle, Dec. 22, 1819, Letters Sent, Vol. I, QMG.

Henry Atkinson (1820)

Illinois Historical Society

William Clark
Portrait by Gilbert Stuart

From William Clark Kennerly, Persimmon Hill

The protest against military spending gained momentum, and on April 7, 1820, the Adjutant General notified Atkinson that Congress had refused to appropriate funds for any further advance up the Missouri. Three days later Calhoun wrote that the Missouri Expedition was over. "The President has decided that the troops shall not progress beyond the Council Bluff . . ." he wrote. Since that post was the point of farthest advance, Calhoun directed Atkinson to strengthen it.[53]

Thus ended the Missouri or so-called Yellowstone Expedition. Instead of reaching the original destination, the mouth of the Yellowstone River in eastern Montana, the troops had to stop at the first intermediate post on the journey. Nevertheless, the expedition was in some measure a success. The troops built a post at Council Bluffs in the Indian country, and from this post the army exerted some influence on the tribes living along the upper Missouri. The efforts of these troops and of those at Fort Snelling, built at the confluence of the St. Peters and Mississippi rivers, surely brought American control of the West one step closer to reality. In these activities in the West as well as others to come, however, the United States Army had less influence on Indian affairs and the opening of the West than it might have had. Continuing man-power shortages, and Congressional refusals to appropriate the necessary funds limited army activity in the West.

Henry Atkinson's part in the Missouri Expedition changed his military career. Before he was chosen to lead the expedition, he was just another obscure regimental commander. Throughout 1819 and 1820 he received both publicity and praise for his leadership, in spite of the fact that the expedition he led failed to reach its destination. As the new commander of the Ninth Military Department, Atkinson directed army activities along the upper Mississippi and Missouri river valleys, an area that included much of the American frontier at the time. He commanded the largest army post in the nation, Cantonment Missouri, with over eleven hundred officers and men. The Ninth Military Department included over three

[53] Calhoun to Atkinson, Apr. 10, 1820, Jackson Papers, 1st series, Vol. 56.

times as many men as his earlier command. Finally, Atkinson had arrived in St. Louis and the West at a time of continuing national expansion. Missouri was at the threshold of statehood, the fur traders had begun to consolidate their position in the Indian country, and the national government had begun to work on the problem of what to do with the Indians. Little did Colonel Atkinson know, during the winter of 1819–20 as he worked at his bachelor quarters in St. Louis, that he was to spend the rest of his life in or near this noisy and colorful entrepôt of the West.

V. Western Command—1819-24

For Henry Atkinson the period between 1819 and 1824 was one of increased administrative duties. He also for the first time devoted a major portion of his efforts to Indian affairs. Throughout the period he learned much about Indian diplomacy and worked with William Clark, superintendent of Indian affairs at St. Louis, to maintain peace with the Indians along the frontier. From 1819 to 1824, while commanding a large and important sector of the army, he gained additional experience as an administrator and acquired the experience and skill necessary for Indian negotiations.

In June, 1819, when Atkinson took command of the Ninth Military Department, it included 1,127 men and seven posts in an area stretching from Fort Crawford at Prairie du Chien in the north to Fort Smith on the Arkansas River in the south; from the arsenal and garrison at Newport, Kentucky, in the east to Fort Osage on the Missouri River in western Missouri Territory in the west. This command involved the usual administrative duties, such as ordering the annual supply of provisions, clothing, equipment, medical supplies, and transportation for the troops and supervising the construction of forts and the training received by the troops. Although Atkinson had faced similar tasks when he commanded the Sixth Infantry at Plattsburg, New York, the size of his new command increased the responsibility and time necessary for meeting these duties. A major addition to his duties, however, dealt with Indian affairs. Before the Missouri Expedition, he had had no experience with the Indians. Now, as a frontier commander, he was ordered to enforce federal laws and treaties dealing with tribes within his department.

During his brief stay in St. Louis in June, 1819, Atkinson had designated Major Thomas Biddle, one of his subordinates, to go up the Missouri, to pay "particular attention to Indian Affairs," and to submit a detailed report of his findings.[1] Now, in November, 1819, Atkinson's personal attention was directed toward Indian affairs. Secretary of War Calhoun asked Atkinson for his views on the factory system, a system of government operated fur trading houses, and on Indian trade. In reply, Atkinson offered two suggestions. First, that "all intercourse by individual traders with the Indians should be prohibited and let [the] government take the whole trade into their own hands . . ." Atkinson, long associated with government actions and regulations, believed that an orderly system of trade operating under government supervision might assure order and stability. He said that well-managed factories might produce enough profits to pay "all the expenses of the military that might be necessary to establish the posts and protect the trade in the Indian country." He concluded with an alternative suggestion: Allow a single company with a large operating capital to have a monopoly of the trade. Then the traders would not find it necessary to trick or rob the Indians to get their peltry ahead of their competitors. Atkinson surmised that employees of such a company, "having but one interest, would find their account in impressing the Indians with a proper regard and respect for the character and views of [the] government."[2] Following either of these suggestions, he believed, would eliminate much of the unregulated competition and, if properly enforced, might lead to peaceful relations with the Indians.

[1] Atkinson to Calhoun, Nov. 26, 1819, ASP:MA, II, 204.

[2] *Ibid.*

Besides offering these suggestions, Atkinson sought to maintain peace by ordering his subordinates at Fort Smith and Council Bluffs to pay particular attention to enforcing the laws regulating Indian trade. "The admission of Citizens into the Indian Country to hunt is forbidden," he informed Major William Bradford, a commander at Fort Smith, "and every means must be taken to prevent it and to recall such persons as may have already gone over [into Indian country] for that purpose . . ." By law, foreigners were forbidden to enter the Indian trade. Atkinson directed his subordinates to post notice to this effect and to arrest violators and turn them over to civil authorities.[3]

Atkinson's attention was frequently directed from Indian affairs to events at Cantonment Missouri. During the winter of 1819–20, the troops there suffered from malnutrition and dysentery. "In this situation, when the most nutritive diet was requisite to restore our exhausted energies," reported Dr. John Gale, surgeon for the Rifle Regiment, "the men were compelled to subsist on salted or smoke-dried meats, without vegetables or groceries of any description." Miscalculation, waste, and dietary ignorance had depleted the supplies. The rations of beans, peas, and vinegar soon had disappeared, and were replaced by Indian corn. The troops and their medical officers complained that the barrels of preserved meat were "decidedly in a putrescant state, and absolutely unfit for issue." One surgeon reported that "the smell and taste both rejected [the meat] with disgust." In addition, several hundred barrels of flour that had been subjected to frequent soakings by rain and river water were spoiled.[4] The troops were forced to supplement their diet at the sutler's store, but the supplies were inadequate.

When the stock of medicine in the hospital was depleted,

[3] Atkinson to William Bradford, Dec. 15, 1819, Jackson Papers, 1st series, Vol. 55.

[4] Thomas J. Mower, "Report, Council Bluffs," Oct. 1, 1820, in Samuel Forry, comp., *Statistical Report on the Sickness and Mortality in the Army of the United States*, 16–17.

Lieutenant Colonel Morgan, commanding officer at the cantonment, asked Doctors Mower and Gale how to improve the health of the troops. They agreed that fresh vegetables, meat, and milk were necessary. These would not be available until spring, so Morgan and his subordinate officers decided to send the sickest men back down-river to Fort Osage as soon as the ice was gone. Here they hoped the medical officers could buy the necessary foods. On March 25 four keelboats filled with one hundred sick men descended the river. This left another one hundred sick troops at the camp. The regimental surgeons moved them to a small stream about three miles away where they lived on fresh game and found enough wild onions to cure all inmates of "Camp Recovery."[5]

Atkinson was "greatly astonished [when he learned] that the troops at the Bluffs should have been affected with the scurvy."[6] His earlier experience with weakened and sick troops had led him to send several hundred head of beef cattle to Council Bluffs along with a large supply of corn meal the preceding autumn. He had assumed these and the existing supply of game, bread, and salted meat would carry them through the winter without sickness. Because of the unexpected sickness among the troops, Atkinson sent two keelboats loaded with fresh flour, beans, corn meal, vinegar, and new pork to Fort Osage, and by April 28, fresh potatoes and bacon had arrived at Council Bluffs.[7]

On June 14, Atkinson himself arrived at Council Bluffs. He was satisfied that the troops had completely recovered from their sickness.[8] He also found that floodwaters, reputedly the highest within memory, had inundated Cantonment Missouri. The troops had packed their possessions and moved to higher ground, about two miles south to Council Bluffs. On June 15 the cantonment was

[5] *Ibid.*, 18; Kavanaugh Journal, entries, Mar. 25 and Apr. 28, 1820, YUL.

[6] Atkinson to Jesup, Apr. 6, 1820, Consolidated File, Atkinson's Expedition, QMG.

[7] Kavanaugh Journal, entry, Apr. 28, 1820, YUL.

[8] Atkinson to Smith, June 20, 1820, Smith Papers, SHSM.

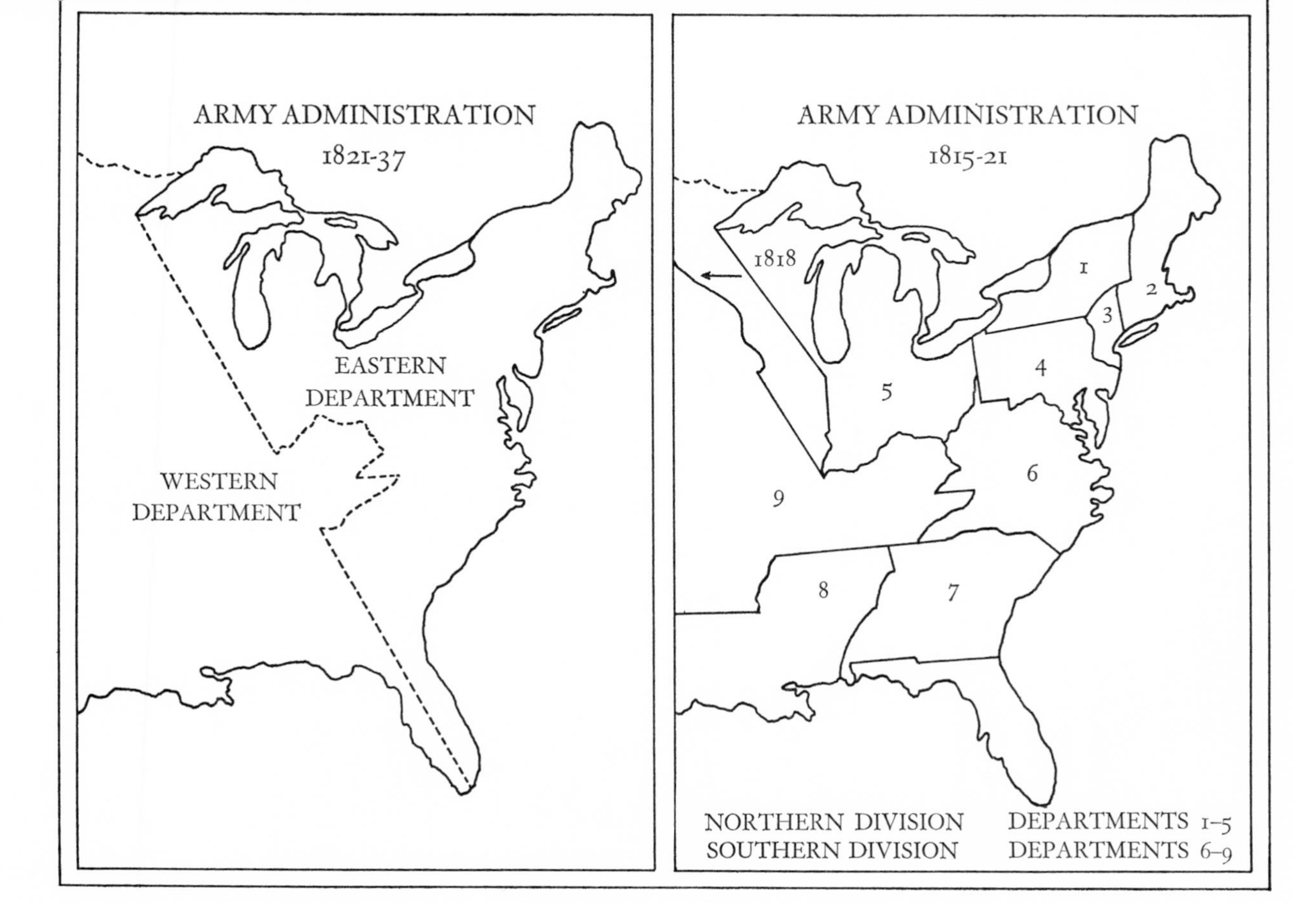
ARMY ADMINISTRATION
1821-37
EASTERN
DEPARTMENT
WESTERN
DEPARTMENT
ARMY ADMINISTRATION
1815-21
1818
1
2
3
4
5
6
7
8
9
NORTHERN DIVISION DEPARTMENTS 1–5
SOUTHERN DIVISION DEPARTMENTS 6–9

flooded by the muddy river, and the front row of barracks had collapsed and fallen into the stream. By July 1 the Missouri receded, leaving a two-foot deposit of sand and mud covering the encampment.[9]

Atkinson and his officers had assumed the cantonment to be only a temporary resting place and a staging area for the push to the Mandan villages that coming summer and, therefore, had built it as near the river as possible to facilitate loading and unloading the transports. The Missouri flood—covering the cantonment, knocking down walls, and washing away several buildings—came after Atkinson had learned the post was to be strengthened. He probably would have relocated his force in the summer of 1820 anyway, but the flood forced him to hurry the decision.

He remained at Council Bluffs through the summer and autumn of 1820 to supervise the building of the new camp. Once again a race against time and the weather forced Atkinson to order temporary rather than permanent quarters. So despite Secretary Calhoun's preference for stone or brick buildings, the command used stone only for the foundations and brick for the fireplaces and chimneys. Logs and plank furnished the building material for the floors, walls, and roofs.

Earlier that year Atkinson had suggested to Calhoun that, whenever possible, troops at frontier posts produce their own fresh-vegetable supply by farming and their meat by hunting game and raising livestock. If the troops could raise much of their own food and thereby reduce the cost of provisions and transportation contracts, they would relieve the War Department from financial embarrassment. Therefore, on April 10, Calhoun had directed Atkinson to raise food at the post. Apparently the Carolina planter himself supervised the planting and care of the crops, and his earlier experience and training as a farmer seem to have been of some advantage. By October, 1820, Atkinson reported harvesting 250 tons of hay, 13,000 bushels of corn, 4,000 bushels of potatoes,

[9] Kavanaugh Journal, entry, July 1, 1820, YUL.

and 4–5,000 bushels of turnips.[10] That autumn he ordered that 700 stock hogs and 62 milch cows be moved to Council Bluffs for fresh meat during the coming winter.[11]

His interest in agriculture extended beyond simply raising food for the troops and animals at the post. During the preceding summer he had experimented with some corn which he had obtained from the Omaha Indians living near the post. He found it "far superior to any other discreption of corn that I have known cultivated anywhere." The Indian corn required only a ninety-day growing season, produced a substantially larger yield, and impressed Atkinson as a more hardy species than "the common gourd seed" then in use. The delighted general sent some to Secretary Calhoun for distribution among his friends. He also sent a barrel of the seed to New York Governor DeWitt Clinton "presuming that it will be a valuable acquisition to the farmers of N. York, the latitude being about the same as that in which the corn thrives so admirably on the Missouri."[12]

Early in August a small party of ten or twelve braves stole five army horses from the plowmen at Council Bluffs. This event, coupled with an Indian attack and murder of two employees of Manuel Lisa, the fur trader, involved Atkinson in his first experience with Indian depredations. Subsequent investigation convinced Atkinson that a wandering band of Sioux was responsible. Later that month, the Sac Indians robbed some frontier settlers and traders in northeastern Missouri. Atkinson sent an officer who was "acquainted with the Indian character" and one hundred men to the Sac village to demand they return all horses stolen that summer, but without result.[13] On August 31 a sentinel at Camp Mis-

10 Atkinson to Calhoun, Oct. 18, 1820, quoted in Franklin *Missouri Intelligencer*, Feb. 5, 1821.

11 Atkinson to Calhoun, Nov. 23, 1820, Letters Received, SW.

12 Atkinson to Calhoun, Dec. 8, 1820, Letters Received, SW.

13 Atkinson to Calhoun, Aug. 21, 1820, in Clarence E. Carter, ed., *The Territorial Papers of the United States*: *Louisiana-Missouri*, XV, 636–37.

souri reported seeing a "few skulking Indians" watching the post from across the river. Atkinson ordered a small mounted party to capture them. However, capturing a band of mounted Indians on the plains proved no simple task, and the quarry escaped.[14] Atkinson, in spite of difficulties with a few nearby bands, was certain the move to Council Bluffs with twelve hundred men the previous summer had guaranteed peace and good feelings between the Americans and most Indians along the Missouri. When he heard reports that the Arikaras and the Mandans farther up the river spoke "lightly of the coming of the troops," he suggested that little confidence could be placed in them. "I have not the least doubt but the presence of 400 troops would be quite sufficient to over-awe them," he stated, "and make as favorable an impression as could be desired . . ."[15] He decided that such a force could produce results unobtainable through simple negotiations. In the summer of 1820, however, he could do no more than negotiate.

Although still a novice in dealing with the Indians, by September, 1820, he showed that he had learned to use pomp and ceremony as part of negotiations. He and Benjamin O'Fallon held council meetings with chiefs and headmen from three bands of Pawnees, the Kansas, Omahas, Poncas, Yanktons, Tetons, and Saone Sioux. Atkinson paraded the brigade before the assembled chiefs and demonstrated infantry and artillery maneuvers. Then he showed the steamboat *Expedition* to the visitors.[16] After this display the chiefs claimed to be friends of the white men and agreed to the treaties submitted to them by Atkinson and O'Fallon.

Atkinson was no Indian hater, as can be seen by his actions toward these unfortunate people during his career. From his first meetings with them at Council Bluffs in 1819, he tried to be open minded about the charges against them, thinking that they demonstrated remarkable restraint in the face of nearly constant white

[14] Atkinson to Calhoun, Sept. 1, 1820, Letters Received, SW.

[15] Atkinson to Jackson, Oct. 18, 1820, Dreer Collection, HSP.

[16] Atkinson to Calhoun, Oct. 18, 1820, quoted in *Missouri Intelligencer*, Feb. 5, 1821.

aggression. In spite of frontier hostility, he continued to enforce the laws of trade and intercourse prohibiting whites from entering Indian territory without permission. At the same time, however, he demanded that the Indians obey the stipulations of treaties they had signed with the United States government.

While Atkinson was at Council Bluffs during the summer of 1820, he received news that on May 15 he had been promoted from the rank of colonel to that of brigadier general. His promotion was unusual in that he had had no combat experience at the head of either militia or Regular Army units and in that it came during a time of peace and of military retrenchment. It was made possible by Brigadier General Eleazer W. Ripley's resignation of February 1. At that time, Henry Atkinson ranked sixth among the ten colonels in the army. Three of those above him—Moses Porter, Daniel Bissell, and James Miller—held brevet ranks of brigadier general.[17] Atkinson's friends and supporters in Congress had submitted his name for consideration for the vacant rank. He had an advantage over the other colonels because of his part in the Missouri Expedition. Although the expedition had failed, Atkinson had received praise for his leadership and organizational ability. Secretary Calhoun, General Andrew Jackson, and even the contractor, Colonel James Johnson, had praised his work. Henry Atkinson was the only colonel who had received widespread publicity and whose name was familiar to most national politicians. His close relationship with John C. Calhoun was an added advantage. As Secretary of War and confidant of President Monroe, Calhoun had chosen the North Carolina colonel to lead the Missouri Expedition. Quartermaster General Thomas S. Jesup, hoping to get the vacant position of brigadier general, asked Calhoun if he might be transferred to an infantry regiment and receive the promotion. "The Secretary of War, however, wished to promote Colonel Atkinson," Jesup later wrote.[18] These advantages, combined with the fact that Atkin-

[17] A brevet (temporary) rank entitled an officer to assume the duties and receive the pay of his higher brevet rank.

[18] Statement of Thomas S. Jesup, Apr. 23, 1823, Thomas S. Jesup Papers, LC.

son had no important personal or political enemies, won the promotion which he accepted on July 25, 1820, only twelve years after he entered the army as a captain of infantry.[19]

Atkinson returned to St. Louis in mid-October, and there learned of Calhoun's continuing support. The Secretary, pleased with his protégé's efforts as commander of the Ninth Military District and impressed by the rapid strides toward self-sufficiency the troops at Cantonment Missouri had made, decided a reward was in order. On January 5, 1821, he wrote Atkinson that the post at Council Bluffs was "sufficiently important to be considered a Fort and in consideration of your indefatigable industry and skillful efforts in accomplishing the objects of the Executive . . . it will be named 'Fort Atkinson.' " Calhoun's letter arrived early in February, and on the seventeenth of that month Atkinson issued Calhoun's directive. Then he and a few friends celebrated his having the largest military installation in the country named after him.[20]

Only two months later, on March 21, 1821, Congress passed an act that reduced the army to six thousand men, to be commanded by one major general and two brigadiers. Thus one of the two major generals and four of the six brigadiers had to be either removed or reduced. Atkinson was surprised when Congress passed the army reduction bill, because he had believed that the Congressional supporters of Generals Jacob Brown and Andrew Jackson would cancel each other in any debate on army reduction. This was correct. Jackson, however, resigned from the army to accept the governorship of Florida Territory, thus breaking the deadlock. Then Major General Jacob Brown received command of the reduced army, which was divided into two major administrative units, the Eastern and Western Departments. These, in turn, were commanded by Brigadier Generals Winfield Scott and Edmund P. Gaines. Brown, Scott, and Gaines comprised a committee to make recommenda-

19 Atkinson to Calhoun, July 25, 1820, Letters Received, AGO.

20 Calhoun to Atkinson, Jan. 5, 1821, in Carter, ed., *Territorial Papers*, XV, 688; Atkinson, Ninth Military Dept., Orders, Feb. 17, 1821, Vol. 93, USAC.

tions to the President concerning the remaining generals and colonels. They transferred Alexander Macomb to the position of Chief Engineer and Daniel Parker to that of Paymaster General. This left Thomas S. Jesup and Henry Atkinson to be fitted into the new administrative framework. After some discussion, the committee proposed retaining Jesup as Quartermaster General and Atkinson as Adjutant General with the rank of colonel.[21]

When Lieutenant Colonel John E. Wool wrote to Atkinson to offer him General Brown's suggestion that he accept the post as Adjutant General of the Army, Atkinson balked. "I cannot go to Washington with degraded rank," he replied. "The only situation, below my present grade, that I would accept of, has been offered to me by the Secretary of War—a regiment, with [rank of colonel and] brevet rank of brigadier." While the generals had deliberated, Calhoun had intimated to Atkinson that he could probably reassume command of his former unit and remain in the West. As a brevet brigadier general, Atkinson would exercise a general's command at least some of the time. If he accepted Calhoun's offer, he wrote, he would be satisfied to "wear out [his] time on a remote frontier till better times . . ."[22]

General Brown, the new commanding general, however, urged Atkinson to become Adjutant General. "As a friend who has rendered you some service," he reminded Atkinson, "permit me to claim your acceptance of this situation in my military family." Brown understood Atkinson's reluctance to surrender his large command in the West for the routine of the Adjutant General's Office, but he expected his subordinate to "be willing to make some sacrifice to meet [his] wishes and the just expectations of the army."[23] Atkinson ignored Brown's plea. His opposition seems to have stemmed from hurt pride. His command on the Missouri, although nominally under the supervision of Andrew Jackson, had

21 *Compilation of Army Registers, 1815–1837*, pp. 182–83, 189–90, 213.

22 Atkinson to Brown, Apr. 6, 1821, ASP:MA, II, 411.

23 Brown to Atkinson, Apr. 13, 1821, ASP:MA, II, 411.

been nearly independent. Atkinson assumed that Brown, a former militia officer and not interested personally in organizational details, wanted him as adjutant to relieve himself of the burdens of his own position as commanding general.[24] Atkinson had served as both an adjutant and an inspector general during the War of 1812 and knew that as Adjutant General he would have more work, closer supervision, less rank and pay, and less opportunity to exercise any personal judgment or command than as a regimental commander in the West. On May 4 he again declined the post.

Although they recognized Atkinson's unwillingness to serve as Adjutant General, the Board of Generals offered him that post, but gave him Calhoun's offer as an alternative. On June 15 Atkinson again wrote to Brown, "I regret that it is not in my power, consistently with my own interest, to oblige you in your repeated requests to take a place on your staff."[25] This ended the exchange of letters, and Brown accepted Atkinson's decision.

On August 16, Henry Atkinson was appointed colonel of the Sixth Infantry. His move back to that regiment caused some inconvenience because other officers had to be shifted to new assignments or to a lower rank. This "unusual, unmilitary procedure" disturbed Andrew Jackson. Voicing his "extreme regret," he complained to President Monroe that "six meritorious officers are to be removed from place to place, reduced from grade to grade, and one driven out of office, to give one favorite officer an election of offices . . . General Atkinson is a favorite of mine, but still general justice is due to all."[26] His criticism stung the President, who replied, "With respect to the army, my effort was to preserve all, that I could . . ." Atkinson enjoyed universal respect from his fellow officers, and "No[rth] Carolina had no one in military or civil stations, of high rank, a circumstance which had weight."[27]

[24] Atkinson to Brown, Apr. 6, 1821, ASP:MA, II, 411.

[25] Atkinson to Brown, June 15, 1821, ASP:MA, II, 411.

[26] Jackson to Monroe, Aug. 4, 1821, in Carter, ed., *Territorial Papers*, XXII, 162–64.

[27] Monroe to Jackson, Sept. 16, 1821, in *Correspondence*, VI, 477.

In January, 1822, when President Monroe submitted the appointments to the Senate for ratification, the Committee on Military Affairs investigated his handling of the reduction. Some senators claimed the President's use of a board of officers to help in making the necessary reductions and relocations had gone beyond the meaning of the law. To their queries, Monroe replied that he felt at liberty to place any officer in the newly created positions. During the investigation, Daniel Parker, previous adjutant and inspector general, testified that General Brown had insisted that Atkinson be made adjutant, even after he received letters from Atkinson declining the post. Parker accused Brown of burning much of the correspondence and some orders from Calhoun and of substituting his own suggestions in their place.[28]

Throughout the investigation Henry Atkinson's military career hung in the balance. Congressman Romulus M. Saunders, Atkinson's long-time friend from North Carolina, reported, "Those [appointments] of an irregular character were rejected, [and] our friend H. Atkinson excaped narrowly."[29] Thus, although the political maneuvering remains somewhat unclear, Henry Atkinson obtained his desired position through a combination of political consideration, pressure applied by the President, the personal support of Calhoun, and his own reputation as an outstanding officer.

Meanwhile, in July, 1821, Edmund P. Gaines, commander of the newly formed Western Department of the Army, had assigned Atkinson to a command in the West. "You will consider the frontier of Missouri and the upper Mississippi as under your immediate charge," he ordered.[30] This command included nearly the same territory as the Ninth Military Department and became known as the "Right Wing" of the Western Department. In December, 1821,

28 Statement of Daniel Parker, Apr. 23, 1822, ASP:MA, II, 410.

29 Saunders to Bartlett Yancy, Apr. 3, 1822, in "Letters of Romulus M. Saunders to Bartlett Yancy, 1821–1828" (ed. by A. R. Newsome), *The North Carolina Historical Review*, Vol. VIII (Oct. 1931), 432.

30 Gaines to Atkinson, July 14, 1821, Ninth Military Dept., Orders, Vol. 93, USAC.

after some confusion arose regarding the limits of his command, Atkinson received a clarification from Gaines. In it Gaines reiterated his previous order and stated that Atkinson's command included Missouri and all territory north and west of it, including Forts Crawford and Edwards on the upper Mississippi.[31] The War Department had not anticipated Atkinson's receiving this command which entitled him to pay and allowances for his brevet rank as a brigadier general. Therefore, Calhoun explained to Gaines that Atkinson could no longer remain at the head of the Right Wing, that his duties should be limited "exclusively to the command of his regiment, and that in future no disposition be made of officers under your command . . . with a view to give effect to Brevet rank . . ."[32] Nevertheless, circumstances were such that Atkinson exercised his brevet command for most of the next twenty years.

His position now redefined, Henry Atkinson assumed the routine duties of his command in St. Louis. On January 18, 1822, while riding with a friend, he suffered a broken leg when the carriage overturned. Thus for the second time in eight years he was in bed with a broken leg. Both times he was fortunate in that he recovered without serious difficulty.[33]

While he was confined to his room, William H. Ashley, lieutenant governor of Missouri, and his partner, Andrew Henry, the fur trader, visited him. They proposed to organize a company of young men to trap, hunt, and trade with the Indians in the Rocky Mountains later that spring. Atkinson reminded his guests that they needed permits from the War Department to enter the Indian country, and since no one at St. Louis could authorize such a trip, suggested they write to Washington. The partners' plans troubled Atkinson because he thought they might enter the Indian country without permission. He also feared that if Ashley and Henry

[31] Gaines Order, included in Atkinson, Ninth Military Dept., Orders, Dec. 6, 1821, Vol. 93, USAC.

[32] Calhoun to Gaines, Apr. 10, 1822, Letters Sent, Vol. 6, AGO; Calhoun to Atkinson, Apr. 10, 1822, Letters Sent, Vol. 6, AGO.

[33] *St. Louis Enquirer*, Jan. 19, 1822.

FORT ARMSTRONG
Drawing copied from the *United States Illustrated* (1854)

State Historical Society of Wisconsin

HERDS OF BISON AND ELK ON THE UPPER MISSOURI
Tableau 47 by Karl Bodmer, 1839

Collection of the Northern Natural Gas Company, Joslyn Art Museum, Omaha, Nebraska

ascended the river, their presence might arouse Indian hostility. Therefore, he wrote Calhoun that the expedition "would greatly retard your views, in opening a friendly intercourse with the upper Tribes." Then he suggested, "If a detachment of troops ascend the river from Council Bluffs, the ensuing spring & the [Fur] company follow after, the difficulties alluded to above, will be obviated." If no troops could be sent on such a mission, then he raised no objections to the company's proceeding at once.[34] Calhoun's answer, if there was one, has not come to light, but that spring Ashley, Henry, and their men proceeded up the Missouri on the first of several expeditions into Indian country to gather furs. Atkinson's fears that Ashley's penetration might lead to further hostilities proved correct. The meetings between traders and Indians brought frequent robberies, murders, and excitement to the St. Louis fur-trading community. In fact, the Arikara War of 1823 and Atkinson's own Yellowstone Expedition of 1825 can be traced to the increasing pressure on the Indians by these fur traders.

During 1822, Colonel Atkinson remained occupied with routine duties of his command. These were varied and minute. He supervised maintenance and training at the posts within the Right Wing, ordered frequent inspections, sent and received orders, and traveled up the Missouri to Fort Atkinson. He ordered specific parts of the food ration, such as beef, flour, or vinegar, sent to a particular post. This may have been simply giving his official seal of approval to many of the orders listed under his name, but often they appear in his own handwriting, so either he had little confidence in his subordinates or he had little clerical help. He co-operated with the Indian agents on the Missouri and upper Mississippi rivers in holding councils with nearby tribes. At these meetings he helped settle trade disputes, obtain the return of stolen goods, and assure the Indians of American efforts to restrain squatters along the borders of Indian lands.

In May, 1823, General Gaines, on the advice of his personal

[34] Atkinson to Calhoun, Jan. 25, 1822, Letters Received, SW.

physician, decided to take a vacation. On May 7 he appointed Henry Atkinson commander of the Western Department in his absence.[35] The Department included all of the United States west of a diagonal line from the western tip of Lake Superior southeast to the tip of Florida. Gaines chose Atkinson because he was the highest-ranking colonel in the department and because of his brevet rank of brigadier general. Atkinson moved from St. Louis to Louisville and there continued to conduct administrative functions similar to his chores as commander of the Right Wing, but now for half of the army.

Early in June, 1823, Atkinson learned from Colonel Henry Leavenworth, commander at Fort Atkinson, that the Arikara Indians, who lived near the Missouri River in northern South Dakota, had attacked William H. Ashley and a party of trappers when they stopped at the Indians' village to trade for horses. The Arikaras surprised Ashley's party, inflicted heavy casualties, and drove the men down the Missouri.

Leavenworth had gathered a party of about two hundred men, had taken four artillery pieces, and had set out for the Arikara villages.[36] No sooner had Leavenworth started up the Missouri than Atkinson received news of a second Indian attack. The Blackfeet had ambushed a party of the Missouri Fur Company near the Yellowstone River, killed seven men, and taken an estimated $15,000 worth of furs.[37] Atkinson remained calm and waited news from Leavenworth's tiny army. He notified General Brown of Leavenworth's move. "It is unnecessary to give any orders touching the matter," he wrote, "particularly as the contest will be long over before reinforcements could reach the scene of action."[38]

[35] Gaines to Adjutant General, May 7, 1823, Letters Received, AGO.

[36] Leavenworth to Atkinson, June 18, 1823, in Doane Robinson, ed., "Official Correspondence of the Leavenworth Expedition of 1823 into South Dakota . . .," *South Dakota Historical Collections*, Vol. I (Aug., 1902), 181–82.

[37] Benjamin O'Fallon to Atkinson, July 3, 1823, ASP:MA, II, 579–80.

[38] Atkinson to Brown, July 12, 1823, Letters Received, AGO.

Nevertheless, Atkinson decided to send more troops to the frontier and ordered Captain John Fowle, then leading a detachment of recruits to Council Bluffs, to march overland from St. Louis with one hundred selected men. This march, Atkinson explained, was necessary to "impress the Indians in that quarter with a just idea of our capacity to chastise every outrage they may commit." He realized that it would have little effect on the actual campaign, but thought it might be useful to check the Indians who watched as their brethren met the whites in battle.[39]

Meanwhile, Leavenworth's troops were reinforced by Joshua Pilcher, an officer of the Missouri Fur Company, who led an irregular force of fur traders, frontiersmen, and a large contingent of Sioux warriors. Leavenworth styled his enlarged force the "Missouri Legion." Pilcher's assistance proved of little value to the army, however, because his Sioux auxiliaries failed to cooperate in attacking the village and because Pilcher refused to help Leavenworth negotiate when the Arikaras sued for peace on August 10 and 11. Colonel Leavenworth hesitated when the Arikara chiefs sued for peace. He dared not risk additional lives and equipment on his own responsibility and accepted the request for negotiations. The Indians, however, stalled through the day of August 12 and that night slipped from their stockade.[40]

Before news of this development reached Atkinson at Louisville, however, General Gaines returned to duty there and sent Atkinson back to St. Louis where he reassumed command of the Right Wing. On July 26, Gaines, who often overestimated the Indian menace, ordered him to the Missouri River "to support the detachment under Colonel Leavenworth, and to give a timely check to the hostile spirit which has recently manifested itself among the Indians of the Upper Missouri . . ." Gaines sent six companies of the First Infantry to St. Louis "to be held in readiness subject to

[39] Atkinson to Fowle, July 13, 1823, ASP:MA, II, 586.

[40] Leavenworth to Atkinson, Aug. 30, 1823, in Robinson, "Official Correspondence . . .," *South Dakota Historical Collections*, Vol. I (August, 1902), 197–98.

[Atkinson's] orders . . ."[41] Gaines feared that the Missouri River tribes would unite and force Leavenworth to retreat to Fort Atkinson without making a lasting impression on his adversaries. Therefore, he advised Atkinson to ready his command by stock-piling supplies, food, and munitions at the Fort and told him that he would send the Fourth Infantry as far as Council Bluffs, where they could remain until spring. Or, in case the Indians defeated Leavenworth, he ordered Atkinson to move into the Indian country that November and harry the tribes during the coming winter.[42]

On the other hand, Atkinson doubted that the Indians would form a coalition. He reminded Gaines that the Arikaras had asked the Mandans, a tribe that lived farther up the Missouri, for refuge earlier. He doubted they would fight Leavenworth in defense of their villages, much less take the offensive. Nevertheless, he wrote Colonel Snelling, commanding the Fifth Infantry at St. Peters on the Mississippi, to report any hostilities among the Sioux in that area, because he thought the Sioux would join any coalition against the Americans. Having done this, he wrote to Calhoun and proposed leading an infantry force up the Missouri each summer to impress the Indians with American military strength. He wanted to lead a force of six or seven hundred men up the Missouri. Of these, four companies would remain at Council Bluffs, and the remaining sixteen would move to either the Mandan villages or the Yellowstone River, where they would construct a cantonment for the First Infantry. Then he would return to Fort Atkinson with what remained of the Sixth Infantry. Each succeeding year "several companies of the sixth might ascend the river, and in conjunction with the first regiment, explore all the upper country intersected by streams navigable for keel-boats, and consequently hold intercourse with all the upper Indians."[43] Each year since the Missouri Expedition he had suggested leading such a force into the Indian

41 Gaines to Atkinson, July 26, 1823, ASP:MA, II, 580–81.

42 Gaines to Atkinson, Ninth Military Dept., Orders, Aug. 8, 1823, Vol. 93, USAC.

43 Atkinson to Gaines, Aug. 19, 1823, ASP:MA, II, 582.

country. Now he wanted to build a post beyond Council Bluffs, although earlier he had not been sure this was a good idea.

His assessment of the Arikara reaction to Leavenworth's moves proved correct. When the marching and countermarching ended, Leavenworth was seen to have made the best of a poor situation, and the War Department had a stronger argument for increased appropriations and further penetration into the West. Atkinson hoped this latest Indian flare-up would enable him to command a force that would go to the Yellowstone. In November, 1823, he ordered the Fort Atkinson quartermaster to buy "one or two substantial keel boats of 30 to 35 tons burden each . . ." for use the next spring. In addition, he resumed experimenting with his idea of propelling the keelboats up river by using man-powered paddle wheels. He submitted a plan of construction for the machinery to Calhoun and asked for permission to continue his tinkering. Secretary Calhoun, still interested in establishing an American military outpost on the Missouri above Council Bluffs, gave his approval and support.[44] Atkinson also submitted a tentative requisition for food and supplies in anticipation of leading his troops up the Missouri in the spring of 1824. In November, 1823, however, he received orders to send two companies of the First Regiment from Bellefontaine back down the Mississippi to New Orleans. This order demonstrated the government's lack of interest and temporarily ended Atkinson's hopes for an expedition up the Missouri and a chance to build another military post farther in the Indian country.

Early in 1824, Generals Gaines and Scott exchanged commands, and the latter moved to Louisville to assume command of the Western Department. In late June, Scott went east, and Atkinson again took temporary command of the Western Department.[45] On June 30 he prepared to shift his operations to Louisville, but news of Indian unrest, this time among the Chippewas along the

[44] Jesup to Atkinson, Nov. 26, 1823, Letters Sent, Vol. V, QMG.
[45] Thian, *Military Geography*, 107.

upper Mississippi, caused him to remain in St. Louis through most of the summer. "I do not apprehend any serious difficulty with the Tribes on the upper Mississippi," he reported, "but as long as they are permitted to wage war against each other at pleasure, their war parties will occasionally kill straggling parties of whites that fall in their way . . ." He suggested that the Indians might refrain from killing frontiersmen if they could be restrained from making war on each other, but added, "how they are to be restrained it is difficult to point out."[46]

During the remainder of 1824, General Atkinson concentrated on the continuing Indian difficulties within the Western Department. These Indian agitations brought about his chance to ascend the Missouri to the Mandan villages and beyond, to the Yellowstone River the next year. In May, 1824, pressure from aroused westerners and humanitarian groups throughout the East persuaded Congress to appropriate $10,000 for an Indian Peace Commission. This commission, accompanied by a military escort, would travel up the Missouri River to negotiate treaties of peace and friendship with the tribes along that stream. News of the appropriation and Atkinson's appointment as one of the two commissioners came too late for action that summer.[47]

The years 1819 to 1824 were ones of change and education for Henry Atkinson. During these years he became a brigadier general, only to be reduced later to the rank of colonel. His military duties, although enlarged in scope, remained similar to those of his earlier command. A new factor, Indian affairs, now took much of his time and attention. Before 1819 he had had no experience with Indians, but during the succeeding years he gained much experience with these people. Atkinson became a close personal friend of William Clark, superintendent of Indian affairs at St. Louis. Together the two men met and negotiated with chiefs from quite a few tribes. As

[46] Atkinson to Charles J. Nourse, Aug. 5, 1824, Letters Received, AGO.

[47] Calhoun to Atkinson, June 1, 1824, Journal of the Treaty Commission, 1825, Record Group 75, Records of the Office of Indian Affairs, National Archives (hereafter OIA).

the highest-ranking officer in the West, Atkinson also attended treaty talks at the posts within his command. Thus he learned to know many Indians and the procedures and problems involved in dealing with them. He tried to give the Indians every chance to meet their treaty obligations and worked to keep squatters and fur traders out of the Indian country. He was a legalist, however, and sought compliance to laws and treaties by Indians and white men alike.

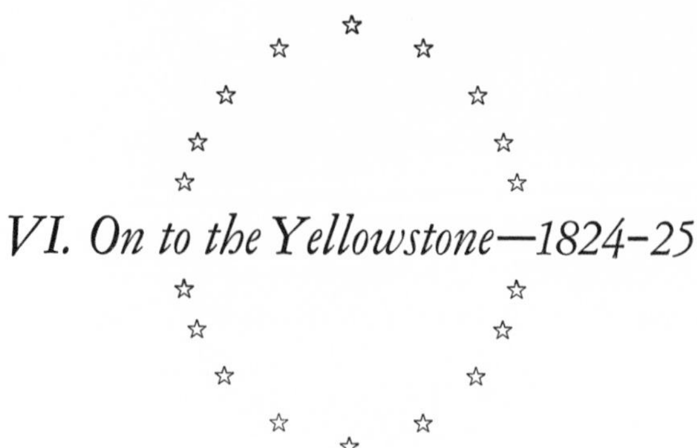

VI. On to the Yellowstone—1824-25

The purpose of the Yellowstone Expedition of 1825 was to make treaties of peace and friendship with the Indian tribes on the northern plains. It was organized in part because of continuing Indian depredations, chiefly along the upper Missouri River. For Henry Atkinson it offered a chance to prove that the bungling and mismanagement evident in the Missouri Expedition of 1819 arose from conditions beyond his control. It also offered an opportunity for him to demonstrate his knowledge of Indian affairs, his organizational skills, and his capacity for leadership.

On May 25, 1824, President Monroe had approved a bill that authorized a commission to sign treaties of peace and friendship with the Indian tribes along the Missouri River, and appropriated money for it and for a military escort. Monroe then appointed Atkinson and Benjamin O'Fallon as joint commissioners to carry on the negotiations.[1]

Early in July, 1824, Atkinson received his appointment and returned from Louisville to St. Louis. Eager to begin, he tried to get trade goods to use as gifts in the coming negotiations as well as food and transportation for the military escort. He was disappointed when he learned these were not available. He had hoped to

[1] *U.S. Statutes at Large*, IV, 37–38; Calhoun to Atkinson and O'Fallon, June 1, 1824, Journal of the Treaty Commission, 1825, OIA.

travel up the Missouri that same summer, but, after discussing his plans with "some of the most respectable Traders," he decided it would be impossible to reach the Mandan villages, in what is now central North Dakota, before winter.[2] Therefore, he delayed his ascent up the Missouri River until the following summer.

In spite of this decision, he continued to prepare for the expedition. In mid-July he ordered a six-month supply of food for five hundred men to be delivered the next spring. He also discussed the Indian situation with Peter Wilson, newly appointed subagent to the Sioux tribes on the upper Missouri. Atkinson believed that although the Sioux remained at peace with the whites, their continuing raids and warfare with neighboring tribes endangered traders. He requested that Wilson move into the Sioux country to arrange for peace talks between the tribes if Major O'Fallon, agent for the upper Missouri, agreed. Three weeks later O'Fallon concurred and Wilson left for the upper Missouri.[3]

Atkinson also renewed his experiments using paddle wheels as a means for propelling keelboats. He had done some work on the paddle wheels in the summer and autumn of 1823. That year he had managed to combine a treadmill with the paddle wheels. To furnish locomotive power, men walked up one side of an inclined, horizontal wheel twenty feet in diameter. This turned a smaller wheel that was connected by a shaft to the paddle wheels. Although the device was workable, the weight of the men walking on the inclined wheel caused frequent breakdowns.[4]

By late in 1824, Atkinson had made several changes in the machinery. Instead of walking on a treadmill to furnish the motive power, the men sat on benches along either side of the boat and pushed horizontal slides in unison. Atkinson placed a horizontal

[2] Atkinson to C. J. Nourse, July 8, 1824, Letters Received, AGO; Atkinson to Calhoun, July 14, 1824, Letters Received, SW.

[3] Wilson to Calhoun, Aug. 3, 1824, in "Letters of Peter Wilson, First Resident Agent Among the Teton Sioux" (ed. by Harry B. Anderson), *Nebraska History*, Vol. XLII (December, 1961), 248–49.

[4] Atkinson to Calhoun, Oct. 11, 1823, quoted in Grant Foreman, "River Navigation in the Early Southwest," *Mississippi Valley Historical Review*, Vol. XV (June, 1928), 35–36.

shaft across the center of the boat with a paddle wheel on each end. The shaft was turned by a gear mechanism, which received the power produced by the men pushing the slides.[5]

After he had tested the new machinery on several trials between St. Louis and Bellefontaine, Atkinson received permission to employ the device on the boats to be used for the coming expedition and also to so equip the keelboats of the First Infantry that was then at St. Louis preparing to leave for Fort Atkinson. The trip to Council Bluffs would provide a rigorous field trial. On September 17, 1824, four companies of the First Regiment under the command of Major Stephen W. Kearny started upriver in four keelboats, *Muskrat*, *Mink*, *Racoon*, and *Beaver*. They carried with them quantities of food, supplies, and equipment. Many spectators lined the bank north of St. Louis to witness the launching of the paddle wheel-propelled boats. Kearny's journal entry that day was laconic: "As we are to attempt to navigate the Missouri, differently from what it has hitherto been, many remarks and observations were made, respecting the feasibility of our plan." After General Atkinson and several junior officers boarded the keelboats and completed the final inspection of the machinery, the boats pulled slowly away from St. Louis and headed north toward the mouth of the Missouri.[6] Atkinson accompanied the boats to Bellefontaine and then returned to St. Louis.

Several weeks later Atkinson rode overland to Council Bluffs to discuss the performance of the machinery with Major Kearny. Kearny reported that the First Infantry had arrived at Fort Atkinson in six weeks with only minor difficulty with the paddle wheels. This convinced Atkinson that the equipment was sound, and he decided to put paddle wheels on all the boats to be used in the expedition the coming summer. He also discussed his plans for the move into the Indian country with his subordinate officers at the post before he returned to St. Louis.[7]

5 Atkinson to Nourse, Oct. 13, 1824, Letters Received, AGO.

6 Journal of Stephen W. Kearny, entry, Sept. 17, 1824, MHS (hereafter Kearny Journal).

7 *Ibid.*, entry, Oct. 31, 1824; Atkinson to Nourse, Dec. 16, 1824, Letters Received, AGO.

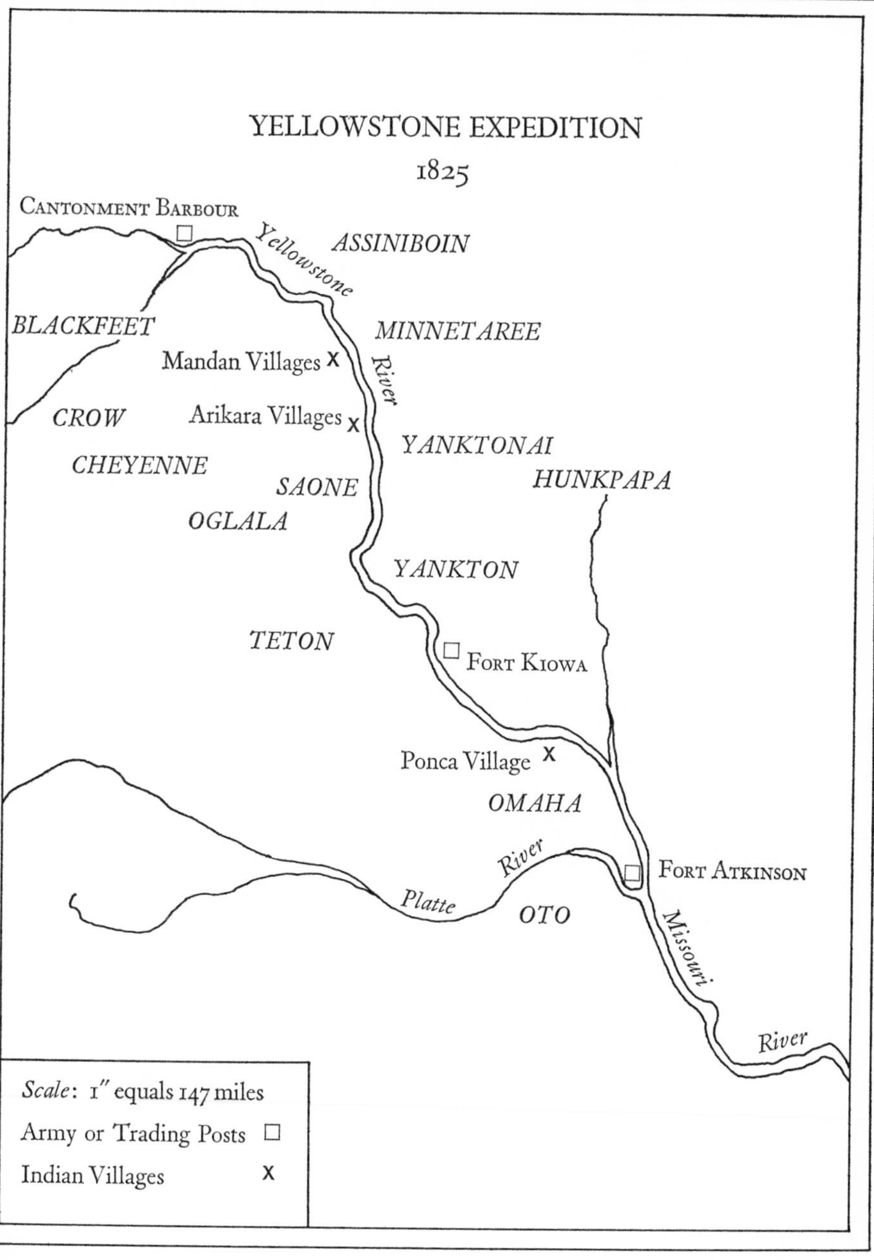
YELLOWSTONE EXPEDITION
1825
Cantonment Barbour
Yellowstone
ASSINIBOIN
BLACKFEET
MINNETAREE
Mandan Villages
River
CROW
Arikara Villages
YANKTONAI
CHEYENNE
HUNKPAPA
SAONE
OGLALA
YANKTON
TETON
Fort Kiowa
Ponca Village
OMAHA
River
Fort Atkinson
Platte
OTO
Missouri
River
Scale: 1″ equals 147 miles
Army or Trading Posts
Indian Villages

After this successful use of paddle wheels on keelboats, the local skeptics admitted grudgingly that Atkinson had indeed made a significant contribution to river navigation techniques. Senator Thomas H. Benton was enthusiastic, perhaps because in his view anything that proved valuable to river transportation aided Missouri and the West. "From the present appearance, the character of the General, the discipline, subordination and harmony of his command," he wrote Calhoun, "we may anticipate a complete success in the objects of the expedition, and that with unprecidented economy."[8]

By March, 1825, Atkinson had completed all arrangements for the expedition. "I shall," he reported, "take with me on the expedition 50 mounted men, and 400 foot in keel boat transportation armed with muskets and rifles & furnished with two pieces of ordnance."[9] He planned to leave St. Louis for Fort Atkinson on horseback about May 1 but, after conferring with co-commissioner O'Fallon and some subordinates, decided to leave early in April. Meanwhile, by April 2 some of the party had reached Franklin, Missouri; on April 19 they arrived at Fort Atkinson.[10]

There Atkinson supervised final preparations. On April 23 he assigned three keelboats to Major Kearny and the First Infantry and five to Colonel Leavenworth and the Sixth.[11] For the next week, packing and loading the keelboats occupied men and officers. During this time Atkinson and O'Fallon conferred on the methods to be used in the coming Indian negotiations. Atkinson also explained to his subordinates the military measures to be followed while the expedition traveled through the Indian country.

On Monday, May 16, the troops were ready to move. The remaining troops and families lined the riverbank to watch, and the

8 Benton to Calhoun, Sept. 22, 1824, Consolidated File, Atkinson's Expedition, QMG.

9 Atkinson to Nourse, Mar. 19, 1825, Letters Received, AGO.

10 Henry Atkinson, "General Henry Atkinson's Report of the Yellowstone Expedition of 1825" (ed. by Roger L. Nichols), *Nebraska History*, Vol. XLIV (June, 1963), 70 (hereafter Atkinson, "Report").

11 Atkinson, Ninth Military Dept., Orders, Apr. 23, 1825, Vol. 93, USAC.

eight keelboats started up the Missouri River.[12] Later that day Captain William Armstrong led a mounted party of forty men from Fort Atkinson to act as cavalry scouts for the expedition. The next day set a pattern for most of the days on the expedition. Roused by the bugler, the men crawled from their dew-laden tents well before sunrise. They packed their tents, boarded the boats, and started upriver at 4:30 A.M. They halted for breakfast at 8:30 A.M. after working their way upstream five or six miles. An hour and one-half later the flotilla started up the river again and traveled another six miles before stopping for dinner at 1:00 P.M. At 2:30 P.M. they again proceeded, traveling another six miles before halting for the night. The soldiers pulled the boats to within ten to thirty feet of each other. Then they disembarked and erected tents to form three sides of a square, with the open rear facing the river but guarded by men on the boats. At 8:00 P.M. the bugler sounded the tattoo over the darkened camp.[13] The daily pattern varied little except when minor accidents, difficulties with the boats or machinery, or bad weather altered the routine. Although often monotonous, river travel included enough danger to keep most of the force alert, and the changing landscape with plentiful wild birds and animals seems to have kept interest high.

Equipped with the paddle wheels designed by Atkinson, the boats moved rapidly, but the strong Missouri current combined, perhaps, with faulty workmanship caused some breakdowns. On May 19 the *Otter*, one of the boats assigned to Major Kearny, smashed into the riverbank. This damaged the machinery and forced Kearny to halt. While his men repaired the apparatus, the remainder of the flotilla continued upriver. After they completed the repairs, Kearny's men hurried upstream with their three boats, but shortly after noon, while the *Otter* was being pulled by the cordelle, the mast snapped off just above the deck. This forced

12 Kearny Journal, entry, May 16, 1825, MHS; Henry Atkinson and Benjamin O'Fallon, "Journal of Atkinson-O'Fallon Expedition" (ed. by Russel Reid and Clell G. Gannon), *North Dakota Historical Quarterly*, Vol. IV (Oct. 1929), 10–11 (hereafter cited as Atkinson-O'Fallon Journal).

13 Atkinson, Ninth Military Dept., Orders, May 15, 1825, Vol. 93, USAC.

Kearny to stop again. He sent word to Atkinson of this new difficulty and dispatched a crew to bring in a cottonwood log as a replacement. His men worked into the night to repair the boat and, after a short rest, set out again long before daybreak in order to rejoin the flotilla.[14]

There was also a continual danger of losing men who went ashore to hunt. On May 25, for instance, Lieutenant William L. Harris went ashore late in the afternoon. He did not return to camp that night, and in the morning Major Kearny organized a hunt for him. He sent two soldiers to track the Lieutenant through the woods and left the *Muskrat* behind, although the rest of the boats set out as scheduled. Kearny also directed the commander of the *Muskrat* to fire a swivel gun occasionally to attract Harris. The hunters failed to find Harris, however, and that night the boat and hunters joined their companions farther upstream. Then Atkinson and Kearny sent another search party, but they also returned without the Lieutenant. On May 26 four men went back to search the riverbank, but could not find a trace of Harris. After dark that evening, just as the officers were ready to give up, they heard a cry from the opposite shore of the river and found the bedraggled officer "nearly worn out."[15]

Other minor difficulties often slowed the flotilla or caused some discomfort. Strong winds occasionally allowed the crews to use sails for a few miles, but often the course of the river turned and twisted so that a favorable wind shortly became a head wind and a hindrance rather than an aid. Sand bars also slowed the progress of the boats, because the men had to tow the boats off the bar with cordelle or towrope. Thunderstorms and sudden rain added to the discomfort. In the small tents, the men, awakened by thunder and hail, often arose to find their clothes and other belongings soaked. Tents, blankets, and even uniforms became musty and moldy from these repeated soakings because, instead of being hung out to dry,

[14] Kearny Journal, entry, May 19, 1825, MHS.

[15] *Ibid.*, May 23–26, 1825; Atkinson-O'Fallon Journal, entries, May 23–26, 1825.

they had to be packed wet and could not be unrolled until the next evening.

On June 5, Edward Rose, one of the interpreters accompanying the cavalry under Captain Armstrong, brought news that the mounted force had reached the Ponca village ten or twelve days earlier. Armstrong's men had found little game, so Atkinson sent a supply of bread and pork back with Rose. News that the tribe awaited their arrival provided fresh impetus for the expedition.[16] Three days later, on June 8, the expedition reached the Ponca village and landed at the mouth of White Paint Creek in what is now northeastern Nebraska. The troops cleared the ground for the encampment, and General Atkinson and Major O'Fallon met with the chiefs during the afternoon, explained their visit, and made arrangements for a council to be held the next morning. The same afternoon the crews unloaded the boats, cleaned them, and repacked the cargoes.[17]

At reveille the next morning the soldiers were told that a brigade review was to be held at 9:00 A.M. They donned their dress uniforms and assembled behind the village of sixty lodges. There, on a broad, grassy plain, sweltering under a clear sky and bright sun, General Atkinson reviewed the troops. After the review, the brigade demonstrated several formations and movements for the Poncas.[18] That afternoon, just before the council meeting began, Atkinson placed his men in ranks on either side of the council area, erected flags, and had the band play. These displays were part of his efforts to impress the Indians with the strength and also the friendship of the United States and of his command.

At the meeting with the Ponca headmen and chiefs, Major O'Fallon explained his work as agent for the Missouri tribes, recognized several Indians as chiefs, and gave them medals and presents.

[16] Kearny Journal, entry, June 5, 1825, MHS; Atkinson-O'Fallon Journal, entry, June 5, 1825.

[17] Kearny Journal, entry, June 8, 1825, MHS; Atkinson-O'Fallon Journal, entry, June 8, 1825; Atkinson to Roger Jones, June 10, 1825, Letters Received, AGO.

[18] Kearny Journal, entry, June 9, 1825, MHS; Atkinson-O'Fallon Journal, entry, June 9, 1825.

After O'Fallon finished his talk, General Atkinson explained his mission as one of peace and friendship. He discussed the treaty that he and O'Fallon presented to the tribal leaders. The Indians, in turn, agreed to sign the document and then circulated a peace pipe. There were no real negotiations because the commissioners had already drawn up the treaty. Their only task was to explain the provisions of the treaty and to convince the chiefs to sign it. After the formal ceremony, the Ponca chiefs were presented several guns, strouding, blankets, knives, tobacco, and a few trinkets.[19] The commissioners used this same procedure whenever they met with the Indians on this trip.

That afternoon a detachment of troops worked to repair some faulty paddle-wheel equipment. The next day, June 10, the expedition left the Ponca village and proceeded up the Missouri. During the next week the hunting parties from the brigade gradually improved their skill. They returned with antelope, deer, and even a few burrowing squirrels or prairie dogs for the officers' fare. Fresh serviceberries and gooseberries also provided welcome additions to the army fare. On June 15, Atkinson met the mounted party along the river. Extreme heat, a shortage of good grass, and poor water had forced the horsemen to abandon their plan to move through the hills, so they remained along the river bottom and kept pace with the flotilla for the next few weeks.[20]

On June 17 the flotilla arrived at Fort Kiowa, the second stop, where the commissioners met Peter Wilson, subagent for the Sioux, who had spent the winter along the Missouri. Wilson explained that the Indians were out on the prairie hunting and dispatched runners to bring them. On June 18 the Teton Sioux arrived, followed the next afternoon by the Yankton Sioux; the Yanktonai Sioux arrived the next day.[21]

19 Kearny Journal, entry, June 9, 1825, MHS; Atkinson-O'Fallon Journal, entry, June 9, 1825; Atkinson to Jones, June 10, 1825, Letters Received, AGO.

20 Atkinson-O'Fallon Journal, entries, June 11–16, 1825; Kearny Journal, entries, June 11–16, 1825, MHS.

21 Atkinson, "Report," June 17, 1825; Kearny Journal, entries, June 17–18, 1825, MHS; Atkinson-O'Fallon Journal, entries, June 17, 18, and 20, 1825.

The councils began on June 21 after a parade of the troops. The commissioners met with the Indians after dinner. After considerable haggling, they got no further that day than organizing the bands—that is, recognizing chiefs and headmen who would later sign the treaties. The next morning Atkinson and O'Fallon met with the chiefs again, and this time the Indians heard the provisions of the treaty and agreed to sign the document. Then they exchanged gifts with the commissioners. Thus three more bands agreed to treaties with the United States.[22] All the treaties Atkinson and O'Fallon signed with the Indians during the summer of 1825 included the same general provisions. The Indians acknowledged the supremacy of the United States over their affairs. They agreed to the regulation of their trade by the President, to allow American traders to enter their country, to protect these traders, and not to trade with unlicensed traders. The Indians also agreed not to trade, sell, or give guns or ammunition to enemies of the United States. Both parties agreed to return stolen property to the other. The United States promised to protect the Indians, to send licensed traders into their country, and to remain at peace with them.[23]

On June 23 the brigade resumed its ascent of the river. They arrived at the mouth of Teton River seven days later, and there established camp and waited for the nearby tribes to gather. On July 3 the Oglala Sioux arrived. As a gesture of hospitality the chiefs invited the commissioners and army officers to a dog feast late the next afternoon. Atkinson's opinion of eating dog is not recorded, but he and O'Fallon realized the importance of following Indian customs and attended the feast. It "consisted of the flesh of 13 dogs boiled in plain water in 7 kettles, much done," accompanied by "water from the Missouri bro't up in the paunches of Buffalo, which gave it a disagreeable taste." After the feast, the Indians placed the commissioners on seats of "Buffalo robes, Beaver skins & some pieces of domestic cloth." Nearby "were

[22] Kearny Journal, entries, June 21–22, 1825, MHS; Atkinson-O'Fallon Journal, entries, June 21–22, 1825.

[23] Charles J. Kappler, comp., *Indian Affairs: Laws and Treaties*, II, 159–61.

arranged 5 entire Buffalo dungs in a row on which a pipe already charged was laid." Chief Standing Buffalo lit the pipe and passed it to Atkinson, who took "a few whifs" and passed it to Major O'Fallon. At the end of the ceremony, the chief knocked the "ashes on the centre dung & presented the pipe to Gen. A." Then the Indians gave the commissioners the robes and skins they had used for seats, and the commissioners returned to their camp.[24]

Meanwhile, the Cheyennes and the Saone or Sione Sioux arrived. On July 6 the commissioners concluded treaties with the chiefs of all three tribes. The next morning the brigade broke camp and embarked. Atkinson decided that the difficulty of finding feed for the horses made the cavalry unit more bother than it was worth, and he sent most of the horses back to Council Bluffs with a detachment of six men. He retained ten or twelve horses and gave a few to the Indians.[25] By disbanding the cavalry unit, Atkinson limited the range of the scouting and hunting parties. He also reduced his ability to demonstrate cavalry maneuvers and mounted artillery drill, which may have lessened the impact of the expedition upon the Indians.

For the next week the troops continued up the river. On July 15 the flotilla arrived at the Arikara villages in northern South Dakota, the scene of the surprise attack on Ashley and his men two years earlier. Atkinson hoped to impress this unruly tribe with American power and paraded the troops longer than usual the next morning. A heavy windstorm caused the council to be postponed until the next morning, but the meeting was successful. The Arikaras signed the treaty. Because of their past misdeeds, however, the tribe received only a few twists of tobacco rather than the usual swords, pistols, powder, lead, and trade goods. Atkinson and O'Fallon also warned the chiefs that future attacks on Americans would surely bring swift retribution, although all past offenses were forgiven.

24 Atkinson-O'Fallon Journal, entry, July 4, 1825; Kearny Journal, entry, July 4, 1825, MHS.

25 Atkinson, "Report," July 7, 1825; Atkinson-O'Fallon Journal, entry, July 7, 1825; Kearny Journal, entry, July 7, 1825, MHS.

When the councils ended, the commissioners seemed to think that the Indians were "impressed with deep & full contrision for their offences" and that they would "behave well" in the future.[26]

After the expedition left the Arikara villages, it progressed with few difficulties other than mosquitoes and bands of howling wolves, that often kept the men awake at night. On July 26 the troops arrived at the Mandan villages in central North Dakota, where they established a camp which they occupied for the next ten days. Atkinson chose this particular site because five Indian villages were situated within a seven-mile area, making it convenient for the Indians and commissioners to arrange councils. On Saturday afternoon, July 30, the commissioners began meeting with representatives from the Mandan and Gros Ventre tribes. The parley lasted most of the afternoon. When the commissioners blamed the Indians for taking part in the attacks on General Ashley's party several years earlier, the chiefs attributed the acts to some of their rash young men. One of their war parties had indeed fired upon the whites, but, the chiefs said, it happened at night and the braves thought they were firing on other Indians.[27] After signing the treaty, the commissioners argued about the Indians' guilt and the number of presents they should receive. O'Fallon objected when Atkinson gave a large number of presents to the tribes.

After they left the Indians, the two men continued to quarrel. At dinner that evening, according to George H. Kennerly, the sutler, "After the most harsh, and angry conversation had taken place, they mutually seized, one a knife, the other a fork, and made [an] attempt to stab" each other. Kennerly claimed to have stopped the fight and blamed O'Fallon for having "provoked the Genl. to this line of conduct, by his continual bad humor, and unnecessary interference with his duties as a military officer . . ." The scuffle ended when O'Fallon denounced Atkinson and threatened

[26] Atkinson, "Report," July 16–18, 1825; Atkinson-O'Fallon Journal, entries, July 16–18, 1825; Kearny Journal, entries, July 16–18, 1825, MHS.

[27] Atkinson-O'Fallon Journal, entries, July 26–30, 1825; Kearny Journal, entries, July 26–30, 1825, MHS.

to go to Washington that autumn and report Atkinson's conduct to the War Department. Later Kennerly wrote, "They have not since spoke to each other, and how it will end God only knows."[28]

This fight might have been the result of their having been in close association too long. More than likely, however, the difference in temperament of the two men was responsible. O'Fallon was eager to punish, but Atkinson usually preferred to settle matters peaceably. Jean P. Cabanné, fur trader and St. Louis resident, characterized the General as more humane and less inflexible than Major O'Fallon when dealing with the Indians.[29] Ever since their negotiations with the Pawnees in 1819, they had disagreed about what method to use when meeting the Indians in council. Atkinson had then given the chiefs sabers and other presents and had joined them for a feast, in spite of O'Fallon's objections. From that first joint session, the different personalities of the two stand out clearly. In spite of their violent quarrel, the commissioners continued to hold joint negotiations and presented a unified front to the Indians. Their continuing disagreement, however, may have been responsible for nearly causing a disaster during the Crow negotiations on August 4.

The Crow Indians, a large and warlike tribe, had reluctantly agreed to negotiate after receiving repeated messages from the commissioners. Described as "Fine looking Indians, and well mounted," a large delegation arrived on August 3. Their camp consisted of three hundred lodges with nearly three thousand Indians, including six hundred warriors. For the first time the Indians had a numerical superiority to Atkinson's brigade.[30]

On August 4, Atkinson and O'Fallon met the chiefs in council, and, after some discussion, they signed a treaty. Then, rather than giving presents as usual, the commissioners began arguing with the Indians over the fate of two Iroquois who were prisoners of the Crows. The Crows had captured these two men from the Blackfeet,

28 George H. Kennerly to James Kennerly, Aug. 1, 1825, Kennerly Papers, MHS.

29 Cabanné to Pierre Chouteau, Jr., Nov. 8, 1824, Chouteau Collection, MHS.

30 Kearny Journal, entry, Aug. 3, 1825, MHS; Atkinson, "Report," Aug. 3, 1825.

and the chiefs refused to release them although Atkinson demanded they do so. The dispute continued. When Atkinson left to get some lunch, Major O'Fallon carried on the argument with the chiefs. The Crows became "very hostile in the conduct" and several of them tried to take presents from the commissioners' tent. O'Fallon lashed out at them with his musket and struck three or four chiefs on the head, gashing one of them severely. At this point Atkinson returned and, through Edward Rose, the interpreter, calmed the enraged Indians. "At one time," Major Kearny remarked, "it was considered, that the result, *Peace or War* was as uncertain, as in throwing up a copper, whether it comes, head or tail . . ." Atkinson got most of the Crows out of camp, and "by some trouble and exertion" effected a partial reconciliation with the chiefs. He ordered his command under arms, but was able to quiet ruffled tempers and the danger subsided.[31] According to one account, some of the officers had left their posts during the negotiations, and the Indians spiked their artillery pieces with wood, grass, and dirt. There may be a kernel of truth in the story, although the army narrators omitted this part of the drama.[32]

There is little reason to believe the Crows intended to attack Atkinson's force because of the two Iroquois prisoners or the lack of presents, since they were usually friendly to the whites. Perhaps Rose's translation angered the chiefs or O'Fallon, but O'Fallon's conduct certainly angered the Indians. O'Fallon may have been dissatisfied with Atkinson's efforts to obtain the prisoners, and tried to use the opportunity to demonstrate that his skill was superior to that of Atkinson. In any case, Atkinson's timely arrival probably prevented a fight, and his conciliatory measures satisfied the Indians for the moment. He invited the chiefs to return for presents to "cover their wounds." The next morning they arrived, accompanied by all the braves. After more talk, Atkinson

[31] Kearny Journal, entries, Aug. 4–5, 1825, MHS.

[32] The latter incident is related in James P. Beckwourth, *The Life and Adventures of James P. Beckwourth* . . . (ed. by T. D. Bonner), 53–54; Capt. B. L. E. Bonneville, *The Rocky Mountains* . . . (ed. by Washington Irving), 216–17.

gave them some presents, and they seemed satisfied. Later he rode to the Crow village for a talk with Long Hair, the head chief, who received him in a friendly manner. After this polite treatment, Atkinson returned to camp, but still maintained the heavy guard he had ordered the previous afternoon. That night the artillery officers fired a series of rockets and shells which they hoped would impress the Indians.[33]

Thus ended the one incident that might have started hostilities and defeated the purpose of the expedition. In this emergency Atkinson not only was able to prevent bloodshed, but also salved the wounds of the Crows. He showed no fear of the Crow warriors, nor did he beg them for peace, but persuaded them that the difficulty had come about through a misunderstanding. Atkinson might have ordered an attack, in which, owing to the organization and heavy firepower of the troops, he probably would have triumphed. Instead, he used the threat of force as a deterrent. In his isolated position, deep within the Indian country, Atkinson's action probably saved many lives and the success of his mission. As it was, news of the incident spread up and down the river far in advance of the flotilla, and because of his firm but peaceable display the expedition was able to continue unmolested.

On August 6 both the Crows and the troops moved up the river separately. By the next evening Atkinson decided that the Indian danger had subsided and reduced the guard detail to normal size. On August 13 they passed the northernmost point of the Missouri, which, according to their calculations, was slightly north of the forty-eighth parallel. From there the flotilla continued west and arrived at the mouth of the Yellowstone in midafternoon four days later. Just beyond the confluence of the two rivers, the flotilla halted, and the men erected their last temporary encampment, Cantonment Barbour, on the north side of the Missouri.[34] Located

[33] Atkinson-O'Fallon Journal, entries, Aug. 4–5, 1825; Kearny Journal, entries, Aug. 4–5, 1825, MHS.

[34] Atkinson-O'Fallon Journal, entries, Aug. 7–18, 1825; Kearny Journal, entries, Aug. 7–18, 1825, MHS.

on a "beautiful & level Prairie," bounded by the two rivers and a forest nearly a mile distant, the area around the camp furnished enough large and small game for all.

On August 19, General Ashley, St. Louis fur trader and acquaintance of both Atkinson and O'Fallon, arrived with twenty-four men and one hundred packs of beaver pelts. Just as the trappers neared shore, one of their boats sank and nearly one third of their fur cargo floated down the river. After much noise and chasing, Ashley and his men recovered the fur packs. They stopped at Atkinson's camp to rest. Atkinson offered to escort Ashley, his men, and cargo back to Council Bluffs, if they could wait a few days while the flotilla went farther up the Missouri. Ashley was happy to accept this offer of protection and had his men camp alongside the army.[35]

Early the morning of August 21, Atkinson and O'Fallon began the trip farther up the river, taking five keelboats, 330 men, and one artillery piece and leaving the rest at camp. Ashley accompanied the commissioners, who still hoped to find either the Blackfeet or Assiniboins and to reach Two Thousand Mile Creek, a point supposedly that distance from the Mississippi. Above the Yellowstone the Missouri narrowed, the current was slower, and high barren hills extended to within a few yards of the river. By mid-morning of August 24, the party reached Porcupine River. Since this was beyond the point they had hoped to reach, they dismantled their paddle-wheel apparatus, and, after giving "three hearty cheers," turned the boats around and began the journey downstream.[36] Two days later the detachment arrived at the Yellowstone. At daybreak on August 27, the flotilla, augmented by Ashley's party, left Cantonment Barbour. Their progress downstream was rapid. On the first day they traveled sixty-five or seventy miles.

The only major accident on the descent was the sinking of the

[35] Atkinson, "Report," Aug. 18–19, 1825; Kearny Journal, entries, Aug. 18–19, 1825, MHS; Atkinson-O'Fallon Journal, entry, Aug. 19, 1825.

[36] Kearny Journal, entry, Aug. 24, 1825, MHS.

Muskrat. The boat, carrying most of the furs, sank in two to four feet of water when she hit a snag that punched a hole in her bottom. Some of the beaver packs went swirling down the river but were soon recovered. The troops spent most of the night repairing the damage, and by morning the *Muskrat* was ready once more. On September 19, twenty-three days after leaving the Yellowstone, the flotilla arrived at Council Bluffs, the Sixth Infantry moved back in the barracks, and the First pitched tents nearby.[37]

On September 20, General Henry Atkinson held a last review of his brigade. He thanked both officers and men "for their indifatigable zeal and perseverance in discharging the fatiguing duties, connected with the expedition, and for the soldierly appearance of the men on the frequent occasions that they were required to appear in uniform." Then he dissolved the command.[38]

For the next several weeks he worked to conclude the routine details of the expedition. He prepared the financial accounts and made copies of the treaties. At Council Bluffs, Atkinson and O'Fallon also held councils with several nearby tribes. The Otoes, Pawnees, and Omahas had all come in by the first week in October. On Friday, October 7, the commissioners, accompanied by three officers, ten invalids, and eight crewmen, boarded a keelboat and left Fort Atkinson for St. Louis.[39] They passed rapidly downstream, stopping at Liberty, Missouri, on October 13 and at Franklin, Missouri, three days later. On October 20 the boat pulled up to the sand bar at the foot of Market Street in St. Louis and the expedition was over. Atkinson and O'Fallon had left St. Louis the previous April for Council Bluffs and now, in midautumn, they returned.[40]

After a short rest at St. Louis, Atkinson went to Louisville where he wrote a dull report of the expedition. In this he listed the stops made along the route of the expedition, discussed the Indian

37 Atkinson-O'Fallon Journal, entries, Sept. 13 and 19, 1825.

38 Atkinson, Ninth Military Dept., Orders, Sept. 20, 1825, Vol. 93, USAC.

39 Atkinson-O'Fallon Journal, entries, September 24–October 7, 1825; Kearny Journal, entries, September 24–October 7, 1825, MHS.

40 Atkinson-O'Fallon Journal, entry, Oct. 20, 1825.

tribes encountered, and described the geography of the river valley. From William H. Ashley he relayed news of South Pass, "an easy passage across the Rocky Mountains . . . indeed so gentle in ascent, as to admit of wagons being taken over." He also discussed the extent of British enterprise and influence among the tribes of the plains. Atkinson wrote that according to Jedediah Smith, one of Ashley's men, "The British traders . . . never, of latter years, visit the Indians residing on the Missouri below the falls of that river, nor do those Indians visit the British establishments on Red river . . ." Because the influence of the British traders was negligible and the Indians were relatively peaceful, Atkinson saw little need for an army post on the upper Missouri. He proposed, however, that the mouth of the Yellowstone was the best location, if the government decided a post was necessary. This, he wrote, was the highest point easily supplied by water, although if adequate protection were to be afforded the fur trappers and traders, the post should be at the forks of the Missouri. He concluded the discussion by suggesting that "An occasional show of an imposing military force in an Indian country produces, in my opinion, a better effect than a permanent location of troops among them."[41] This report, although it does include some interesting material, shows Henry Atkinson unaware of the possible historical importance of the expedition or of his comments about it. He included only a minimal narrative and seemed to take the importance, danger, excitement, and drudgery in stride. Atkinson's unimaginative prose makes him appear as just another colorless, frontier army officer.

Atkinson's report seems to have received scant attention. The expedition, however, accomplished its purpose of signing treaties with the Indians along the upper Missouri. Commissioners Henry Atkinson and Benjamin O'Fallon concluded twelve treaties with sixteen bands of Indians during the eighteen-week journey. They traveled between 1,600 and 2,000 river miles up the Missouri. The expedition did not produce any lasting protection to the Americans in the Indian country.

[41] Atkinson to Brown, Nov. 23, 1825, ASP:MA, II, 657.

For Henry Atkinson, the Yellowstone Expedition of 1825 was one of the most successful assignments in his military career. When he organized it, he profited from his earlier difficulties with navigation on the Missouri. His careful planning and the vigilance of his subordinates made it possible for the brigade to spend an entire summer in the wilderness without losing a single man or incurring serious damage to the flotilla. Because this was a rare feat in an era when most commands of between 450 and 500 men experienced some loss of life nearly every month, Atkinson received praise from the War Department. His efforts to adapt paddle wheels for propelling the keelboats also added to the success of the expedition. Using his invention, the keelboats did indeed travel faster than those paddled or pulled along by the usual methods. By tact and diplomacy he ended a quarrel with the Crows and insured the peaceful continuation of the expedition. Unlike the Missouri Expedition of 1819, the Yellowstone Expedition of 1825 accomplished the goals of the War Department. This success demonstrated Atkinson's organizational abilities and his qualities of leadership.

VII. *New Command: An Infantry School—1825–27*

Early in 1826, Henry Atkinson, now forty-three or forty-four years old, got married. Later that year he was chosen to help pick a site for an infantry school, to superintend its construction, and to become the first commander. Atkinson also retained command of the Right Wing of the Western Department of the Army and continued to play an important part in keeping peace with the Indians.

Shortly after his return to St. Louis, Atkinson was asked by Jacob Brown, commanding general of the army, for his opinion of Indian removal, the necessity for forts along the frontier and the protection of the Santa Fe trade. Before giving his answer to these questions, Atkinson solicited opinions from experienced travelers and Santa Fe traders. He favored removal of more Indians to the West, but only if "a cordon of posts along that whole extent of country" could be provided "to preserve peace among the multiplied number of tribes, and to give protection to our frontier." Troops, he declared, were as necessary to keep peace among the various tribes as to protect frontier settlers. A line of forts, he felt, would protect the Indians from exploitation and abuse by whites.[1] He also suggested that a post be located on "the Arkansas at the north bend of that river" about three hundred miles from Cantonment Gibson. This spot was nearly midway on the route to Santa Fe

1 Atkinson to Brown, Nov. 23, 1825, ASP:MA, II, 657.

and had water and some forage for the animals. Atkinson cautioned, however, that a post would be of little value to caravans unless the army used mounted patrols rather than infantrymen as escorts. He wrote that eighty to one hundred men should be used "to escort the caravans, and make fresh pursuit of depredating parties of Indians." Because of the enormous cost for maintaining such a post and because of the size and nature of most Santa Fe caravans, Atkinson declared that the caravans should be willing and able to protect themselves.

> When we take into view the limited number of troops scattered along our extensive frontier, and which appear necessary for the protection of our frontier settlements, I could hardly recommend that any of them should be withdrawn from that service to establish the contemplated post.[2]

The army did not need to match the Indians man for man. It should, however, maintain a force large enough to make them wary of attacking. In general, army planners seemed to agree.

Atkinson wrote this report to General Brown while he was in Louisville. He had gone there, however, to make final plans for his coming marriage to Miss Mary Ann Bullitt, eldest daughter of the late Thomas Bullitt, a wealthy merchant of that city. Atkinson's position as an army general and his social grace had brought him and the Bullitts together at Louisville social events. During his frequent stays in Kentucky, particularly when commanding the Western Department of the Army in 1823, 1824, and 1825, Henry had often visited the Bullitt family. His surviving papers fail to contain a single hint of his romance with Mary Ann. By the fall of 1825, however, it is certain they were thinking of marriage.

In late December, Atkinson had received an order to come to Washington.[3] This gave no hint of why he was being called to the national capital, but fit well with his plans. If he married soon, he could travel to Washington, combining official duties and a honey-

[2] Atkinson to Brown, Nov. 23, 1825, ASP:MA, II, 656–57.

[3] Jones to Atkinson, Dec. 20, 1825, Letters Sent, Vol. 7, AGO.

moon. In fact, he hoped to obtain a furlough at Washington and return to North Carolina to introduce his bride to his family and friends.

On January 15, 1826, Henry Atkinson and Mary Ann Bullitt exchanged marriage vows before the Reverend Henry M. Shaw, rector of Christ Church, a small Episcopal church in Louisville.[4] Henry was forty-three or four; his new wife, twenty-two. They had similar backgrounds of hard-working, well-to-do families, who were among the social leaders in their respective communities. After the ceremony friends and relatives overflowed the Bullitt homes on Jefferson Street. Both the General's friends and those of his bride considered the match a good one.[5]

A few days after the wedding, Atkinson, Mary Ann, and the General's friend and co-worker, William Clark, began a leisurely trip east by way of the National Road. They arrived at Washington together late in February. There they visited friends in Congress as well as War Department and Indian Office officials. To his disappointment, Atkinson learned he could not obtain a furlough.

On March 4, 1826, Atkinson received new orders. He and General Gaines were "to select a suitable position near the mouth of the Missouri river for an infantry school of instruction . . ."[6] During the winter of 1825–26, War Department officials had instituted two changes for better co-ordinating the scattered segments of the western army. The rotting buildings at Bellefontaine were no longer serviceable for storage of arms and clothing, so the War Department decided to construct a new arsenal in or near St. Louis. At the same time the Department, with the approval of the President, decided to build an infantry school of instruction at some convenient place in the West.

Atkinson's orders regarding the school specified no date of execution, so he and Mary Ann took a sight-seeing tour of the

[4] St. Louis, *Missouri Republican*, Feb. 2, 1826.

[5] Saunders to Yancy, April 17, 1826, in "Letters of Romulus M. Saunders to Bartlett Yancy, 1821–1828," *North Carolina Historical Review*, Vol. VIII (Oct., 1931), 456.

[6] Quoted in Jesup to James Barbour, Jan. 17, 1827, ASP:MA, III, 588.

eastern coast. They visited New York City, where Atkinson probably had friends from his stay after the War of 1812, and from there sailed up the Hudson to West Point before returning to Washington. On March 26 they reached Baltimore where they met William Clark and took "the accommodation stage" for St. Louis.[7]

Traveling slowly and perhaps stopping for a brief visit at Louisville, the Atkinsons and Clark reached St. Louis in April, 1826. There the General received a letter from General Gaines including copies of orders and correspondence that were intended to keep Atkinson abreast of current army policies and actions. Gaines reminded Atkinson to "Consider your command to be in all respects similar to what it would be if the troops of my department were on duty in the field, charged with the defence of a specific and more limited section of the frontier . . ."[8] To Gaines, frontier defense and promptness in meeting crises were of first importance. He wanted his subordinate to act first and notify him of the action later rather than to wait for his instructions. Apparently Gaines assumed that Atkinson would retain his duties with the Right Wing in spite of his new assignment in connection with the infantry school.

Anticipating construction of the new school in the vicinity of St. Louis and Bellefontaine, either Atkinson or Gaines ordered Major Kearny to return his detachment of four companies of the First Infantry from Council Bluffs to Bellefontaine.[9] In mid-May, Jacob Brown, commanding general of the army, arrived at St. Louis on a tour of inspection. He discussed his ideas about the school with Atkinson and perhaps made suggestions to help Atkinson choose the site.[10]

[7] William Clark to Meriwether L. Clark, Mar. 26, 1826, Clark Papers, MHS; G. H. Kennerly to Alziere Kennerly, Apr. 1, 1826, Kennerly Papers, MHS.

[8] Gaines to Atkinson, Apr. 18, 1826, Dept. of the West, Letters Sent, Letter Book 99, USAC.

[9] Journal of James Kennerly, entries, May 1–2, 1826, MHS (hereafter Kennerly Journal).

[10] Entry, May 14–15, 1826, in "William Clark Diary" (ed. by Louise Barry), *Kansas Historical Quarterly*, Vol. XVI (May, 1948), 8.

Henry Atkinson and his wife spent the next few months living "on the mound" in the home that formerly belonged to Colonel William Rector, surveyor general for Illinois and Missouri. While Atkinson awaited further orders from the War Department, he examined the surrounding countryside for a suitable site. By June 4 he chose the bluffs about three miles south of "Vide Poche" or Carondolet, an old French settlement nine or ten miles south of St. Louis. This location had a good harbor. The ground, underlaid by limestone, offered a position of some elevation, and there was plenty of "good oak timber on the spot for building." Atkinson proposed to begin construction that summer if General Gaines agreed to the choice.[11]

Later that month Gaines arrived from Louisville and, together with Atkinson, William Clark, and Governor John Miller, rode from St. Louis to examine possible sites. The party spent several days examining a number of spots along the tree-studded banks of the Mississippi. Beginning with the old post at Bellefontaine, they proceeded down-river seeking a suitable place on the bluffs north of the city, but to no avail. They examined the area across the river near Alton, Illinois, but the land there was too expensive. Finally, they rode to Carondolet to examine the site recommended by Atkinson. Much of this land was still in the public domain, and the villagers promised to relinquish their claims to what was not. The elevation, nearness to the river, and thin, sandy soil atop limestone bluffs all pointed to a healthful spot; besides, the available clay and limestone would furnish cheap building materials. On July 3, 1826, General Edmund P. Gaines agreed to the choice of site for the future Jefferson Barracks. The two submitted their suggestions to General Brown, who approved them.[12]

On July 10, 1826, Major Stephen W. Kearny brought four companies of the First Infantry from Bellefontaine to Carondolet,

[11] Wm. Clark to M. L. Clark, June 4, 1826, Clark Papers, MHS; Atkinson to Jesup, June 12, 1826, Letters Received, QMG.

[12] Gaines and Atkinson to Brown, July 3, 1826, Dept. of the West, Letters Sent, Letter Book 100, USAC.

where they erected temporary quarters named Cantonment Adams in honor of the former President. These structures furnished housing for Kearny's men later, when they helped erect permanent buildings at nearby Jefferson Barracks. Three weeks later, Atkinson received orders from General Brown to begin construction. "The general-in-chief places you in charge of the whole scheme of construction," wrote the Adjutant General. "He accordingly directs that you will commence operations without delay." General Brown had only two suggestions: that "substantial and comfortable barracks for two complete infantry regiments be speedly erected," and that Atkinson employ the men of the First and Third Infantry Regiments to do all the carpentry, blacksmith, and masonry work on the post.[13]

Atkinson was not entirely free to devote himself to the construction of Jefferson Barracks. Reports of unrest and possible intertribal wars along the Arkansas River between the Little Osages on one side and the Delaware, Kickapoo, Piankashaw, Wea, and Shawnee tribes on the other required his attention. Fortunately, he and William Clark, superintendent of Indian affairs at St. Louis, could operate effectively together. Neither thought any troop movement to that area was necessary. These difficulties stemmed from the policy of removal under which the government forced tribes from states east of the Mississippi to move west. Once settled on their new lands, friction with the local tribes quickly ensued, usually over hunting privileges. After some haggling in this case, the disputing tribes agreed to meet in council at Clark's agency house in September, 1826. In early October the tribes agreed to live in peace.[14]

In September, 1826, Atkinson left Major Kearny in command and with Mary Ann went to Louisville. There he conferred with General Gaines and relaxed for several weeks. During his absence, Colonel Henry Leavenworth arrived at St. Louis from Green Bay

[13] Jones to Atkinson, July 28, 1826, Letters Sent, Vol. 7, AGO.

[14] Atkinson to Gaines, Aug. 7, 1826, Letters Received, AGO; Atkinson to Gaines, Oct. 7, 1826, in Carter, ed., *Territorial Papers*, XX, 294.

with the Third Infantry, and on September 17, Leavenworth's command moved south to the construction site. There they encamped, near but not with the First Regiment, and named their temporary encampment Camp Miller in honor of John Miller, governor of Missouri.[15] On October 2, Atkinson and his wife returned to St. Louis, and he reassumed supervision of the building. The General ordered some of Leavenworth's men to erect temporary log barracks for the coming winter. The rest of the troops worked with the First Infantry, constructing more permanent buildings.

The work continued throughout the autumn and early winter. Atkinson, now the head of the first army infantry school, did not know how his new duties would affect his command of the Right Wing. General Gaines clarified his position. He assured Atkinson that his command of the Right Wing remained intact even after he assumed personal command of the infantry school. Gaines declared that any recurrence of Indian hostilities made it imperative for Atkinson to keep informed and ready to take prompt measures. His administrative duties, however, were not to interrupt his duties as commandant of the infantry school, a post Gaines considered "of the highest importance that can be assigned to any officer under my command next to those which actual or threatened hostilities would require."[16]

In late February, Mrs. Atkinson traveled to Louisville to be at her parents' home for the birth of her first child. Several weeks later, Henry, Junior, was born. Atkinson spent much of his time that spring traveling between St. Louis and Louisville, while he tried to supervise construction at Jefferson Barracks and still be with his wife and son. In early April he brought his family back to St. Louis where they lived with the Clarks for nearly a month before moving to new quarters at the Barracks. Their new home was built of hewn logs. It had four rooms, eighteen by twenty feet each,

15 Kearny Journal, entry, July 10, 1826, MHS.

16 Gaines to Atkinson, Dec. 24, 1826, Dept. of the West, Letters Sent, Letter Book 99, USAC.

and a twelve-foot hall down the center. Although large by military standards, it certainly was less spacious and elegant than the Bullitt home in Louisville and the Atkinsons' earlier home in St. Louis. The post itself was built atop a gently rolling limestone bluff that sloped toward the Mississippi. The buildings formed three sides of a quadrangle, with the fourth remaining open and facing the river. They included officers' quarters, enlisted men's barracks, a hospital, mess buildings, and storage space for guns and ammunition. The entire camp lay within a "wood of slender oaks, without underwood" and was surrounded by open prairie.[17]

In the spring of 1827, the War Department ordered a part of the Sixth Infantry moved from Fort Atkinson to Jefferson Barracks. Atkinson suggested to the Adjutant General that Fort Atkinson be abandoned and the entire regiment be brought to Jefferson Barracks. He also suggested that the army establish a new post farther down the Missouri. Possible sites for any new post, he said, were the land at the mouth of the Little Platte River just north of the Missouri boundary or the land near the mouth of the Kansas River. The War Department accepted his first proposal. By May 15 the first units of the Sixth reached St. Louis, and only one month later the entire regiment arrived at Jefferson Barracks. Thus, with little publicity or excitement, the army closed what had been its largest post west of the Mississippi.

On June 19, 1827, shortly after the arrival of the last units of the Sixth Infantry, General Jacob Brown stopped at St. Louis for a week of inspections, discussion, and rest. Brown, Scott, and others had long worked for an army infantry school, and the new barracks met their expectations. Brown seemed pleased with the progress shown at the post, both in construction of the buildings and in the quality and amount of training the men were receiving.[18] Rather than scattering recruits among the dozens of tiny posts

[17] Atkinson to Henry Stanton, Jan. 6, 1839, First Military Dept., Letter Book 106, USAC; Maximilian, Prince of Wied-Neuwied, *Travels in the Interior of North America* (Vol. XXII *Early Western Travels*, ed. by R. G. Thwaites), 229–31.

[18] *Missouri Republican*, June 28, 1827.

along the coasts and frontier, the new school allowed the army to organize and train complete units up to brigade size. Previously, the posts often consisted of only a platoon of twenty to thirty men, and recruits never experienced company-sized exercises and training. Now, entire regiments could be trained under a competent staff with a planned schedule. Incentives and competition might be employed, and more standardization of drill and training could be achieved. The new school represented a distinct advance in military thinking within the army.

Troops at Jefferson Barracks received training with rifle and musket, target practice, company, battalion, and regimental formations and maneuvers from time to time. It soon became apparent, however, that keeping troops at Jefferson Barracks was a luxury which the army could not often afford, and the units stationed there for training often had to be moved to the frontier to quell Indian disturbances or build roads or new posts. Even before the post was entirely finished, during the summer of 1827, Colonel Leavenworth took a detachment of the Third Regiment up the Missouri to begin work on a new post while the First and Sixth Regiments remained at the Barracks.[19] Atkinson's new command proved both interesting and challenging. Experienced at constructing military posts, he had no qualms about ordering that the buildings be constructed of stone and brick rather than the less permanent wooden materials suggested by his superior. With such materials the army could expect much longer use of the buildings, although the original cost was greater than it would have been for frame structures. By midsummer the buildings were nearly finished.

Several officers involved in the building of Jefferson Barracks have erroneously received credit for the tasks carried out by Henry Atkinson. General Jacob Brown has been suggested as having chosen the site. It is true that as commanding general of the army, Brown did have the final say, but he merely accepted Atkinson's recommendation. It has been claimed that Major Stephen W. Kearny constructed the early buildings and was the first com-

[19] Atkinson to Jones, Jan. 21, 1827, Letters Received, AGO.

mander of Jefferson Barracks. This may be supported only if one assumes that the temporary shelters Kearny's men built during July, 1826, were part of Jefferson Barracks. They were not. Kearny's only command was over the men within his own unit, and even this came under Atkinson's jurisdiction as commander of the Right Wing of the Western Department. As Atkinson's subordinate, Kearny did take charge on several occasions when his superior was absent on army business. Colonel Henry Leavenworth has also received credit for building and commanding this post. As in the case of Kearny, Leavenworth was merely a subordinate officer exercising a temporary command while Atkinson, his superior, was absent. All of the records clearly indicate that Henry Atkinson chose the site, superintended the building, and was the first commander of the army infantry school established at Jefferson Barracks.

The years 1825–27 were full of changes for Henry Atkinson, personally and professionally. He married, and his first son was born. He built and took command of Jefferson Barracks and the infantry school there. That Henry Atkinson should receive the command of the school is not surprising. His long experience in both field and staff positions, his strict attention to organization and detail, his reputation for maintaining his command in top military form, and his position as commanding officer in the West, all helped to bring about his appointment.

VIII. Red Bird Takes Some Scalps—1827

DURING THE SUMMER OF 1827, Henry Atkinson demonstrated his knowledge of Indian affairs and his skill as a military leader in pacifying the Winnebago Indians after the Red Bird Massacre and their attack on two keelboats near Prairie la Crosse. His actions in the circumstances show that he considered it more important to maintain peace than to gain fame as an Indian fighter. Instead of using the army to attack and perhaps destroy the Winnebagos, he employed the threat of force to end the difficulties peacefully. Atkinson's response to the Indian disturbance also showed the wisdom of General Brown's idea of maintaining a large reserve force at a central point near the frontier.

The Atkinsons had hardly settled down in their new quarters at Jefferson Barracks, when, on July 10, 1827, they received news that the Winnebago Indians had killed several people near Prairie du Chien and were threatening war against the miners in northern Illinois. The murders in Prairie du Chien, later called the Red Bird Massacre, merely added another to a series of depredations committed by the Winnebagos. In 1820, Winnebago braves had killed two soldiers near Fort Armstrong, at Rock Island, Illinois. Earlier, members of the tribe, living at the mouth of the Fox River near Lake Winnebago in Wisconsin, had charged tolls on boats of travelers passing their villages. In March, 1826, Winnebagos had murdered Francis Methode, his wife, and three children near Prairie du Chien.[1] Colonel Willoughby Morgan, commanding officer at Fort Crawford, on learning of the murders, had arrested leaders from the nearest Indian villages. He soon released them but demanded that they surrender the murderers. They eventually gave up six men, all of whom claimed to be innocent. After a public hearing, Morgan released all but two of the six.[2] Although these two men eventually gained their freedom, they were held in jail for a long time, first at Fort Crawford and then at Fort Snelling. Rumors circulated among the Indians that these men had been killed while in captivity. This did nothing to quiet the Winnebagos.

The encroachment of miners into the lead-mining area of northern Illinois and southern Wisconsin, beginning in 1816, also disturbed the Indians. Conflicting Indian claims and contradictory treaties caused confusion about what land belonged to the Indians. The Winnebagos hunted and traveled in the area between Rock Island in the southwest and Lake Winnebago in the northeast. They showed no disposition to yield their rights simply because the Sac and Foxes or the Chippewas had ceded the land to the Federal Government.

In mid-August, 1826, Thomas Forsyth, Indian agent at Rock Island, reported that miners were, even then, digging lead on Indian lands, and he complained that the Superintendent of the Mines at St. Louis had no authority to lease "Indian lands to any people whatever."[3] He correctly predicted a flood of hundreds of miners into the Winnebago country, and by January, 1827, Winnebago bands sent "war clubs, belts, and pipes to the neighboring tribes, as well as to some of the tribes in the South . . . for the purpose of making war on our frontiers."[4]

[1] Peter L. Scanlan, *Prairie du Chien: French, British, American*, 160.

[2] John Kinzie to Cass, July 15, 1826, Cass Letter Received, No. 171, State Historical Society of Wisconsin (hereafter SHSW); Thomas Forsyth to William Clark, July 13, 1826, Draper Collection, T–6: 51–52, SHSW.

[3] Forsyth to Clark, Aug. 15, 1826, Draper Collection, T–6:54, SHSW.

[4] *Ibid.*; Atkinson to Gaines, Sept. 28, 1827, in 20 Cong., 1 sess., Senate Doc. No. 1, 160.

Meanwhile, the War Department had decided that Fort Crawford was unnecessary, and in October, 1826, ordered the troops stationed there north to Fort Snelling.[5] This withdrawal may have seemed an American admission of weakness to the Indians. Fort Dearborn at Chicago had been closed some months earlier. This left all of northern Illinois and, in particular, the area between Galena and Chicago unguarded by a regular army force. The nearest military posts were at Fort Howard at Green Bay and Fort Armstrong at Rock Island.

In late May, 1827, Sioux Agent Lawrence Taliaferro went to Fort Snelling to meet the Sioux in council. There was trouble immediately. A Chippewa band of thirty braves with their women and children was attacked by the Sioux while camped near the fort. Two Chippewas were killed. Colonel Snelling captured nine of the Sioux offenders and promptly turned them over to the Chippewas, who shot two in retaliation for the murders. The others were released. Atkinson approved the act as "proper and just and in accordance with the spirit of the treaty of Prairie du Chien."[6]

After this incident, rumors circulated among Indians and whites. According to Joseph M. Street, new Winnebago agent at Prairie du Chien, several Sioux emissaries told the Winnebagos that the white men were responsible for the deaths of the two Sioux. The Winnebagos later told Street that a Sioux named Wawzee-Kootee, a known "babbler," also reported that Colonel Snelling had killed the two Winnebago prisoners who were being held at Fort Snelling for the Methode murders. The Winnebagos had offered the Sioux a string of wampum as an invitation to join in a war party against the whites. The Sioux refused, but Wawzee-Kootee repeated his story and urged the Winnebagos to "go strike the first blow and the Sioux will then help you." Street wrote that, although the Sioux had refused to join them, the Winnebagos were con-

[5] Bruce E. Mahan, *Old Fort Crawford and the Frontier*, 103.

[6] Snelling to Atkinson, May 31, 1827, Indian Office Files, Box 1, No. 10, SHSW; Atkinson to Gaines, June 15, 1827, Indian Office Files, Box 1, No. 8, SHSW.

vinced that the Sioux would join them once fighting began.[7] Wawzee-Kootee and the other Sioux with him had misled the Winnebagos by not stating their intentions more clearly. In addition, a rumor that the United States and Great Britain were moving toward war had circulated among the Indians during the winter of 1826–27.[8] Perhaps this led the Indians to assume they could attack frontiersmen without fear of reprisal.

Another incident, although only reputed to have occurred, may also have given an added stimulus to the Indians. According to John Reynolds, later governor of Illinois and a well-known Indian hater, the crewmen of two keelboats, going up the Mississippi to Fort Snelling with supplies for the garrison, had stopped at a Winnebago village and had got the Indians drunk. Then "they captured some six or seven squaws, who were also drunk. These squaws were forced on the boats *for corrupt and brutal purposes . . .*" The keelboatmen then proceeded northward, taking the Indian women along.[9] Western editors repudiated this tale vociferously, but it seems unlikely that Reynolds would have included it without some basis, particularly in view of his known hostility toward the Indians.

Whatever the rumors and schemes, the Indians were uneasy and restless. The miners were beginning to occupy land in northern Illinois, and more and more white men were passing through their

[7] Joseph M. Street to Secretary of War, Nov. 15, 1827, in 20 Cong., 1 sess., *House Exec. Doc. No.* 277, 14–15; Street to Edwards, Nov., 1827, in Ninian Edwards, *The Edwards Papers* (ed. by E. B. Washburne), *Chicago Historical Society Collections*, III, 315–16; James H. Lockwood, "Early Times and Events in Wisconsin," *Wisconsin Historical Society Collections*, Vol. II (1903), 156; William J. Snelling, "Early Days at Prairie du Chien, and Winnebago Outbreak of 1827," *Wisconsin Historical Society Collections*, Vol. V (1907), 142–44. Snelling also claimed that Red Bird had just returned from an unsuccessful raid against the Chippewas when he met the Sioux and, after being taunted for his failure by his tribesmen, was more easily influenced by the Sioux blandishments. *Ibid.*, 143.

[8] Lockwood, "Early Times and Events in Wisconsin," *Wisconsin Historical Society Collections*, Vol. II (1903), 155; Forsyth to Clark, May 24, 1827, Draper Collection, T–6: 265, SHSW.

[9] John Reynolds, *Reynolds' History of Illinois, My Own Times*: *Embracing also the History of My Life*, 177–78.

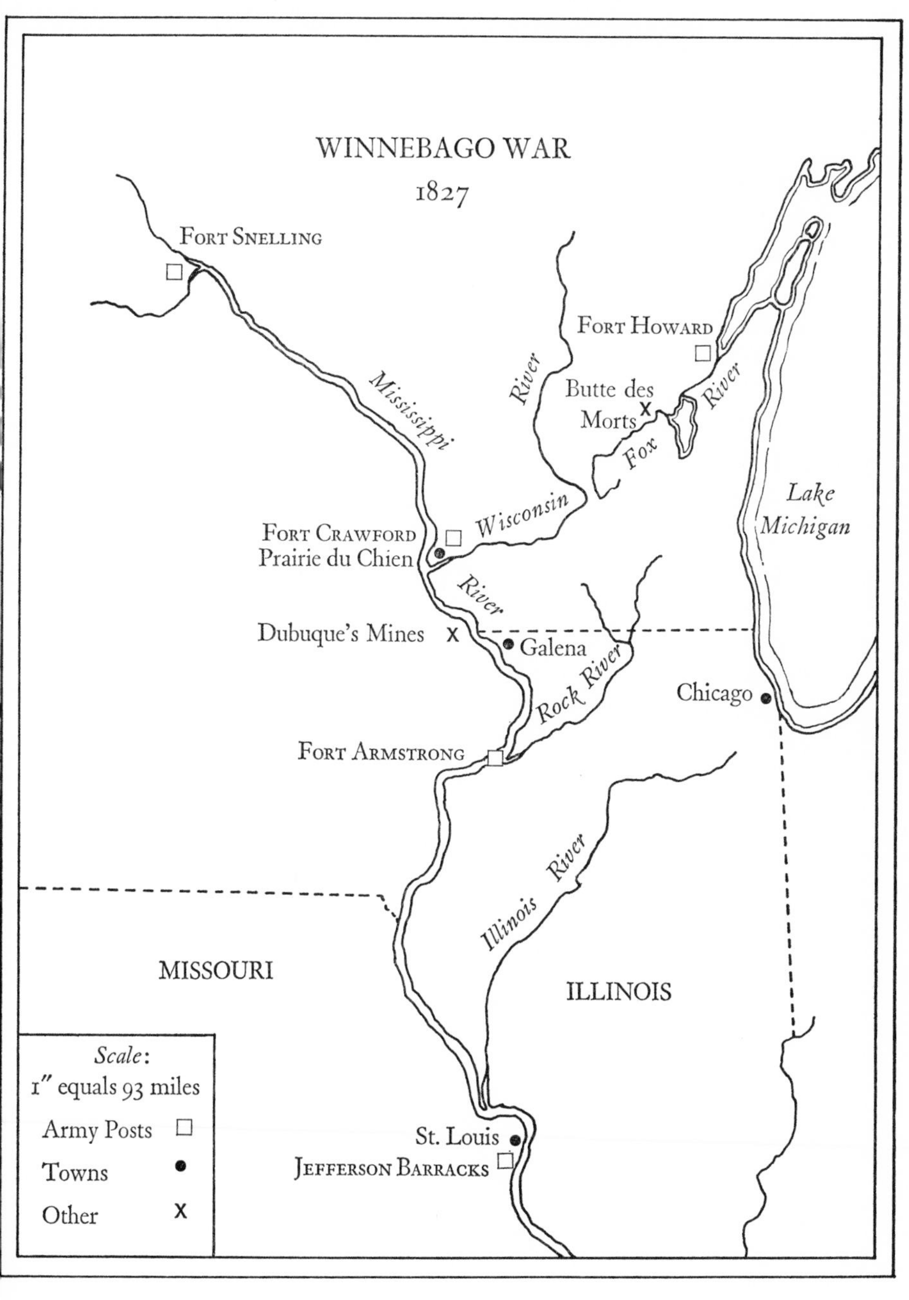
WINNEBAGO WAR
1827
FORT SNELLING
Mississippi
River
FORT HOWARD
Butte des
Morts
Fox
River
Lake
Michigan
Wisconsin
FORT CRAWFORD
Prairie du Chien
River
Dubuque's Mines
Galena
Rock River
Chicago
FORT ARMSTRONG
Illinois
River
MISSOURI
ILLINOIS
Scale:
1″ equals 93 miles
Army Posts
Towns
Other
St. Louis
JEFFERSON BARRACKS

country. Protests to their agent seemed to be of no avail. In this situation, acts of violence occurred, perhaps unrelated except in time. The first was the murder of Registre Gagnier and Solomon Lipcap and the scalping of one of the Gagnier children at Prairie du Chien in late June, 1827.[10] The murders, known as the Red Bird Massacre, were committed by Red Bird, a noted Winnebago warrior, and three companions. They had stopped at the trading post of James H. Lockwood in Prairie du Chien, and, after threatening Lockwood's wife and her brother, the Indians left the village. From there they went to McNair's Coulee, two or three miles from the village and entered the home of Registre Gagnier, a French half blood who lived there with his wife, two children, and Solomon Lipcap, a hired man. The Gagniers had known Red Bird and, like the whites in the vicinity, thought him trustworthy. Therefore, when the Indians asked for food, Mrs. Gagnier began to prepare some. At this moment Red Bird shot her husband, a second brave shot Lipcap, and Wekau, a third, tried to shoot her. She wrestled the gun away from him and chased the startled Indian from the cabin. When the gun misfired, she grabbed her boy of three and ran to the village to spread the alarm. The other Indians found her infant daughter still in the cabin and scalped but did not kill the child. Red Bird and his followers then fled northward to the Prairie la Crosse village where they displayed the fresh scalps to their friends and urged them to attack the whites.[11]

A second act of violence occurred on June 30, shortly after the Red Bird Massacre. The two keelboats whose crews had reputedly

[10] There is much confusion about the exact date of the murders. John Marsh, Indian subagent at Prairie du Chien, reported it variously as June 24, 26, 27, and 28, 1827. The parish register noted Gagnier's death as June 28. For a further discussion of this question see, Scanlan, *Prairie du Chien*, 129–31.

[11] Lockwood, "Early Times and Events in Wisconsin, *Wisconsin Historical Society Collections*, Vol. II (1903), 161–62; Thomas L. McKenney, "The Winnebago War of 1827," *Wisconsin Historical Society Collections*, Vol. V (1907), 199–200. Other accounts of the attack differ slightly. One says that the Indians attacked the family after the meal was finished. Another that Lipcap was shot while out in the garden rather than at the cabin. In any case, the Indians scalped and killed Gagnier and Lipcap, and scalped one of the children.

kidnapped the Winnebago squaws returned from Fort Snelling on their way to St. Louis. When the boats passed near the shore in front of the Winnebago village at Prairie la Crosse, the Indians opened fire. Taken by surprise, the crewmen dropped below decks and allowed the craft to drift. When the current carried one of the boats close to shore, the Indians leaped into their canoes and paddled toward it. By this time the crew began replying with a heavy fire of their own. They drove off all but two of the attackers, who clambered aboard and fired into the hold where most of the crew remained. The two braves steered the first boat to a nearby sand bar before the crew killed them. Then, amid a hail of balls from Indian muskets, the crew spilled out of the boat and pushed it from the sand bar back into the current, and soon they drifted beyond the range of the Indian guns.[12]

News of these attacks spread panic along the frontier. In Green Bay, Lewis Cass, governor of Michigan Territory, learned of the murders at Prairie du Chien and set out down the Fox-Wisconsin waterway to investigate. He arrived at Prairie du Chien on July 4, appointed militia officers, inspected the local defensive measures, and ordered Captain Thomas McNair and his militia company on active duty.[13] Then he sent messages to the peaceable Winnebago chiefs, urging them to keep away from their more refractory brethren. He also notified the guilty bands to go to the council at Butte des Morts to settle their grievances. Finally, he asked the Sioux, Menominees, and Sac and Foxes to remain at peace. In this way he sought to isolate the troublesome Winnebagos from the nearby tribes.[14]

Then Cass left Prairie du Chien for Galena. On his way down the Mississippi, he stopped at Dubuque's mines and asked John

[12] Snelling, "Early Days at Prairie du Chien," *Wisconsin Historical Society Collections*, Vol. V (1907), 147–51; Lockwood, "Early Times and Events in Wisconsin," *Wisconsin Historical Society Collections*, Vol. II (1903), 162–63.

[13] Cass to Thomas McNair, July 4, 1827, *Michigan Pioneer and Historical Collections*, Vol. XXXVI (1908), 547–48; Cass to James Barbour, July 4, 1827, Carter, ed., *Territorial Papers*, XI, 1094–95.

[14] *Ibid.*, 1095.

Connelly, the subagent to the Fox tribe, to persuade some of them to go to Prairie du Chien and aid the citizens in its defense. Cass also held a council with the Foxes and repeated his request.[15] Whether or not they went is unknown. From Dubuque he continued south to Galena. The miners there had fled to the city where they hoped to protect each other, but they had neither arms nor ammunition. Cass feared that Prairie du Chien was in more danger than Galena and asked the Galena militia for volunteers to relieve Prairie du Chien. They agreed, and Colonel Abner Field led a part of the local militia north. From Galena, Cass hurried down to St. Louis, arriving there on July 10. There he met with William Clark and Henry Atkinson. That afternoon Cass outlined to them the situation and the steps he had taken.[16]

The three men came from the meeting with these general plans. Atkinson would move a part of his force north to Prairie du Chien and then, if necessary, continue farther into the Indian country and force the Winnebagos into submission. Cass would return to Green Bay and hold the scheduled councils, hoping to settle the difficulties before Atkinson's force arrived. Clark would write his subordinates to try to keep their charges at peace so that, if Atkinson had to fight, he would face only the Winnebagos and not a combination of dissatisfied warriors from all tribes in the area. After the meeting Cass traveled back to the treaty grounds at Butte des Morts.

For the next few days the officers and men at Jefferson Barracks hurried to pack personal things and military equipment for the coming campaign. At 6:00 A.M., July 15, Atkinson and 580 men boarded three steamboats—*Indiana*, *General Hamilton*, and *Essex*—and headed for the upper Mississippi thirty minutes later.[17]

15 Cass to John Connelly, July 5, 1827, Carter, ed., *Territorial Papers*, XI 1097–98.

16 "William Clark Diary," *Kansas Historical Quarterly*, Vol. XVI (May, 1948), 30; Cass to Barbour, July 10, 1827, Carter, ed., *Territorial Papers*, XI, 1102–1103.

17 Kennerly Journal, entry, July 15, 1827, MHS; "William Clark Diary," *Kansas Historical Quarterly*, Vol. XVI (May, 1948), 30; John O'Fallon to T. A. Smith, July 15, 1827, Smith Papers, SHSM.

Atkinson led the force north and arrived at the Des Moines Rapids in three days. From there he went to Rock Island and Fort Armstrong, where he stopped to meet with the Sac and Fox chiefs. After declining their offer to help against the Winnebagos, he gave them a few gifts. Atkinson and the force left the post on July 26. The next day they arrived at Galena, where Atkinson inspected the local defense measures and supplied the Committee of Safety with arms and munitions before again moving north toward Prairie du Chien.[18]

Governor Ninian Edwards of Illinois, meanwhile, alerted a part of the Illinois Militia. He empowered Colonel Thomas M. Neal, commanding officer of the Twentieth Illinois Regiment, to accept the services of up to six hundred volunteers for thirty days. They were to be mounted and rendezvous at Fort Clark, Peoria, and then move to Galena. Neal was to co-operate with any Regular Army officers there. Thus two columns of armed men moved northward toward the mining area in northern Illinois.[19]

Meanwhile, troops led by Colonel Josiah Snelling traveled south from Fort Snelling toward Prairie du Chien. Leaving St. Peters late on July 9 or early the next morning, Snelling brought four companies to Fort Crawford by July 12, There he found the Galena militia company unmanageable and discharged them. Then he seized several Winnebago chiefs and braves as hostages.

General Atkinson arrived at Fort Crawford on July 29 and halted, waiting to learn the outcome of the Indian council being held by Cass and McKenney at Butte des Morts. He sent three companies of infantry to "scour the country" near Prairie du Chien. They failed to find any Winnebagos or, for that matter, any Indians. On August 2 he again sent out a patrol, but with the same result. Atkinson claimed to have doubted the presence of Indians, but said he dispatched the search parties because "the French

[18] Atkinson to Clark, July 24, 1827, Letters Received, St. Louis Superintendency, OIA; Atkinson to Gaines, July 30, 1827, Letters Received, AGO.

[19] Proclamation of Ninian Edwards, July 14, 1827, in N. W. Edwards, *History of Illinois from 1788 to 1833*, 348; Edwards to Neal, July 14, 1827, *ibid.*

inhabitants affected to have seen them on every hill."[20] He held six of the Winnebago chiefs arrested by Colonel Snelling as hostages.

Up to this point, Henry Atkinson had acted in the efficient fashion he frequently demonstrated. Now he hesitated. He could not attack the Indians while some of the tribe were holding councils with Governor Cass at Butte des Morts. Besides, Atkinson was not eager to fight the Winnebagos. He merely brought his force to serve as a threat to the Indians that they must submit to American demands and surrender those responsible for the murders at Prairie du Chien and for the attack on the two keelboats. Atkinson believed that the army should act to preserve peace rather than spread death.[21]

When he had not heard from Cass by August 1, Atkinson sent two half-blood messengers to the council grounds at Butte des Morts to ask whether or not the Winnebagos had agreed to a treaty and had also promised to surrender the murderers. The same day he sent an express to the Winnebagos, demanding that those not meeting in council with Cass and McKenney come to Fort Crawford to meet with him. He warned them that failure to come immediately would cause the whites to "consider them enemies."[22] This note, however, brought no response.

Many people in Illinois, including Governor Edwards, clamored for military punishment and rapid removal of the tribe, but Atkinson took no action. His strategy was to strengthen his force, isolate the Indians, and move toward them from two directions. While he worked to implement this policy, the Winnebagos learned that their supposed allies, the Sioux, were not going to help them, that the Potawatomi were restless but unco-operative, and that the Sac and Foxes were willing to aid the whites. This news and the knowledge that Atkinson's force numbered many hundreds brought results. Thomas L. McKenney, negotiating with the tribe, wrote

[20] Atkinson to Gaines, July 30, 1827, Letters Received, AGO; Atkinson to Clark, Aug. 3, 1827, Illinois Governors' Correspondence, Letter Book 2, No. 756A, Illinois State Archives, Springfield, Illinois (hereafter ISA).

[21] Atkinson to Gaines, July 30, 1827, Letters Received, AGO.

[22] Atkinson to Clark, Aug. 3, 1827, Governors' Letter Book 2, No. 756A, ISA.

Atkinson that the Winnebagos "appear to be all peaceably disposed, and disown any agency in the late murders . . .," but the letter took several weeks to arrive.[23] While the negotiators waited for word from the General, he waited for news from them.

On August 5, Wabokieshiek or White Cloud, the Winnebago prophet, led a party from his village on the upper Rock River to Rock Island where they met with their agent, Thomas Forsyth. The Indians claimed they had heard many rumors and wanted to know the truth. After telling them of Atkinson's movements into the Winnebago country and giving exaggerated figures of army strength, Forsyth told them that the "White Beaver [Atkinson] was at Prairie du Chien with his soldiers and . . . he and his young men were not there to eat and drink only." Forsyth claimed that his talk sobered the Indians and that they asked him to tell Atkinson they favored peace. Forsyth then suggested they go to Fort Crawford and tell him themselves. The Prophet replied that the Indians preferred to await the return of their tribal leaders from the treaty talks, and then travel with them to meet Atkinson.[24]

By this time Atkinson decided that Fort Snelling needed additional supplies. Therefore, he sent Colonel Snelling and his four companies of infantry back to their post with the necessary provisions. After reaching the fort, Snelling was to send another four companies, under Major John Fowle, to Prairie du Chien with any light boats they had. The main concentration of Winnebagos was at the Fox-Wisconsin portage, and many boats would be necessary to ferry the command that far up the Wisconsin.[25]

During early August, Atkinson continued to wait for news from Cass and for the Indians to answer his call for a council. "If I were to act against the Prairie le Crosse Band the nation would consider all responsibility on their part for the offences committed abrogated," he wrote to Clark. "I do not intend by any act of mine

[23] McKenney to Atkinson, Aug. 3, 1827, Indian Office Files, Box 1, No. 26, SHSW.

[24] Forsyth to Clark, Aug. 7, 1827, Draper Collection, T–8:67–68, SHSW.

[25] Helen D. Dick, "A Newly Discovered Diary of Colonel Josiah Snelling," *Minnesota History*, Vol. XVIII (Dec., 1937), 403.

to destroy that responsibility . . ."[26] By August 17, Atkinson had learned from Forsyth that the Winnebagos wanted to push the responsibility for the murders and attacks on the Prairie la Crosse band. To this he replied, "All of this is very pretty but I do not believe half of it. One of the Ouisconsin Indians was of the number who killed the family here recently."[27]

Although most of the tribe seemed frightened into submission, the Prairie la Crosse band continued to be defiant. Lawrence Taliaferro, Indian agent at St. Peters, wrote that the Sioux of his agency had told him that between 150 and 200 Winnebagos were cultivating their corn fields at their village along the Mississippi opposite the mouth of the Iowa River. According to the Indian messengers, the Winnebagos were prepared to harvest their crops or "to die in the attempt." They kept small armed parties on all the islands and along the shore to protect their village and to attack any whites passing up or down the Mississippi. Taliaferro feared that a major Indian war was imminent.[28]

Reports from the council at Butte des Morts indicated that the danger of Indian war was nearly over. At Chicago the militia unit which had marched northward only days before promptly disbanded. At Galena the miners began moving back to the mines.[29] Thus by August 10, Atkinson, with nearly seven hundred men, remained at Fort Crawford, and the Winnebagos continued their negotiations with Cass. While awaiting further developments, Atkinson received orders from General Gaines that he "inflict on them [the Winnebagos] exemplary punishment," and that he demand a cession of the entire lead-mining region as a price for their bad conduct. Gaines also directed Atkinson to purchase or rent "a sufficient number of horses to mount two or three of his companies," because without a mounted force Atkinson would be unable to

[26] Atkinson to Clark, Aug. 8, 1827, Governors' Letter Book 2, No. 756B, ISA.

[27] Atkinson to Snelling, Aug. 17, 1827, Army Papers, MHS.

[28] Taliaferro to Clark, Aug. 8, 1827, Letters Received, St. Peters Agency, OIA.

[29] McKenney to Atkinson, Aug. 3, 1827, Indian Office Files, Box 1, No. 26, SHSW; John Kinzie to John Dixon, Aug. 7, 1827, included in Dixon to Edwards, Aug. 21, 1827, Governors' Letter Book 2, No. 761, ISA.

A Bird's-Eye-View of the Mandan Village
1,800 miles above St. Louis on the west bank of the Missouri River
From a painting by George Catlin

Smithsonian Institution

Black Hawk and Followers
in Balls and Chains—Jefferson Barracks, 1832
From George Catlin, *Souvenir* . . . (London, 1850), I, pl. 29

The New York Public Library

pursue or meet the Indians "except at times and in places of their own selection."[30] These orders reflect their author's attitude toward the Indians, but they were not in agreement with government policies or with Atkinson's attitude. Therefore, he took no action on them.

On August 19 the express sent to Butte des Morts two weeks earlier returned with several letters from Cass. The Governor wrote that "he had not effected any adjustment of our difficulties with the Winnebagoes." He also feared that they might attack the miners near Galena and advised Atkinson to move his troops up the Wisconsin River to the portage between it and the Fox River because nearly four hundred Indians had encamped there.[31] Two days later Major John Fowle, leading four companies of the Fifth Infantry, arrived from Fort Snelling. He brought two keelboats and nine smaller Mackinaw boats. With these reinforcements and boats, Atkinson prepared to lead his command up the Wisconsin River as soon as possible.[32]

He planned to take nearly 600 men in thirteen companies of infantry, two six-pound artillery pieces, and, if possible, 150 mounted volunteers from Galena. The mounted troops would act as scouts and flank guards. On August 20, Atkinson sent a messenger to Galena asking for a mounted force. Henry Dodge, one of the Galena militia leaders, agreed to send the militia on the condition that a small force of regulars guard the town during the expedition.[33] Atkinson agreed to Dodge's terms and told Dodge to meet him at English Prairie nearly eighty miles up the Wisconsin River from Prairie du Chien.[34]

30 Gaines to Barbour, Aug. 16, 1827, in 20 Cong., 1 sess., *House Exec. Doc. No. 2*, 147–48.

31 Atkinson to Gaines, Sept. 28, 1827, in 20 Cong., 1 sess., *Senate Doc. No. 1*, 161–62.

32 *Ibid.*

33 Dodge to Atkinson, Aug. 26, 1827, William Henry Papers, SHSW.

34 Samuel Whitesides to Edwards, Aug. 25, 1827, Governors' Letter Book 2, No. 765, ISA; Atkinson to Gaines, Sept. 2, 1827, in 20 Cong., 1 sess., *House Exec. Doc. No. 2*, 150.

Meanwhile, Major William Whistler started down the Fox River from Green Bay with a force of 100 regulars, 50 mounted militia, and 250 Indian auxiliaries. On August 29, Atkinson sent a detachment of 150 men to Galena, loaded his remaining force on keel and Mackinaw boats, and started northeast up the Wisconsin. After traveling nearly eighty miles in two days, he met Colonel Dodge with 130 mounted militia from Galena. The next morning he employed these newly acquired mounted troops as scouts and ordered them to range along the north side of the river.[35]

On September 1, while Atkinson and his force pushed their way north and east up the river, Major Whistler and his command arrived at the Fox-Wisconsin portage. Early that afternoon an express from Atkinson arrived with orders for Whistler to fortify his position and await the General's arrival.[36] The proximity of these two large bodies of troops seems to have frightened the Indians. About noon on September 2, a Winnebago warrior came to Whistler's camp at the portage bearing the message "do not strike; when the sun is there tomorrow (pointing to about three o'clock) they will come in." Thomas L. McKenney, who had accompanied the troops, asked whom the brave meant, and he replied, "Red Bird and We-Kau." Later that same afternoon and again that evening, two other braves repeated the performance.[37] This repetition demonstrated a fear that the soldiers might attack before the offenders could be surrendered.

About 3:00 P.M. the following day, just as they had promised, some Winnebagos arrived at Whistler's camp. Red Bird and We Kau, carrying a white flag, flanked by chiefs carrying American flags and accompanied by about one hundred braves, entered the army camp. Meanwhile, the soldiers had formed a long line with a

[35] *Ibid.*; Clark to Edwards, Sept. 3, 1827, Governors' Letter Book 2, No. 775, ISA.

[36] McKenney, "The Winnebago War of 1827," *Wisconsin Historical Society Collections*, Vol. V (1907), 178.

[37] McKenney, "The Winnebago War of 1827," *Wisconsin Historical Society Collections*, Vol. V (1907), 179.

small band on one flank. The chiefs stopped near the center of the army formation and held a short talk with their subagent, John Marsh, and with McKenney. They wanted to surrender the two braves to the civilian authorities rather than to Major Whistler, but finally agreed to surrender Red Bird and We Kau to the army. The two braves stepped forward and were placed in a small tent under guard. The chiefs explained that they could not surrender a third murderer because he had left the village.[38] Thus Atkinson's policy of waiting and of putting pressure on the entire tribe proved successful.

Late that afternoon McKenney left Whistler's command and canoed down the Wisconsin to meet Atkinson. Shortly after dark he reached the camp at Le Petit Roche, about forty-five miles from the portage. There he explained to Atkinson the results of the council at Butte des Morts and discussed the surrender of the Winnebago braves.[39] On September 6, Atkinson arrived at the portage. The next day he sent runners to the Winnebagos demanding they meet him in council two days later. They assembled, and after some discussion surrendered two more braves. When Atkinson asked for several others, the chiefs told him that it would take some time to bring them. The meeting ended with the issue still in doubt, so they agreed to meet again the next day. After more talks Atkinson decided the chiefs would fulfill their promises and agreed to allow them more time to bring in the other braves. He kept several hostages, however, to remind the Indians of their obligations.[40]

With the murderers at least temporarily taken care of, Atkinson worked toward a settlement of a more basic issue—that of American miners trespassing on Winnebago lands. He ignored orders from General Gaines that he force the Winnebagos to cede

[38] McKenney, "The Winnebago War of 1827," *Wisconsin Historical Society Collections*, Vol. V (1907), 182–83.

[39] Thomas L. McKenney, *Memoirs, Official and Personal*, 122.

[40] Atkinson to Gaines, Sept. 28, 1827, in 20 Cong., 1 sess., *Senate Doc. No. 1*, 162.

their lands as a prelude to peace. Atkinson wrote to Gaines, "I have required no cession of land from the Winnebagoes, because at the time, I did not feel authorized to make a treaty of that nature." Instead he concluded a provisional treaty with only two articles. The first promised the Indians that the President would appoint a commission to study conflicting claims to the mining lands during the next year; the second provided that until an agreement was reached, the Indians were not to molest the whites or their mining operations south of the Wisconsin River.[41]

After the council Henry Atkinson led the army back down the river to Prairie du Chien, where the chiefs had promised to bring the remaining braves. His force arrived at Fort Crawford on September 13 and waited for the Indians. His deadline, September 20, came and went.[42] Late the next evening several chiefs arrived. After a brief meeting they surrendered the last two fugitives and, in return, received their nine tribesmen. The next morning, September 22, Atkinson issued the following proclamation of peace:

> Know ye, that the Winnebago nation, having surrendered up all of the offenders, in the late transgressions that have been demanded of them, and showing an entire submission to the authority of the United States, I have granted them peace.
>
> Their country is opened to licensed traders, and they are to be treated as friends, so long as they demean themselves peaceably.[43]

Later that afternoon the troops boarded two steamboats and began the trip back to Jefferson Barracks. Before leaving, however, Atkinson regarrisoned Fort Crawford, with the four companies of the Fifth Infantry under Major Fowle, and left them a twelve-month supply of provisions, arms, and munitions. The strength of this post and the complete submission of the Winne-

41 Atkinson to Gaines, Sept. 28, 1827, in 20 Cong., 1 sess., *Senate Doc. No. 1*, 156, 162–63; Provisional Treaty, Sept. 9, 1827, *ibid.*, 157–58.

42 Provisional Treaty, Sept. 9, 1827, in 20 Cong., 1 sess., *Senate Doc. No. 1*, 156.

43 Atkinson Proclamation, Sept. 22, 1827, in 20 Cong., 1 sess., *Senate Doc. No. 1*, 159.

bagos led him to comment that the "frontier is in a state of tranquillity that will not be shortly interrupted."[44] He proved to be a poor prophet.

The six Winnebago prisoners were put in the Fort Crawford guardhouse with their two brethren surrendered a year earlier for the Methode murders. The braves fared badly and Red Bird died on March 16, 1828. Although the other seven survived the winter, their fellow tribesmen doubted the wisdom of surrendering so easily to the White Beaver. Agent Street reported, "the Indians are much dissatisfied with the delay, and would have been perfectly content that they should have been shot at the time. Now I apprehend something unpleasant from a reaction arising out of the delay."[45] His observations were accurate and Indian depredations continued.

The Winnebago braves who were surrendered to Atkinson during the campaign eventually were tried and sentenced to death, but a few weeks before their scheduled execution President Adams pardoned them.[46]

Henry Atkinson's efforts in this campaign were praised by army officers and officials in the Indian Office. Generals Gaines and Scott both expressed their satisfaction, and Governor Cass and Thomas L. McKenney added their praise and agreement. Voicing the opinions of many contemporaries, Stephen Watts Kearny, an officer serving under Atkinson, wrote, "The Genl. in the management of this affair, displayed much good judgement, combined with his usual military firmness . . ."[47]

Jacob Brown, the commanding general of the army, also expressed his pleasure with Atkinson's actions. Brown had been working for a concentration of troops at a reserve post from which they might be rapidly dispatched to put down Indian depredations.

[44] Atkinson to Gaines, Sept. 28, 1827, in 20 Cong., 1 sess., *Senate Doc. No. 1*, 162; *Niles Register*, Nov. 10, 1827.

[45] Street to Edwards, Mar. 27, 1828, in *The Edwards Papers*, (ed. by E. B. Washburne), *Chicago Historical Society Collections*, III, 332.

[46] Peter B. Porter to Clark, Nov. 3, 1828, Letters Sent, Vol. 5, 468–69, OIA.

[47] Kearny to John McNeil, Nov. 14, 1827, Kearny Papers, MHS.

Jefferson Barracks, although created as an infantry school, served as this troop center as well. By his successful use of force to intimidate the Winnebagos, Atkinson reinforced Brown's contentions. Relaying Brown's thanks, a subordinate wrote, "If an occasion were to be created in order to exemplify [Brown's] views with regards to a [settlement] of Indian aggressions as connected with the School of Practice it would not have been more aptly circumstanced than by this demonstration against the Winnebagoes."[48]

Although Atkinson's campaign may seem cautious and slow-moving, he never intended it to be anything else. His strategy, planned in conference with Lewis Cass and William Clark and, to a lesser extent, under orders from General Gaines, was simple: Locate and isolate the Winnebagos, then move into their country with an overwhelming force and demand the surrender of the murderers, at the same time refraining from acts that might start fighting. This forced the Indians to choose between a peace under which they had to surrender several braves and chiefs or a war in which they would have to fight without allies.

Atkinson's tactics were likewise simple. After his arrival at Prairie du Chien, he notified the Indians that he was ready to negotiate. When they failed to heed his call, he moved six hundred well-armed men up the Wisconsin River, placing much of the tribe between his force and that under Major Whistler then descending the Fox River from Green Bay. Fortunately for the Winnebagos, Atkinson was not eager to make or expand his reputation for military prowess. Instead, his humane views assured them a chance to talk and to meet his demands. His moves had been calculated to avoid provoking the Winnebagos into a war, a policy that succeeded in every detail.

[48] J. R. Vinton to Atkinson, Oct. 16, 1827, Letters Sent, Vol. 8, AGO.

IX. *Administrative Interlude—1827–32*

After the Winnebago War, Henry Atkinson returned to Jefferson Barracks and his command of the infantry school there. During the next few years he continued to work for peace with the Indians, a task that became more difficult each succeeding year. Increasing American penetration into the Indian country and the removal of more Indian tribes from the eastern United States to lands west of the Mississippi caused continuing conflict between whites and Indians and between eastern and western tribes. In addition, the period was one of continuing change and stress within the army. As one of the high-ranking officers, Henry Atkinson became involved in several of these controversies.

In the fall of 1827 the buildings at Jefferson Barracks were still unfinished, and the troops were still scattered. The Third Infantry cantonment remained on the first hill. On a second hill about a quarter of a mile beyond them were the tents of the Sixth Infantry. Partially completed "extensive stone barracks" stood on a third hill, and beyond these lay the camp of the First Infantry. Among and around these groups of buildings and tents "some staff and other officers, with their families, were in huts in various detached situations . . ."[1] During the winter of 1827–28 most of the troops

[1] Philip St. George Cooke, *Scenes and Adventures in the Army*, 17–21.

left their temporary encampments and moved into the nearly completed barracks.

The trouble in the Winnebago country in 1827 was only a prelude. The rich lead deposits continued to attract miners, who ignored Indian rights if they knew about them. In the winter of 1828, Henry Dodge led a well-armed party of 130 men far into Winnebago country, north of the treaty line in northwestern Illinois, and established a stockaded camp in the lead area. Indians and whites alike realized this act was a violation of the agreement that Atkinson had made with the Winnebagos in 1827. The troubled chiefs, aware that further intrusions might cause renewed violence, consulted their agent, Joseph Street. "We promised not to interupt the white people at the F[ever] river lead-mines," one chief said. But, the Indians complained, large parties had come far into their country to dig lead "where Indians have made lead many years. We want to know where they will stop—the hills are covered with them, & more & more are coming, and shoving us off our lands, & taking them to make lead. We want our father to stop this before blood may be shed."[2]

Both Indian Agent Street and Major John Fowle, commander at Fort Crawford, demanded that Dodge leave the Indian country and he agreed to go "as soon as he conveniently could." Dodge was slow to leave, so Street asked Major Fowle for 180 men from the fort to force Dodge and his followers to leave. Fowle claimed that his force was too small to send even half of it into Indian country, so Dodge and his associates continued to dig lead.[3] In July, 1828, William Clark, Street's superior, asked Atkinson for a detachment of one officer and six or eight privates to accompany the Indian agent when he again ordered the miners off the Indian lands. Accordingly Atkinson ordered Colonel John McNeil, the new commander at Fort Crawford, to assign a detachment for that purpose.

[2] Quoted in Street to Clark, Jan. 26, 1828, Letters Received, St. Louis Superintendency, OIA.

[3] Street to John Fowle, Feb. 7, 1828, Letters Received, St. Louis Superintendency, OIA; Fowle to Street, Feb. 7, 1828, *ibid.*

Atkinson believed that the government should enforce the treaties and laws. Like many army officers, he thought squatters and intruders on Indian lands disrupted Indian affairs, complicating the tasks of the army, and that these people were criminals and should be treated as such. Therefore, he wrote telling McNeil that "should the intruders refuse to withdraw you will at once employ such force as may be necessary to effect the object, and keep the specified lands free from such intrusion."[4] As was usually the case, when the soldiers arrived, the miners left.

In December, 1828, however, Agent Street complained to the War Department that white intruders were continuing to cause unrest among the Winnebagos. When Atkinson received this information, he again ordered the commanders of Fort Crawford and newly built Fort Winnebago to assist the agent in removing squatters, which they apparently did.[5]

In 1827, Atkinson had promised the Winnebago chiefs that the President would send commissioners to settle the conflicting claims to the mining land. This had been done in 1828, but Congress had failed to appropriate funds for the purchase of Indian lands arranged by the commissioners. Thus in 1829 when miners again entered Winnebago country, the Indians objected to what they thought was double-dealing and treachery. Because of warnings of possible violence from Street, Atkinson ordered three companies of the First Regiment to remain at Fort Winnebago at the Fox-Wisconsin portage.[6]

During 1828, Henry Atkinson had become concerned over a threat to his position within the army. Former Brigadier General Daniel Bissell had been released from his command during the army reduction of 1821. Each year after that he had attempted to obtain reinstatement to his position as commander of the Second Artillery at his former rank and pay. Atkinson heard rumors that

[4] Clark to Atkinson, July 7, 1828, Indian Office Files, Box 2, No. 44, SHSW; Atkinson to John McNeil, July 7, 1828, *ibid.*, No. 45.

[5] Atkinson to Porter, Dec. 15, 1828, Dept. of the West, Letters Sent, Letter Book 101, USAC.

[6] Atkinson to Macomb, Apr. 18, 1829, Letters Received, AGO.

Bissell might be reinstated and that certain infantry colonels had promised to exchange their commands with him if he regained his former position. If Bissell re-entered the army and then was transferred to the infantry, Atkinson's position as second-ranking officer in the West would be in jeopardy. According to army usage, because Bissell had held his rank and brevet from an earlier date, he would supersede Atkinson as commander of the infantry school at Jefferson Barracks. The possible loss of his command as a general and the resulting loss of social prestige probably distressed Atkinson more than any possible loss of pay.

In January, 1828, he wrote the War Department to complain. He objected to Bissell's probable transfer, citing paragraph 1299 of the *Army Regulations*, "that no officer shall be transferred to a Regiment to the prejudice of any officer thereof." Although a transfer such as was being proposed for Bissell was not among the examples cited in the *Regulations*, Atkinson maintained "the same rule and principle [was] applicable in the case in question." He claimed his position would be "materially prejudiced" by Bissell's transfer to either the Third or Fifth Infantry Regiments. He noted that "it would suppress the exercise of my rank & deprive me of commands to which I have been assigned and now exercise." In fact, Atkinson objected to any move under which Bissell might be transferred to the infantry because his own rank might be affected at some future date by having to serve with Bissell.[7] Whether Atkinson's letter had a direct effect is uncertain, but the President rejected Bissell's plea for reinstatement.[8]

On February 28, 1828, the long-ailing Jacob Brown, commanding general of the army, died, leaving a vacancy on the army general staff. Atkinson wrote to Lewis Williams, member of the North Carolina Congressional delegation, and asked for his assistance in obtaining the appointment.[9] Nominally General Brown's death left

[7] Atkinson to Jones, Jan. 18, 1828, Letters Received, AGO.

[8] For additional information on this point see Howard M. Ryan, "Daniel Bissell—'Late General,'" *Bulletin of the Missouri Historical Society*, Vol. XV (Oct., 1958), 20–28.

[9] Atkinson to Lewis Williams, Mar. 11, 1828, Letters Received, AGO.

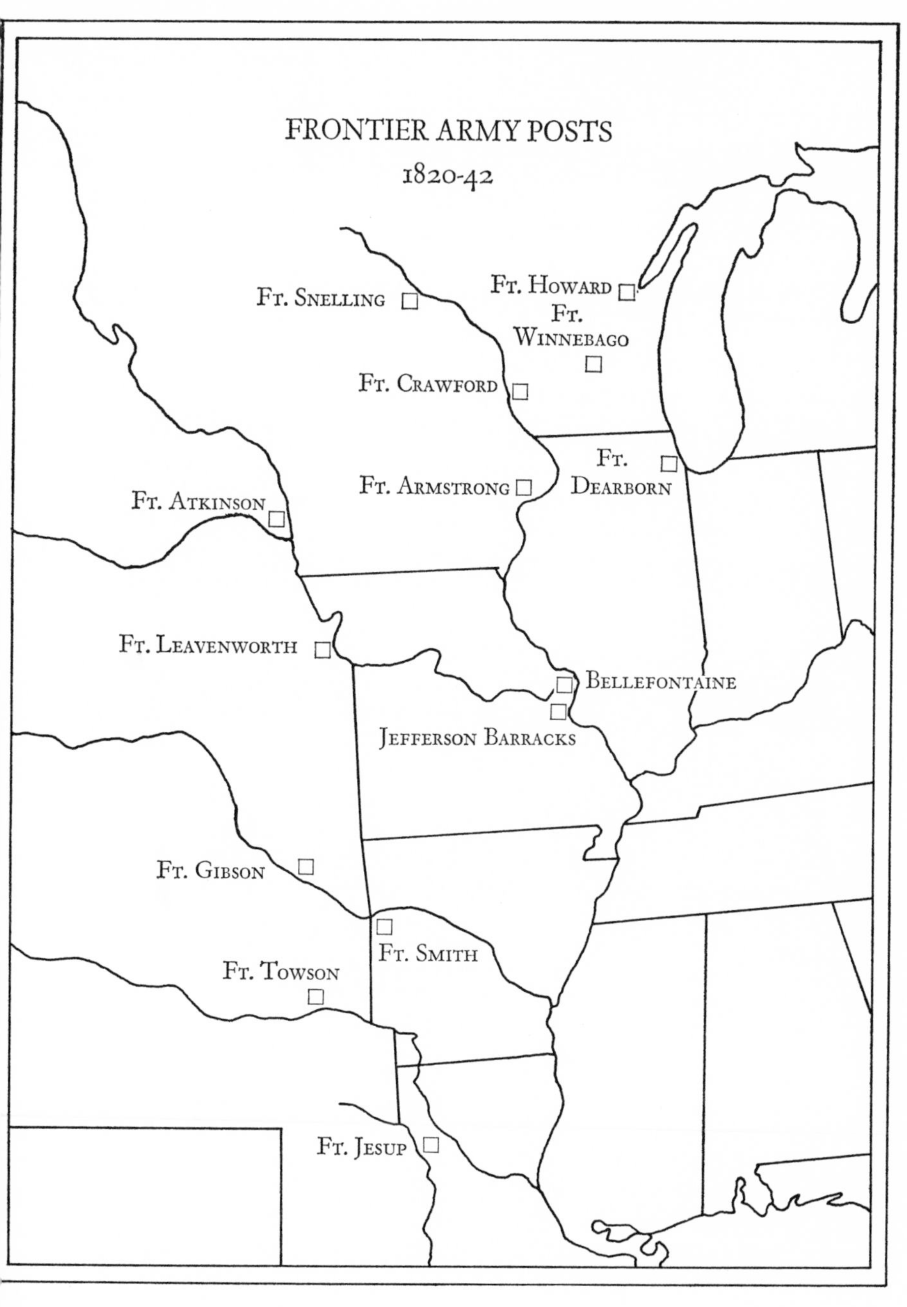
FRONTIER ARMY POSTS
1820-42
Ft. Snelling
Ft. Howard
Ft. Winnebago
Ft. Crawford
Ft. Armstrong
Ft. Dearborn
Ft. Atkinson
Ft. Leavenworth
Bellefontaine
Jefferson Barracks
Ft. Gibson
Ft. Smith
Ft. Towson
Ft. Jesup

the vacancy as commanding general open to only two men, Generals Gaines and Scott. Their bitter personal rivalry and continuing disputes over precedents and rank, however, made the choice of either difficult. If Scott gained the position, Gaines was almost sure to resign; in the event Gaines received the appointment, his rival would leave the army. To avoid an almost certain resignation by either candidate, President John Quincy Adams chose Colonel, but Major General by brevet, Alexander M. Macomb as the new commanding general. By moving beyond the two men next in line on the *Army Register*, the President was within his powers as commander in chief, but his action added to the controversy. General Gaines, although disappointed, was mollified by the fact that his arch rival Scott had failed to get the appointment. Scott, on the other hand, refused to obey Macomb's orders and threatened to arrest him for presuming to issue orders to his superiors.[10]

For Atkinson, Macomb's appointment meant there was no opening on the general staff because both his immediate superiors retained their positions. Thus he had to remain at his present rank and post. General Scott's refusal to obey Macomb was to Atkinson's advantage, however, because Scott remained in Washington rather than assuming command of the Western Department. On May 28, the day General Macomb assumed his new duties, President Adams suspended Scott from duty. Because of this suspension, Atkinson commanded the West for the next year.[11]

General Macomb had little personal experience with Indian affairs, having been an engineer and having worked chiefly in Washington since 1821. So when he received reports of Pawnee difficulties in the Southwest, he referred them to Atkinson. Macomb thought that Atkinson's "knowledge of the Indians would enable [him] to judge and determine what steps it would be best to pursue," and told him to use his discretion.[12] Meanwhile, Atkinson had

10 See also Elliott, *Winfield Scott*, 244–56.

11 Macomb Orders, Nov. 27, 1828, quoted in *Niles Register*, Dec. 6, 1828.

12 Macomb to Atkinson, Nov. 28, 1828, Letters Sent, Vol. 2, Record Group 108, Records of the Headquarters of the Army, National Archives (hereafter HQA).

received complaints about depredations by the Pawnees and other tribes along the Arkansas River and the route of the annual caravans of the Santa Fe traders. Since the Plains Indians fought on horseback, Atkinson reminded Macomb that "it would be difficult to reach them with foot soldiers owing to their remote situation & their facility of movement." He again suggested using mounted men, but Congress failed to furnish adequate funds to purchase the horses at this time.[13]

News of the success of both the Comanches and Pawnees against the Santa Fe traders spread among the plains tribes. According to the *Missouri Republican*, runners sped between the various bands to create excitement and to seek an offensive alliance against the whites.[14] On January 11, 1829, Atkinson ordered Major John Bliss, commander at Cantonment Leavenworth, with the help of the local Indian agent to investigate the disturbances and to report their findings to him. In the midst of the excitement, Atkinson remained calm and tried to obtain the facts before sending troops against the Indians. By the time this order reached Bliss, however, the Pawnees had left their villages for their annual winter hunt, and the possibility of war faded.[15]

In the spring of 1829, Atkinson recalled the troops from Cantonment Leavenworth and left only a small detachment there to guard the buildings. Then he sent a detachment of four companies from the Sixth Infantry to escort the caravan of Santa Fe traders to the Mexican border. The troops were to spend the summer on the plains waiting for the return of the traders and to escort them back to Missouri.[16] The Santa Fe traders, although they had often asked for government protection, showed little enthusiasm for their infantry escort. The foot soldiers impeded their movement and could not go beyond the Mexican border where most Indian depredations occurred.

13 Atkinson to Macomb, Jan. 1, 1829, Dept. of the West, Letters Sent, Letter Book 101, USAC.

14 Jan. 6, 1829.

15 Atkinson to John Dougherty, Jan. 11, 1829, Indian Papers, MHS.

16 Atkinson to John Bliss, Apr. 15, 1829, Dept. of the West, Letters Sent, Letter Book 101, USAC.

In order to provide protection in Mexican territory, John Miller, governor of Missouri, asked Atkinson for sabers, pistols, and a fieldpiece, to be used by a mounted civilian guard organized to defend the caravans in Mexican territory. Atkinson agreed to the proposal.[17] In May, 1829, Hezekiah Niles, Baltimore publisher, denounced Atkinson and Governor Miller and asked his readers what their response might be to a similar move by the governor general of Upper Canada. What if he armed traders of the "British north west company" then roaming through the Rocky Mountains?[18] "Would not a body of Englishmen, so armed, even if ascertained to be on the Rocky mountains, give birth to a feeling that could be quieted only by their expulsion?" he demanded.[19]

Such criticism brought a prompt response from the War Department. John H. Eaton, then secretary of war, demanded an immediate explanation from Atkinson. He replied that Governor Miller had asked for assistance, and he had agreed to furnish it. Atkinson had assumed that the armed party "could not be considered or viewed in a belligerent light by the Mexicans, as the caravans in the Mexican trade always go armed."[20] When Eaton ordered that the arms be withheld, Atkinson complied. Obviously he had gone too far.

In November, 1829, after the Sixth Infantry had returned to Jefferson Barracks from escorting the traders, Major Bennett Riley, commander of the escort, reported to Atkinson "that he [had been] much annoyed by parties of hostile Indians who infested the neighbourhood of the position he occupied on the Arkansas River."[21] This report and his own observations caused Atkinson to ask for mounted troops again. Five or six companies stationed at

17 Atkinson to Smith, Apr. 18, 1829, Smith Papers, SHSM.

18 Niles probably meant the Hudson's Bay Company, because the Northwest Company had merged with it in 1821.

19 *Niles Register*, May 23, 1829.

20 Atkinson to Eaton, June 12, 1829, Dept. of the West, Letters Sent, Letter Book 101, USAC.

21 Atkinson to Jones, Nov. 24, 1829, Letters Received, AGO.

or near Cantonment Leavenworth could do the job. The mounted troops, he said, should be issued "swords, pistols, and a rifle, or short musket." Such a command, he claimed, could protect the frontier inhabitants and trading caravans.[22] Nothing came of Atkinson's suggestions that year, however.

During the summer of 1829, Atkinson had moved his residence from Jefferson Barracks to Louisville, leaving General Henry Leavenworth in command at the Barracks. In July when a war party of Iowa and Sac braves plundered some settlers on the frontier, Leavenworth moved most of his command up the Missouri, and Governor Miller activated one thousand Missouri militiamen.[23] When Atkinson learned of the incident, he ordered Leavenworth not to pursue the braves to their villages "unless circumstances should render it imperative." He was merely to protect the settlers. Atkinson told him to work with the Indian agents and to settle the difficulty peaceably. He was sure the Indians had "no premeditated intention . . . to commence hostilities, but to plunder, as is too frequently their habit."[24] This particular scare proved similar to most others. Rumor and fright had magnified a small raiding party looking for easy plunder into an all-out Indian war. Atkinson, however, was again successful in maintaining peace by keeping the whites and Indians apart.

By November, 1829, the quarrel between Generals Macomb and Scott ended. Scott agreed to serve under Macomb in his former capacity as a departmental commander. On November 20, Scott was ordered to take command of the Eastern Department, and Gaines the Western. Gaines, however, was to complete his tour of inspection before reporting to Washington. Thus Atkinson retained command in the West for two more months. On January 23, 1830, General Gaines formally assumed command of his department and

22 *Ibid.*

23 Leavenworth to Atkinson, July 23, 1829, Letters Received, SW.

24 Atkinson to Macomb, July 31, 1829, Dept. of the West, Letters Sent, Letter Book 101, USAC; Atkinson to Macomb, Aug. 2, 1829, *ibid.*

ordered Atkinson back to Jefferson Barracks and his command of the Right Wing.[25]

Before he could leave Louisville, however, Atkinson received orders to report to Washington as the president of a court martial to try Adjutant General Roger Jones. By mid-February he had arrived at the capital, where the trial opened on February 25. The court investigated a dispute between Jones and Macomb. Jones was charged with disobedience of orders, conduct subversive of good order and military discipline, and disrespect toward his commanding officer. The court ruled him guilty of the first and third charges and sentenced him to a reprimand in general orders.[26] On March 13 the proceedings ended, and Atkinson returned to St. Louis in late April, 1830.[27]

At Jefferson Barracks, Atkinson received news from Rock Island that some of the Sac and Foxes had refused to leave their homes at the mouth of Rock River. Although by 1830 many of the tribal leaders seem to have accepted the inevitability of moving across the Mississippi, disgruntled elements within the tribes gathered under the leadership of Black Hawk, a brave with a reputation as a great warrior. This group refused to remain west of the Mississippi, and in spite of threats of military action, returned annually to their old lodges and fields at the mouth of the Rock. In April, 1830, Agent Thomas Forsyth told William Clark that the time for talk had passed and that for action was at hand. "I told [the Indians] that I am done speaking to them on that subject," he wrote, "and in my opinion you would turn this affair over to the American Braves, commanded by the White Beaver [Atkinson]—whom all the Indians in this country know very well."[28] Apparently Clark took no action.

[25] AGO Order 74, Nov. 20, 1829, quoted in *Missouri Republican*, Dec. 15, 1829; Gaines Order, Jan. 23, 1830, quoted in *St. Louis Beacon*, Feb. 3, 1830.

[26] ASP:MA, IV, 450–79.

[27] Entry, Apr. 30, 1830 in "William Clark Diary" (ed. by Louise Barry), *Kansas Historical Quarterly*, Vol. XVI (May, 1948), 392.

[28] Forsyth to Clark, Apr. 30, 1830, Draper Collection, T–8:110, SHSW.

RUINS OF THE MILITARY POST AT COUNCIL BLUFF [FORT ATKINSON]
at 11:00 A.M., May 25, 1833
From a painting by Karl Bodmer

Collection of the Northern Natural Gas Company,
Joslyn Art Museum, Omaha, Nebraska

Fort Atkinson, erected in 1840
From Benjamin F. Gue, *History of Iowa*

State Historical Society of Wisconsin

In June, Clark told Atkinson of new intrusions on the mineral lands that belonged to the Fox Indians at Dubuque's mines in northeastern Iowa. Atkinson issued a proclamation warning the squatters to leave the Indian country. He told them that if they refused, soldiers would destroy their property and force them to leave.[29] He realized that most of the squatters would ignore the proclamation, but issued it so that arrested squatters could not plead ignorance when taken into court.[30]

On June 26 he ordered Major Stephen W. Kearny to take four companies of the Third Regiment to Prairie du Chien and there co-operate with the troops under Colonel Morgan at Fort Crawford. William Clark and Colonel Morgan were then holding a council with most of the tribes of the upper Mississippi at Prairie du Chien. They hoped to settle boundary disputes and persuade the tribes to accept American arbitration in their frequent quarrels. Kearny's troops would thus serve a twofold purpose. They would reinforce the garrison at a time when many Indians were present and could also be used to remove the squatters on the western side of the Mississippi at Dubuque's mines. Atkinson ordered Kearny to stop at the mines on his way to Prairie du Chien and to warn the intruders they would be arrested and turned over to the civil authorities of Michigan, Illinois, or Missouri if they refused to leave the Indian country.[31] In this, Atkinson expected more from the processes of civil law and government than they deserved. Frontier courts had usually released squatters, and army arrests did little to deter the squatters.

Atkinson realized that Kearny's troops were needed at Fort Crawford and said nothing at that time about leaving a force at the mines for the remainder of the summer. On July 6, however, he ordered Kearny to leave a detachment of one officer and twenty men at the mines for the next six weeks. He thought this would

29 Atkinson Proclamation, June 21, 1830, Letters Received, AGO.

30 Atkinson to Eaton, Aug. 2, 1830, Dept. of the West, Letters Sent, Letter Book 102, USAC.

31 Atkinson to Kearny, June 27, 1830, Dept. of the West, Letters Sent, Letter Book 102, USAC.

make it difficult for the squatters to re-establish themselves during that season.[32]

During the summer of 1830, the tribes along the frontier caused some trouble by raiding each other's villages. On May 5 a band of Menominees ambushed a band of about twenty-five Foxes, killed ten, and scattered the rest across the Mississippi.[33] No further attacks occurred that summer, but in August of 1831 the friends and relatives of the slain Foxes retaliated. This attack on the Menominees brought government intervention because in the summer of 1830 both tribes had signed the Treaty of Prairie du Chien. This pact allowed the government to arbitrate such disputes. After repeated but unsuccessful efforts to obtain those responsible for the attack in 1831, Atkinson planned an expedition early in 1832 to keep the tribes apart and to settle the difficulty. Rather than ending the Indian fighting, this expedition culminated in the Black Hawk War of 1832.

Late in 1830, General Macomb asked Atkinson for his views on the number of troops necessary for Western defense and a pacification of the Indians. Atkinson offered a plan that included four regiments of infantry to be stationed on the upper Mississippi, on the Missouri, on the Arkansas, and on the Red River. This was the arrangement then in operation, with Jefferson Barracks and Cantonments Gibson and Jesup containing troops that could be moved to endangered frontier areas. These men could also be moved to the defense of New Orleans or the Gulf Coast if necessary.[34]

Macomb had also asked Atkinson for his ideas on the possibility of reducing the number of officers in the army, a measure then under consideration in Congress. As the officer charged with frontier defense from the Arkansas River to Lake Superior, Atkinson opposed any reduction in the size of the army. "I have looked upon the army, under the organization of 1821 as wisely adapted to

[32] Atkinson to Kearny, July 6, 1830, Dept. of the West, Letters Sent, Letter Book 102, USAC.

[33] Street to Clark, May 7, 1830, Letters Received, St. Louis Superintendency, OIA.

[34] Atkinson to Jones, Feb. 23, 1831, Letters Received, AGO.

the interest of the country in a time of peace," he wrote. He favored skeleton or cadre regiments that could be expanded rapidly in time of emergency and were inexpensive. He indicated that a reduction of line officers could be made only at the "manifest injury to the public service."[35] Atkinson's comments reveal that he was not seriously worried about further reduction of the army.

Between 1827 and 1841, Atkinson became involved in a controversy with the Treasury Department about his claims for brevet pay. When he commanded the Right Wing of the Western Department, he claimed the pay and allowances of his brevet rank—that of brigadier general. The second auditor of the Treasury, however, rejected his claims for double-rations allowances, beginning in 1827, whenever he was not actually in command of a particular post. During Atkinson's command in the "Winnebago War" of 1827, for example, the auditor claimed that Atkinson was not entitled to double rations for the time he was absent from Jefferson Barracks, because he was not then commanding that post. This meant that Atkinson had to refund the pay he had already drawn. He countered angrily that, whether at Jefferson Barracks or not, he exercised command over it and the other six posts within the Right Wing.[36] While he was in Washington for the trial of Colonel Jones, in 1830, he had submitted an appeal to the Treasury, but received no satisfaction at the time.

On March 30, 1830, William B. Lewis, second auditor, rejected Atkinson's appeal and demanded that he refund the money he had drawn for double rations in 1827. "Before complying with this demand," Atkinson answered stubbornly, "I must insist upon waiting to know the President's decision upon my claims."[37] The day he replied to Lewis, Atkinson also sent an appeal to President Jackson, but the President declined to act on the petition.

A month later Atkinson received another demand to refund the money. He again refused and wrote, "It is not the amount of the

[35] Atkinson to Macomb, Sept. 28, 1830, ASP:MA, IV, 650.

[36] Atkinson to Jackson, May 25, 1830, Letters Received, unregistered series, SW.

[37] Atkinson to Lewis, May 25, 1830, Letters Received, unregistered series, SW.

sum disallowed that alone urges me to combat the decision made in your office. It is the principle involved in the question."[38] The controversy continued until 1840, and at one point Atkinson went without his pay for three and one-half years because of his insistence that he was entitled to receive brevet pay. During this time he borrowed from friends and business associates, sold several slaves, and used some of his wife's income to meet his expenses. Eventually he compromised with the Treasury, but as late as 1840 he still had to repay $1,500 in pay that he had drawn but was not entitled to receive.[39]

Atkinson had few disputes with his subordinate officers. One of these, however, occurred during the spring of 1831 when he was in Louisville. General Henry Leavenworth passed through that city on his way to Washington. He intimated that while at the capital he would ask to have the Western commands shifted so that he would be the senior officer on the Missouri and Mississippi frontier. Atkinson considered that area as almost a personal domain because he had commanded the military defenses on both rivers almost continuously since 1819. As a result he protested to the Adjutant General. "I cannot believe for a moment that the government will remove officers & corps to gratify individual inclination . . ." he wrote. He pointed out that Leavenworth had made frequent moves which he ascribed to "apparent impatience and restlessness." He continued, "and now, forsooth, it would seem that he wishes myself, his senior, & my regiment removed to subserve his further views." Atkinson opposed any such arrangement. He claimed to have no intention of detracting from Leavenworth's reputation or merits, "but merely [to appeal] against his being indulged to the prejudice of myself & my Regt." In this case Atkinson worried without cause. No changes were made.[40]

38 Atkinson to Lewis, Aug. 17, 1830, Letters Received, unregistered series, SW.

39 Atkinson to Lewis, May 7, 1836, Right Wing Letter Book 106, USAC; Mary Atkinson to Thomas L. Alexander, Jan. 19, 1840, Mary Atkinson Letters, in private collection of Gen. B. W. Atkinson, San Diego, California (hereafter B. W. A.).

40 Atkinson to Jones, May 16, 1831, Letters Received, AGO.

While he faced the difficulties of keeping peace on the frontier and administrative problems within the army, Atkinson had retained command of Jefferson Barracks. He continued to operate that post as an infantry training school. In spite of necessary troop movements that frequently increased or decreased the number of men at the post, the troops got some regularly scheduled training. During September of 1831, for example, they received rifle and musket instruction and target practice.[41] Perhaps the urgency of deteriorating Indian relations on the upper Mississippi stimulated this particular training.

Between 1827 and 1832, Atkinson's efforts to maintain peace had been largely successful. There were no major Indian-white clashes or serious intertribal wars. By 1832, however, it was becoming more difficult to keep settlers and Indians apart, as well as to curb intertribal conflicts.

[41] Atkinson Order, Sept. 19, 1831, Jefferson Barracks Order Book 161, USAC.

X. The Black Hawk War—1832

HENRY ATKINSON'S PART IN THE BLACK HAWK WAR, although not the most important event in his military career, received much publicity. The "war" itself resulted in part from vacillation, slow communications, treachery, political opportunism, and the rashness of frontier militia. It proved to be the only time that Atkinson failed to prevent a major outbreak of violence between Indians and white men during his twenty-three years as a frontier commander.

Events leading to the war had begun in November of 1804 when five members of the Sac and Fox tribes signed a treaty at St. Louis by which they ceded to the United States government all the tribal land east of the Mississippi.[1] The irregular negotiations, the small annuities given the Indians, and the clause that allowed them to remain on the ceded land until it was sold to settlers by the government caused not a few difficulties later. According to the Sac and Foxes, the Indians who had signed the treaty had not been authorized to do so, but had been in St. Louis merely to arrange the release of an Indian prisoner who had killed a trespasser on their Missouri lands. Therefore, some of the tribesmen denied the validity of the treaty and said those men responsible for it were "all dead"; that is, they had lost their voice in tribal councils.[2]

1 ASP:MA, I, 693–94.

2 Black Hawk, *Ma-Ka-Tai-Me-She-Kai-Kaik: Black Hawk, an Autobiography* (ed. by Donald Jackson), 60.

Nonetheless, white settlement had increased, and squatters even moved into the principal Sac village on the Rock River, just a short distance from the Mississippi. Stories that these settlers had beaten and robbed some Indians who remained in the village caused resentment among the tribe.

By spring, 1829, Illinois settlers petitioned Governor Edwards for relief and protection from the "depredations of these irritated and bloodthirsty savages" and demanded that the Indians be removed. The Indians asked their agent at Rock Island to stop further white encroachment. Thus on the one hand were the white squatters, supported by the Governor, who were illegally on land reserved for the Sac and Foxes; on the other, were the Indians, or at least a part of the tribe, trying to retain their homes and land.

In the fall of 1829, Congress ordered that the land along the lower Rock River be surveyed and sold. Many tribal leaders recognized their treaty obligation to leave the area and began building new villages in Iowa. A group of dissidents, however, continued to deny the treaty cessions and rallied under Black Hawk. For the next two years this band returned to the tribal lands at the mouth of the Rock River to plant new crops of corn. The settlers objected when the Indians returned in 1831. John Reynolds, governor of Illinois, called out seven hundred mounted militia and joined forces with General Gaines to drive the Sac and Foxes back across the Mississippi, but the Indians fled before the armed troops arrived. On June 30, 1831, Black Hawk and his chiefs signed the so-called Corn Treaty under which they agreed to submit to the authority of Keokuk, to remain west of the Mississippi and not return without permission from American authorities, and to abandon all meeting with the British. In return, the United States agreed to accept their claims to land west of the Mississippi and promised to give the Indians corn to replace what they had lost by moving.[3]

There were other troubles in the summer of 1830. A band of Sioux and Menominees, traditional enemies of the Sac and Foxes,

[3] Gaines to Hugh L. White, July 6, 1831, in 22 Cong., 1 sess., *House Exec. Doc. No. 2*, 186; "Articles of Capitulation," *ibid.*, 187–88.

ambushed and killed ten Fox chiefs and braves on their way to Prairie du Chien. A year later, on July 31, 1831, the Foxes attacked a band of Menominees near Prairie du Chien, killing twenty-five.[4] Joseph Street, Indian agent at Prairie du Chien, demanded action:

> The pacification of July 1830 has been violated under the guns of Fort Crawford; and if some immediate course is not taken to chastise these violators of that solemn arrangement, the influence of the officers of the United States will be destroyed and the power of the Government disregarded by the Indians.[5]

William Clark and Henry Atkinson both ordered their subordinates at Rock Island to demand that the Sac and Foxes surrender those responsible for the Menominee murders at Prairie du Chien. Accordingly, Felix St. Vrain, Sac and Fox agent, and Colonel Willoughby Morgan, commandant at Fort Armstrong, met with tribal leaders on September 5, 1831, and demanded the surrender of the murderers. Keokuk, spokesman for the councils of the chiefs of both the Sac and Fox tribes, explained that the chiefs had no authority to hand over the offenders, that the guilty men had to surrender voluntarily. He claimed that the government was picking on the Sac and Foxes and asked, "Why do you not let us be as the Great Spirit made us? and let us settle our own difficulties?"[6] Thus no agreement had been reached when the Indians went to western Iowa for their winter hunt, but Atkinson and Clark hoped the chiefs would be able to arrange the surrender of the murderers in the spring.[7]

During the winter of 1831–32, however, the Indians became more determined to return to their old farms and homes. One reason for this was news from Neapope, a Sac chief who returned from the

4 Clark to Secretary of War, Aug. 9, 1831, in 22 Cong., 1 sess., *House Exec. Doc. No. 2*, 191–92.

5 Street to Clark, Aug. 1, 1831, in 22 Cong., 1 sess., *House Exec. Doc. No. 2*, 193.

6 "Journal of a council held with the chiefs and warriors of the Sac and Fox Indians at Fort Armstrong," Sept. 5, 1831, in 22 Cong., 1 sess., *House Exec. Doc. No. 2*, 203–204.

7 William T. Hagan, *The Sac and Fox Indians*, 137.

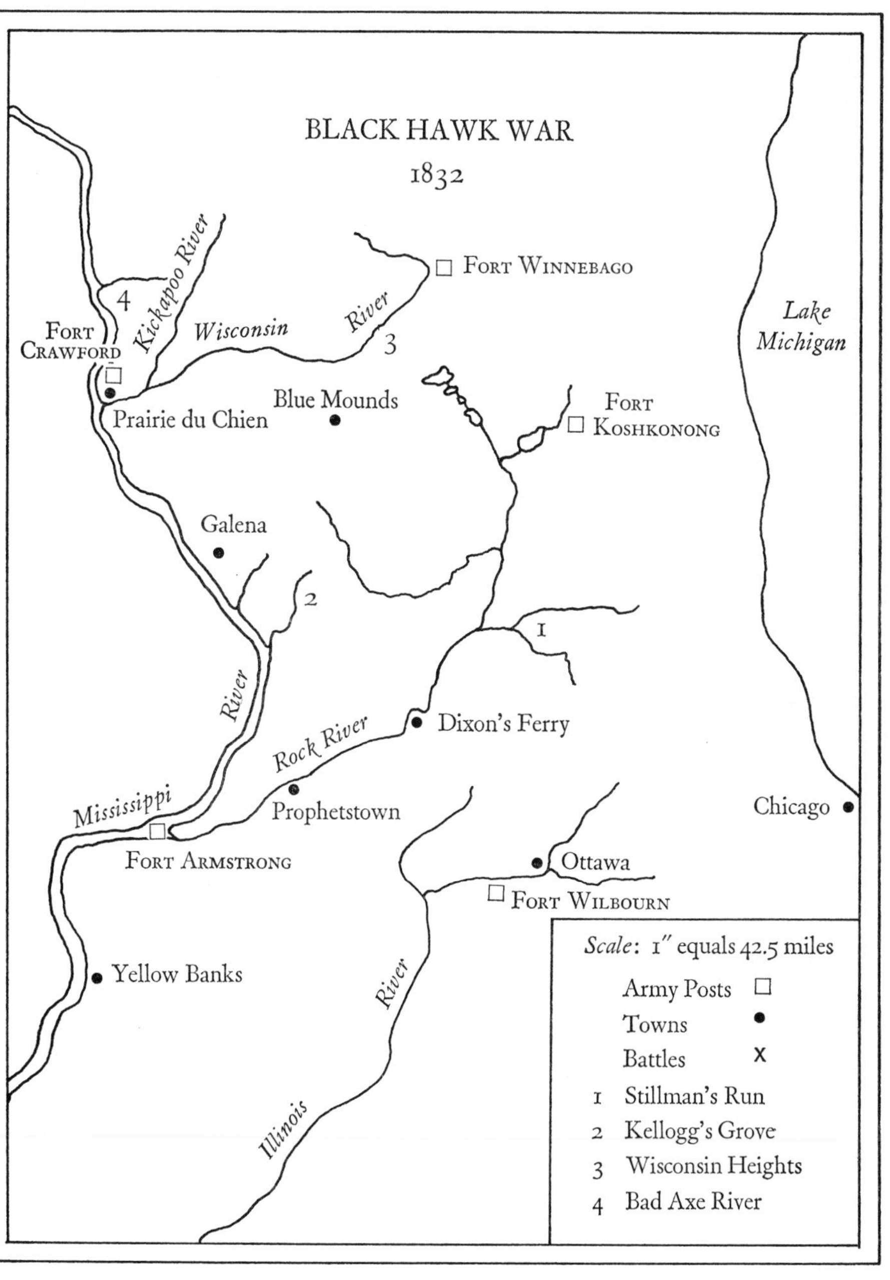
BLACK HAWK WAR
1832
Fort Winnebago
Lake Michigan
Kickapoo River
4
Fort Crawford
Wisconsin
River
3
Prairie du Chien
Blue Mounds
Fort Koshkonong
Galena
2
1
River
Dixon's Ferry
Rock River
Mississippi
Prophetstown
Chicago
Fort Armstrong
Ottawa
Fort Wilbourn
Yellow Banks
River
Illinois
Scale: 1″ equals 42.5 miles
Army Posts
Towns
Battles X
1 Stillman's Run
2 Kellogg's Grove
3 Wisconsin Heights
4 Bad Axe River

British post of Malden. He reported to Black Hawk that a British agent had told him that if the Indian claim that they had not sold their land was true, then the United States could not take their land, and that, "in the event of a *war*, we should have nothing to fear! as they would stand by and assist us."[8] At the same time he brought an invitation from Wabokieshiek (the Winnebago prophet) for Black Hawk and his band to come to Prophetstown, where they could "make corn." According to Black Hawk, Neapope also told him that the Prophet said that the British would send them "guns, ammunitions, provisions, and clothing, early in the spring. The vessels that bring them will come by way of Mil-wa-ke. The prophet has likewise received wampum and tobacco from the different nations on the lakes—Ottowas, Chippewas, Pottowatomies; and as for the Winnebago, he has them all at his command. We are going to be happy once more!"[9]

Recalling this conversation with Neapope that winter, Black Hawk later said, "[I] was pleased to think that, by a little exertion on my part, I could accomplish the object of all my wishes." At any rate, after Neapope left, Black Hawk dispatched messengers to the various bands to recruit more supporters. These he gathered at the location of Fort Madison in southeastern Iowa where he began the move that eventually destroyed most of his one thousand followers.

Meanwhile, news of the Fox attack on the Menominees in July, 1831, and reports from the Indian agents telling of the Indians' preparations for war caused apprehension at the War Department. On March 17, 1832, General Alexander Macomb ordered Atkinson to take the troops at Jefferson Barracks north to Fort Armstrong and there demand that the Sac and Foxes surrender eight or ten of the leaders in the attack. If they refused, Atkinson was to capture the murderers by force or to take hostages

[8] Black Hawk, *Autobiography*, 132.

[9] Neapope's evidence, August 20, 1832, in "Minutes of an Examination of Indian Prisoners taken by order of Major-General Scott," Black Hawk War Papers, ISHL; Black Hawk, *Autobiography*, 132.

from among tribal leaders. At the same time, Macomb suggested that Atkinson move in such a manner that the Indians would realize the United States wanted to punish the guilty, not to hurt the innocent. Atkinson received full discretionary powers.[10]

In April, 1832, Atkinson prepared to ascend the Mississippi with the two hundred men then at Jefferson Barracks. He assumed he would have no difficulty persuading the Sac and Foxes to surrender a number of hostages and thus satisfy the War Department and the Sioux and Menominees. He qualified his optimism, however, by saying, "in this [getting the Indians to surrender the offenders] I may be mistaken." Atkinson hoped his trip would be brief, but, planning for any contingency, he ordered that summer uniforms be packed so that they could be shipped later that season if necessary.[11]

The equipment and supplies were loaded on the evening of April 7, and early the next morning Henry Atkinson took six companies of infantry aboard the steamboats *Chieftain* and *Enterprise* and began the trip to Fort Armstrong. After a four-day cruise, broken only by marching around the Lower or Des Moines Rapids (at present Keokuk, Iowa), the troops arrived at Fort Armstrong on Rock Island at midnight, April 11. Before he started upriver, Atkinson had learned that Black Hawk's band had returned to their old lands along Rock River. "It is probable," he complained, "that I shall have more trouble in adjusting the difficulties in that quarter, than I first anticipated." The General assumed that Black Hawk had no serious intention of reoccupying the old village, but with only sketchy information, he had little idea of where the Indians were or what they were doing.[12]

Black Hawk and his followers were even then moving slowly up the Rock River toward the Prophet's village. Some of the band may have wanted war, but there is no clear evidence that the In-

[10] Macomb to Atkinson, Mar. 17, 1832, Letters Sent, Vol. 9, AGO.

[11] Atkinson Order, Apr. 5, 1832, Black Hawk War Papers, ISHL.

[12] Atkinson to Macomb, Apr. 7, 1832, Letters Received, AGO.

dians had any plans other than to settle among either the Winnebagos or Potawatomi.[13] According to Black Hawk, they were afraid that Atkinson's force would attack them at the mouth of the Rock. Atkinson, however, did not attack. At this point he committed the first in a series of mistakes. Although he thought his force was too small to stop the Indians, he knew them well enough to realize that he could have asked for a parley. Instead of talking with Black Hawk, Atkinson negotiated with the friendly Sac and Fox chiefs near Fort Armstrong. They again refused to surrender any hostages and said that the men involved in the Menominee massacre were with Black Hawk's band. Thus Atkinson was in a quandary. He could not insist that the friendly chiefs surrender some of the murderers because doing so might cause them to join the hostile band. He also had to convince Black Hawk and his followers to abandon their hope of living east of the Mississippi.[14] At this point a meeting between Atkinson and the leaders of Black Hawk's band might have convinced the Indians that they had to remain west of the Mississippi and, thus, might have prevented the war that followed.

Atkinson's second blunder was a letter he sent to John Reynolds, governor of Illinois. In it he described the frontier as being "in great danger" and promised to co-operate with Reynolds in taking action for the protection and defense of frontier settlements. He did not, however, ask the Governor to call out the militia, but described the situation in such a way that Reynolds thought the letter was a formal request for troops.[15] As a result, Reynolds mobilized a mounted militia force on April 17, before it was needed or even was expected. This brought Henry Atkinson the additional difficulties arising out of a premature call up of the militia.

On April 14 he took his staff upriver to Fort Crawford. At this

[13] Black Hawk, *Autobiography*, 137–38; Neapope's evidence, Aug. 20, 1832, Black Hawk War Papers, ISHL; Atkinson to Reynolds, Apr. 13, 1832, ISHL.

[14] See also Roger L. Nichols, ed., "The Black Hawk War: Another View," *Annals of Iowa*, Vol. XXXIV (Winter, 1963), 525–33.

[15] Atkinson to Reynolds, Apr. 13, 1832, Black Hawk War Papers, ISHL; Reynolds, *My Own Times*, 223.

time neither Atkinson nor Black Hawk seems to have had any definite plans. Atkinson, however, hoped to meet the Indians and persuade them to surrender the murderers and to return west of the Mississippi, but he made no move to meet with the Indian leaders in person. Instead, on April 15, he sent François Labuissier and Appenoose, a Fox brave, up the Rock to ascertain the Indians' plans. They returned the next day and reported that Black Hawk's band was only eighteen miles above Rock Island and was moving slowly toward the Prophet's village. The Sac and Foxes had threatened the two men Atkinson sent after them, and some of them had bragged that they were ready and eager to fight the Americans.[16] On April 17, Governor Reynolds ordered twelve hundred mounted militia into service. The next morning Atkinson wrote that he feared the Indians were "so hostile, that nothing short of punishment [would] bring them to a proper sense of their misconduct." In spite of this statement, he still hoped that a peaceful removal of the Indians was possible.[17]

While awaiting further information, Atkinson, on April 19, again met with the friendly Sac and Fox chiefs at Rock Island. This time they agreed to surrender three of their number which satisfied Atkinson. He thought that to demand more might cause further defections to Black Hawk.[18] On April 23, Captain Gustavus Loomis, stationed at Fort Crawford, reported rumors that the Sioux and Menominees had agreed to join forces at the mouth of the Wisconsin River and from there move down the west side of the Mississippi to the Sac and Fox country. Loomis also claimed that they were determined to attack the Sac and Foxes and would resist any attempts to stop them. He suggested that Black Hawk's band feared the Sioux and had moved east of the Mississippi to escape this danger.[19] Although two thirds of the members of the Sac and Fox tribes and all of the leading chiefs were still west of the Mis-

[16] Entry for Apr. 16, 1832, Journal of Felix St. Vrain, Black Hawk War Papers, ISHL.

[17] Atkinson to Gaines, Apr. 18, 1832, Black Hawk War Papers, ISHL.

[18] Atkinson to Macomb, Apr. 19, 1832, Black Hawk War Papers, ISHL.

[19] Loomis to Atkinson, Apr. 23, 1832, Black Hawk War Papers, ISHL.

sissippi, this report seems to have increased fears among the whites of a general Indian war.

On April 24, 1832, Atkinson sent Wacomme and Pachanoi, two Sac braves, to Black Hawk and the chiefs in the band with a message to return across the Mississippi. Atkinson also wrote, "It is not too late to do what is right . . . If your hearts are good I will send an officer to talk with you in three or four days."[20] It is strange that Atkinson, knowing these Indians as well as he did, sent these braves as messengers rather than respected men such as one of his officers, the Sac agent, Felix St. Vrain, or one of the friendly chiefs.

When they heard Atkinson's message, the chiefs with Black Hawk protested that they had "no bad feelings," but they refused to return. Black Hawk claimed "I do not command the Indians—the village belongs to the chiefs—why do they want to know my feelings—I have no bad feelings."[21] Atkinson's message, however, nearly convinced some of the Indians to return across the Mississippi, but White Crow, a one-eyed Winnebago chief sometimes called "The Blind," convinced the Sacs to remain east of the Mississippi.[22] As a result, the Sac and Foxes continued up the Rock River and continued to maintain that they would not attack anyone.

Atkinson learned of this two days later. Meanwhile, Henry Gratiot, subagent to the Winnebagos, accompanied by White Crow, had also visited Black Hawk's camp to inquire about the intentions of the Indians. Gratiot received discourteous treatment, and for a time there was some question whether or not he would be allowed to leave. He was released, however, and went down the Rock to Fort Armstrong, arriving a day after Atkinson's Indian messengers had delivered Black Hawk's message that he would not return but had only peaceful intentions.[23] Gratiot reported Black Hawk's reply was "that his heart is bad and he will not return."

[20] Atkinson to Black Hawk *et al.*, Apr. 24, 1832, Black Hawk War Papers, ISHL.

[21] Black Hawk *et al.* to Atkinson, Apr. 26, 1832, Black Hawk War Papers, ISHL; Black Hawk, *Autobiography*, 137–38.

[22] Wee Sheet's evidence, Aug. 27, 1832, Black Hawk War Papers, ISHL.

[23] Atkinson to Reynolds, Apr. 27, 1832, Black Hawk War Papers, ISHL.

This was a direct contradiction of the report by the Indian messengers the day before. These differences, the Sacs later claimed, were the result of White Crow's talk and of poor translation.[24] After he received these conflicting replies, Atkinson still could have sent a responsible officer or even gone to talk with the Sac himself with a good interpreter and other Sac and Fox chiefs. His failure to do so was a third error and was probably one of the factors leading to the fighting later. Instead, he accepted Gratiot's report and decided that war was imminent. These errors of judgment are inexplicable. Atkinson knew the Indian leaders personally and had taken part in councils with them. Thus he found himself caught between two equally unacceptable alternatives. Should he take no action and a frontier Indian war result, he would receive the blame. On the other hand, if he moved to force the Sac and Foxes back west of the Mississippi, a war might also result. In these circumstances Atkinson wrote General Macomb, "The conduct of Black Hawk and his associates renders it necessary that I should at once take the field, and as far as possible prevent them from doing any mischief . . ."[25]

Meanwhile, Black Hawk's band discovered that the promises they had received the previous winter had been modified. The Winnebago chiefs seemed reluctant to allow the Sac and Foxes to settle in their country. They altered their earlier invitation by saying that "if the white people did not interfere, they had no objection." However, they wanted the Sacs to remain in the lower river valley near the Prophet's village.[26]

Black Hawk decided that he had been tricked, but attempted to hide these facts from the band. He discussed their position with the chiefs and leading braves. They agreed to ask the Potawatomi if they, too, had changed their minds about welcoming the Sacs to their country. When the Sac leaders met with several Potawatomi

[24] "Minutes of an Examination of Indian Prisoners . . .," Aug. 19, 20, and 27, 1832, Black Hawk War Papers, ISHL.

[25] Atkinson to Macomb, Apr. 27, 1832, Black Hawk War Papers, ISHL.

[26] Black Hawk, *Autobiography*, 139.

from bands living between Dixon's Ferry and Chicago, they learned that this tribe also refused to aid them. After this council Black Hawk realized that continuing flight was impossible. He later said, "I concluded to tell my people, that if the White Beaver came after us, we would go back—as it was useless to think of stopping or going on without provisions."[27]

Atkinson, meanwhile, unaware of Black Hawk's decision, gathered men and supplies. On May 8 he mustered the Illinois Militia into the service of the United States. Once he organized the volunteers, his army of 340 regulars and approximately 1,700 militia began ascending the Rock in pursuit of the Indians. Here Atkinson made his most serious mistake in the campaign. He allowed the 1,500 mounted militiamen under the command of General Samuel Whiteside to ride ahead of the infantry, which was traveling by keelboat. Black Hawk and his chiefs had said that they would leave the whites alone and fight only if first attacked. This is precisely what happened. Atkinson's order to Whiteside contained the following clause: "should Genl. Whiteside . . . be of opinion that it would be prudent to come up with the enemy with as little delay as possible he will move upon him, and either make him surrender at discretion or coerce him to submission."[28]

When the militia moved ahead of the regulars, Governor Reynolds, acting as commander in chief, accompanied them up the Rock River to Dixon's Ferry. There he met Colonel Isaiah Stillman, who commanded an independent mounted battalion that had not been mustered into federal service. Reynolds ordered Stillman to "proceed without delay . . . to the head of 'Old Man Creek' where it is supposed there are some hostile Indians, and coerce them into submission."[29] Had Atkinson kept the troops together, he would have mustered Stillman's battalion into federal service. Once this happened they would have been subject to his command rather than to that of Reynolds. As it was, when Reynolds ordered Stillman's

27 *Ibid.*, 140–41.

28 Atkinson Order, May 9, 1832, Black Hawk War Papers, ISHL.

29 Reynolds to Stillman, quoted in Hagan, *The Sac and Fox Indians*, 156–57.

battalion to find the Indians, he overruled General Whiteside, who wanted to keep the militia together at Dixon's Ferry. So Governor Reynolds must also bear some blame for Stillman's attack on the Indians which started the actual hostilities.

Isaiah Stillman and his party of 275 mounted volunteers arrived at Old Man's Creek (now called Stillman's Run) on the evening of May 14. Soon three flag-bearers from Black Hawk's band arrived at their camp. These braves, sent by Black Hawk to discuss a return down the river, greatly excited the militia. The officers had no interpreter and were uncertain how to proceed. When other Indians were seen watching from a nearby hillside, some of the militiamen rushed after them, fired on them, and killed several. One of the flag-bearers was shot, but the other two escaped. Most of the Sac and Foxes who had been watching to see how the flag-bearers would be treated fled back to their own camp. There the chiefs rallied their men, probably only forty or fifty because the main body of the band was encamped several miles away, and prepared to ambush the onrushing militia. The Indians' ambush worked, and the Sacs killed twelve militiamen and drove the rest back to Dixon's Ferry twenty-five miles away.[30] This act of stupidity and violence marked the beginning of the Black Hawk "War."

Ever so many accounts describe this battle. Colonel Zachary Taylor, then attached to Atkinson's force, reported:

> [A] detachment of militia, about three hundred strong . . . who had been several days at Dixon's watching the movement of the Indians . . . attacked them, but on the Indians joining battle with them & killing one white man, they became panic struck & fled in the most shameful manner that ever troops were known to do . . .[31]

Although the battle had little military significance, it was of the utmost importance in shaping the following events. Before Stillman's defeat, Atkinson claimed a peaceful settlement was still possible. After the battle, however, frightened settlers, Indian

[30] Black Hawk, *Autobiography*, 141–45.

[31] Taylor to Dr. Thomas Lawson, Aug. 16, 1832, Black Hawk War Papers, ISHL.

haters, and aspiring politicians all clamored for Indian blood. Atkinson regretted that Stillman's defeat "not only encouraged the Indians but closed the door against settling the difficulty without bloodshed."[32]

Atkinson hoped to move after the Sacs, but this took several days because the militia was so disorganized. On May 19 the combined force of regulars and volunteers left Dixon's Ferry and started up the Rock River in pursuit of Black Hawk's band. Meanwhile, the Indians had retreated up the Kishwaukee River, looking for a way back to the Mississippi through Wisconsin. From time to time, however, they sent out small war parties, apparently joined by Winnebagos and Potawatomi still living in the Illinois-Wisconsin area, that attacked and plundered the whites. On May 22, Atkinson, unable to locate the main body of Indians and disturbed by the reports of continuing depredations, led the unmounted militia and regular infantry back to Dixon's Ferry. Here he established his supply depot and operational headquarters. He then sent the mounted troops under General Whiteside farther up the Rock to "scour the country," but they failed to find the Indians.[33]

Meanwhile, reports of Stillman's defeat moved east. According to the *National Intelligencer*, "the whole frontier was in a complete state of alarm and confusion."[34] On May 22, General Macomb received information that Black Hawk and his band were willing to surrender the Menominee murderers and return west of the Mississippi. This information was false and probably stemmed from Atkinson's reports of the surrender of some of the murderers by the peaceful tribesmen a month earlier. Macomb did not know the information was incorrect, but, after consulting with President Jackson and Secretary of War Lewis Cass, he decided that such a surrender was no longer sufficient. Macomb reported Jackson's distrust of Black Hawk to Atkinson and relayed Jackson's order to demand the surrender of Black Hawk and other leaders of the band that had returned to Illinois. If the Indians refused to surrender

[32] Atkinson to Dodge, May 17, 1832, Black Hawk War Papers, ISHL.

[33] Atkinson Order, May 22, 1832, Black Hawk War Papers, ISHL.

[34] June 12, 1832.

Black Hawk and other hostages, Macomb wrote that Jackson ordered "that you attack and disperse them . . ."[35] This order left Atkinson little freedom of action. The Indians were not likely to surrender their chiefs without a fight.

Meanwhile, at Dixon's Ferry, the Illinois Militia clamored to return to their farms. Since they had not enrolled for a definite term of service, they were discharged. Accordingly, on May 25, Atkinson asked Governor Reynolds to call up another two thousand state troops. A few days later Atkinson asked Agent Street at Prairie du Chien for a group of Sioux and Menominee braves for scouts. He also wrote asking General Hugh Brady to join him. A few days later he called for an additional one thousand state troops.[36]

None of these troops had arrived by May 26 when Governor Reynolds discharged the first levy of the Illinois Militia. Atkinson realized that he would have to cease all operations unless he obtained some mounted troops, so he and his staff went from Dixon's Ferry south to Ottawa. There they re-enlisted six companies of the militiamen, who agreed to serve an additional twenty days. Besides these militiamen, Atkinson had slightly over three hundred regulars.[37] Thus a two-month period of planning and work ended in failure. The army, now reduced to a mere defensive force, was unable to check sporadic Indian attacks along the Illinois-Wisconsin border or to locate the Indian camps.

Nevertheless, Atkinson apparently did not consider sending messengers to Black Hawk and the band of nearly one thousand Sac and Foxes to negotiate an end to the hostilities. Perhaps he did not think his messengers could locate the Indians. Thomas Owen, Indian agent at Chicago, however, sent chiefs and braves from the Potawatomi tribe under his jurisdiction to spy on the hostile band throughout the campaign. Although Owen and the Potawatomi were able to find the Sac and Fox band, Atkinson and

[35] Macomb to Atkinson, May 22, 1832, Letters Sent, Vol. 2, HQA.

[36] Atkinson to Reynolds, May 25, 1832, Black Hawk War Papers, ISHL; Atkinson to Loomis, May 26, 1832, *ibid.*; Atkinson to Brady, May 27, 1832, *ibid.*; Atkinson to Reynolds, May 29, 1832, *ibid.*

[37] Atkinson to Macomb, May 30, 1832, Black Hawk War Papers, ISHL.

his scouts were not. On June 3, Owen wrote that the Sacs said "that they were preparing to march and if they could get across to the West side of the Mississippi, they would do so immediately." Owen believed that the hostile band would take advantage of Atkinson's inability to patrol the entire frontier and slip west before he could rebuild his force.[38] The Indians, however, remained and continued to attack outlying settlements, travelers, and supply trains while Atkinson seemed to do nothing.

Inactivity during a military campaign rarely escapes censure, and Atkinson's case proved no exception. A contemporary observer denounced "the tardy operations of our chief officers" and complained that their ineptitude allowed the "nimble footed Indians to ravage" the frontier.[39] The *National Intelligencer* also criticized the campaign, but suggested that reliance upon "multitudinous bodies of citizens" being moved in an "undisciplined and unprovisioned" fashion might not be the proper way to defend the nation's frontiers.[40] Through his acting secretary of war, John Robb, President Andrew Jackson pointed to Atkinson's singular lack of success in ending the war promptly and concluded, "Some one is to blame in this matter, but upon whom it is to fall, is at present unknown . . ."[41]

Consequently, on June 15, President Jackson appointed General Winfield Scott to move west with one thousand regulars and to subdue Black Hawk's band. Before this news reached the frontier, however, Atkinson organized a new militia force. These troops assembled at Fort Wilbourn near Ottawa, Illinois. While the volunteer units assembled, Atkinson sent search parties to investigate reports of Indian depredations and to locate the Indians' camp. Then, between June 18 and 23, he organized the new army. One usually competent observer, Lieutenant Philip St. George Cooke,

38 Owen to Stevens T. Mason, June 3, 1832, Indian Office Files, Box 5, No. 7, SHSW.

39 Stephen Mack to Mrs. Lovicy Cooper, June 13, 1832, quoted in William D. Barge, *Early Lee County*, 18–19.

40 June 16, 1832.

41 John Robb to Atkinson, June 12, 1832, Letters Sent, Military Affairs, SW.

a Regular Army officer accompanying Atkinson, described the militia camp as being filled with a "multitude of citizen volunteers, who were as active as a swarming hive; catching horses, electioneering, drawing rations, asking questions, shooting at marks, electing officers, mustering in, issuing orders, disobeying orders, galloping about, 'cussing and discussing' the war, and the rumors thereof."[42]

After Atkinson mustered the last Illinois troops into federal service, he probably had too large a force. The army now included three brigades of mounted militia of nearly 1000 men each. These were commanded by Generals Alexander Posey, James D. Henry, and Milton K. Alexander. Atkinson also had nearly 400 regulars and 200 dismounted militia commanded by General Hugh Brady. In addition, Colonel Henry Dodge had organized a mounted battalion of 350 miners at Galena and in the Wisconsin lead-mining area.[43] Not only did Atkinson have too many men for the campaign, but his lines of supply stretched back to St. Louis. Although Mississippi River steamboats could deposit supplies at Galena, roving bands of Indian warriors attacked settlements, making the route between there and his base of operations at Dixon dangerous. Two other routes were available for supplies. Some supplies came directly up the Rock River, which by midsummer was too low for heavy boats. The remainder had to come up the Illinois River and then overland from Ottawa.

On June 25 reports of a large Indian force near Kellogg's Grove induced Atkinson to send General Alexander Posey and the First Brigade to the lead district to co-operate with Dodge. However, Atkinson correctly surmised that this Indian attack was a ruse "in order to draw my attention from a pursuit of the main body up Rock River."[44] At this point, he had no specific plan of attack, and his efforts were chiefly reactions to Indian thrusts rather than positive movements.

[42] Cooke, *Scenes and Adventures in the Army*, 158.

[43] Atkinson to Macomb, June 23, 1832, Black Hawk War Papers, ISHL.

[44] Atkinson to Posey, June 25, 1832, Black Hawk War Papers, ISHL; Journal of Albert S. Johnston, entry, June 26, 1832, *ibid.* (hereafter Johnston Journal).

When he received no news to the contrary, Atkinson decided that Black Hawk's band was still hidden in the swampy area along the upper Rock, so he moved his forces slowly in that direction. On this move he further divided his force. With Henry's brigade and Dodge's battalion that had just arrived from Galena and the infantry, he moved up the east side of the Rock River. He sent General Alexander's brigade to the other shore to go up the river on the west side in a parallel column. For days the army struggled through bogs, over hills, into marshes, and around tangled thickets. The Indian scouts with Atkinson were either treacherous or incompetent, and the frontiersmen knew little about the area, so the troops moved at a snail's pace. Atkinson's cautious moves during late June and early July brought continuing criticism of him by the militia, by newspaper editors, and by some politicians.

While the army moved up the Rock River, the regulars and volunteers established separate camps, and on the evening of June 29 the militiamen stampeded their own horses by firing noisy volleys into the night air. Lieutenant Cooke described this event:

> a singular scene; a whole brigade was regularly paraded and firing in the air as regularly as they knew how, while their General, mounted on a tall stump, was endeavoring to argue them out of it; but their perseverance was not more extraordinary than their commencement . . . their General finally damned them to all posterity, and resigned his commission in violent disgust.[45]

With most of his army consisting of such troops, it is no wonder Henry Atkinson moved slowly.

By July 6 his force was searching for the Indians on both sides of Lake Koshkonong in south central Wisconsin. Here reports of President Jackson's displeasure reached Atkinson and stung him into an even greater effort to find the Sacs. Army scouts and spies often reported finding one- or two-day-old Indian camps, but they were unable to find the Indians in the tangled swamps and marshes of southern Wisconsin. The Sac warriors were scattered in small

[45] Cooke, *Scenes and Adventures*, 161–62.

parties, so Atkinson had little choice but to hunt the remainder of the band. After moving through rain and marshes for a week, the army halted. Atkinson realized the Indians could continually elude his force simply by moving a few miles through the swamps and by further scattering in small bands. On July 10, with food scarce because of the militia's waste and carelessness with supplies, Atkinson abandoned further offensive action and sent most of the volunteers to Fort Winnebago for more provisions. He recognized the difficulty of continuing dependence on supply wagons and ordered the volunteers to return with one hundred loaded pack horses.[46] While waiting for their return, he wrote to General Scott, who had then reached Chicago, asking that new tactics be employed. He complained about "the most difficult country to operate in imaginable," and recommended that the artillery be abandoned as of no use "unless the Indians fortify" which was unlikely. By this time he also realized he had too many troops and wrote that if he were sure Scott's plans were not based on a large force, he "would at once discharge at least a third or even a half of them."[47]

General Scott, however, had his own troubles. While his troops were en route via the Great Lakes, they were incapacitated by Asiatic cholera. When Atkinson heard this, he urged Scott to keep the infected troops away from the frontier army. Scott needed no urging. Thus, although Scott had been sent to replace Atkinson, the White Beaver remained in command until the fighting was over.

The volunteers' trip to Fort Winnebago on July 10 inadvertently ended this campaign. Generals Alexander and Henry and Colonel Dodge received reports that the Sacs were moving toward them. Henry and Dodge—with their commands—ignored Atkinson's order to return directly from Fort Winnebago with the supplies and, instead, pursued the Indians. General Alexander alone rejoined Atkinson near Lake Koshkonong. Meanwhile, the force under Dodge and Henry sought the Indians in vain, and the embarrassed commanders sent messengers with reports of the Indians'

[46] Johnston to John Plympton, July 10, 1832, Black Hawk War Papers, ISHL.

[47] Atkinson to Scott, July 9, 1832, Black Hawk War Papers, ISHL; Atkinson to Scott, July 11, 1832, *ibid.*

supposed location to Atkinson. Only a few miles from camp, however, the messengers discovered the broad, plain trail left by the retreating Sacs and raced back to Dodge and Henry with the news.[48] The militia commanders now had a reason to ignore their previous orders.

Atkinson learned of their discovery late on July 20 and sent a small detachment farther up the White Water Creek (Bark River) to make sure all the Sacs were gone. Then he marched his command through a cold rain and across flooded creeks back to Fort Koshkonong, at the confluence of White Water Creek and the Rock River. There they left one company of regulars to protect the extra equipment and the sick, who remained at the fort.[49] Anticipation of a chance to meet the Indians seems to have inspired the troops, and, on the morning of July 21, Atkinson led his command west. He wrote General Posey, then patrolling northwestern Illinois, of Black Hawk's movement and ordered him to block the Indians' escape route if they should turn south and to join him at Blue Mounds.[50]

By July 25 the regulars and attached militia units arrived at the Wisconsin River near Blue Mounds. During this forced march, the much ridiculed regulars easily outmarched their mounted tormentors. In spite of gaining on Black Hawk, however, many of the volunteers complained about Atkinson's leadership. Others turned their disgust and frustration toward their fleeing adversaries. Voicing what may have been a common opinion, William B. Archer, one of the militiamen, wrote, "Rest assured if we come up [against the Indians] there will be fighting, our men have become desperate against them—and no troops can be more elevated in spirits than ours when we come near them."[51]

48 Dodge to Atkinson, July 19, 1832, Black Hawk War Papers, ISHL; Henry to Atkinson, July 19, 1832, *ibid.*

49 Johnston Journal, entry, July 20, 1832, Black Hawk War Papers, ISHL; Atkinson to Scott, July 21, 1832, *ibid.*

50 Johnston to Posey, July 22, 1832, Black Hawk War Papers, ISHL.

51 Archer to Jacob Harlan, July 25, 1832, William B. Archer–Jacob Harlan Letters, ISHL.

Meanwhile, on July 21, Dodge and Henry caught up with the fleeing Sacs near the Wisconsin River. Some of the braves fought a rear-guard action, while most of the women and children swam the river or built crude rafts or canoes for crossing. This action, known as the Battle of Wisconsin Heights, was a defeat for the Indians who lost between forty and eighty men; the whites had only one man killed.[52] In spite of the heavy losses, most competent observers considered the Indians' tactics superb. Lieutenant Jefferson Davis, although not a participant in the war, later described their action as a "most brilliant exhibition of military tactics . . . a feat of most consummate management and bravery in the face of an enemy of greatly superior numbers."[53] On July 25, after this victory, the militia came into Atkinson's camp at Blue Mounds for more ammunition and provisions. Lieutenant Cooke commented sarcastically:

> After all their boasting, the simple fact was, that Black Hawk, although encumbered with the women, children, and baggage of his whole band, covering himself by a small party, had accomplished that most difficult of military operations,—to wit, the passage of a river,—in the presence of three regiments of American volunteers![54]

Early on the morning of July 26, Atkinson's force of thirteen hundred troops began crossing the Wisconsin by rafts. The troops first had to fell and trim trees, and they also tore down an old cabin to obtain material for the rafts. It took the army two days to cross the river. This gave the Indians at least a five-day start in their race for the Mississippi. By the time the troops had crossed the Wisconsin, the Indians had been forced to abandon wounded and sick

[52] The discrepancy in figures for Indian casualties comes from an incomplete count by the Indians. Many braves wounded at Wisconsin Heights later died of their wounds.

[53] Quoted in Mrs. John H. Kinzie, *Wau-Bun, the "Early Day" in the North-West* (ed. by Milo M. Quaife), 509.

[54] Cooke, *Scenes and Adventures*, 170–71.

along the trail, drop kettles, blankets, and other camp equipment, and begin eating bark and roots and killing their horses for food.[55]

Once across the river, Atkinson's army soon found the Sacs' trail. Black Hawk led his weary pursuers through the most difficult country yet traversed. The troops complained of heavy brambles and underbrush, steep bluffs, dark and marshy valleys, poor grass for the horses, and hordes of mosquitoes. In fact, the country was so rough and broken that Lieutenant Cooke thought the Indians made a grievous blunder by not sending back small bands of warriors to further harass and disrupt the stumbling whites. "Here a small force could have retarded pursuit at every step," he stated, and "an ambush might have been formed every mile." Fortunately for Atkinson and his army, Black Hawk faced too many other difficulties to try this tactic. Cooke reported that the officers and men were relieved when they emerged from the "gloomy forests into the gladsome light of the sun" on July 31, near the Kickapoo River.[56]

After marching until late in the evening on August 1, the army reached the Sacs' camp of the previous day. Atkinson hoped to overtake the Sacs early the following morning, and ordered a brief rest. He set marching time for 2:00 A.M. As usual, however, the militia complicated his operations. They had already turned their horses loose when they received Atkinson's early marching orders. So when the bugler's notes roused the sleeping troops, those brigades under Generals Posey, Alexander, and Henry were left to search for their mounts in the darkness. The regulars and Dodge's battalion led the chase. Three miles away from camp, Dodge's advanced scouts met the Indian rear guard near the confluence of the Bad Axe and Mississippi rivers, and the final "battle" of the war began.[57] When his scouts located the almost leaderless Sacs (Black

[55] Atkinson to Scott, July 27, 1832, Black Hawk War Papers, ISHL; Charles Whittlesey, "Recollections of a Tour Through Wisconsin in 1832," *Wisconsin Historical Society Collections*, Vol. I (1903), 79.

[56] Cooke, *Scenes and Adventures*, 176–77.

[57] Atkinson to Scott, Aug. 9, 1832, Black Hawk War Papers, ISHL.

Hawk and the Winnebago prophet had deserted the band the night before the battle and Neapope disappeared before the Battle of Wisconsin Heights), Atkinson rushed to the front and deployed his forces. He placed the regulars in extended order with Dodge's battalion to their right. As the other militia brigades caught up, he ordered them to fill in on the left of the skirmish line. At first the army followed the Indian rear guard, which momentarily succeeded in leading the troops north of the main body of the Indians. However, when the men encountered only light resistance, Atkinson sent some of Dodge's scouts farther to the left, and they with some of Henry's men encountered the rest of the Indians. Once found, the Sacs had little chance, and by the time the sun burned off the morning mists in the Mississippi River bottoms, Black Hawk's band no longer existed. During the fierce skirmishing, often with spear and clubbed musket, most of the Indians were either captured or killed. Casualty estimates vary, but even the most conservative indicate at least 150 Indians were killed and another 50 captured.[58] Thus the war ended at Bad Axe. This slaughter, usually called a battle, completely broke the Sacs' resistance.

When the fighting ended, Atkinson sent several Winnebago braves after Black Hawk and the Prophet. The Winnebagos captured these two Sacs and brought them to Fort Crawford. Then Atkinson arranged transportation for the troops to Fort Crawford, from where the militia was to be marched south and then mustered out of federal service. Several days later the troops boarded the *Warrior* and steamed south to Fort Crawford.

When the war ended, Atkinson's army, the largest he ever commanded, dispersed rapidly. What had begun as a simple maneuver to keep several hostile Indian tribes apart and to capture a few murderers from the Sacs had expanded into a bloody, expensive war. Some blame, of course, falls on Black Hawk and those Indian advisers who misled the aging warrior. The Indians did not start

[58] Atkinson to Scott, August 9, 1832, Black Hawk War Papers, ISHL; Johnston to Samuel Stambough, Aug. 7, 1832, *ibid.*; Henry Smith, "Indian Campaign of 1832," *Military and Naval Magazine*, Vol. I (Aug., 1833), 330–31.

the fighting, however, and had tried to parley, only to have their flags of truce met by musket fire. Governor Reynolds, too, must bear some responsibility for this fighting. He ordered the Illinois Militia for duty against the Sacs before Atkinson expected or called for them. Later he ordered Colonel Stillman's regiment after the Indians instead of placing them under Atkinson's command. This move started the fighting. Atkinson, however, was not blameless. His vague, alarm-filled letter to Reynolds convinced the Governor that the militia were needed. By failing to keep the militia and regular troops together while they traveled up the Rock River, Atkinson gave Governor Reynolds the opportunity to order Stillman's regiment after the Indians. Throughout the spring and summer he overlooked chances to send qualified messengers and negotiators to talk with the Indian leaders.

Atkinson was too hesitant. At first he moved slowly because he accepted the Indians' word that they would not fight unless first attacked. When the fighting did begin, however, he failed to increase the speed of his actions against them. During the campaign he apparently accepted wild rumors and scare stories from frontier editors and local politicians. At times he seems to have taken no action, either because he did not know what to do or because he feared the possible adverse publicity.

Atkinson's strategy to isolate and then follow the Sacs until they either sued for peace or could be cornered and forced into battle was sound. He erred, however, by gathering too large an army and by remaining with the slow-moving infantry simply because they were regular troops. If he had mounted several companies of them or had gone with the militia, the war might have been averted or ended sooner.

It is easy, however, to criticize in retrospect what proved to be a frustrating and complex military operation. Contemporaries agreed on the difficulties of transportation and of maintaining enough provisions for a large and poorly disciplined force in this wilderness. There were no roads, the army had few trustworthy scouts, and much of the campaign was through hilly, wooded, or swampy areas that made marching and moving supply wagons difficult. Regular Army officers, although obviously biased against the militia, were unanimous in their denunciations of the Illinois Volunteers. They claimed they disobeyed orders and wasted food and ammunition. In fact, the unpreparedness of the militia on the morning of August 2, when the final battle with the Sacs occurred, seems to have been only one in a long series of mishaps and ignored orders throughout the campaign.

Atkinson's handling of the day-to-day movements of troops and supplies was adequate. He used forward scouts, flank guards, and rear guards and specified the defensive measures to be taken each night to prevent surprise attack. In spite of considerable difficulties he usually kept the troops supplied with both provisions and ammunition. It must be remembered, however, that Henry Atkinson, like many American generals, had obtained his rank during a period of peace and had never held a field command during wartime. In spite of his success as a leader and organizer in several large troop movements, this was his first experience as a leader during a campaign. Perhaps significantly, when Atkinson was being criticized both on the frontier and in Washington, General Scott wrote from Chicago, "I do not know—I cannot flatter myself that I might have done better."[59]

Throughout his career, Henry Atkinson had tried to deal peaceably with the Indians. He often led troops to trouble spots, but prior to this campaign he had successfully avoided warfare with the Indians. He was criticized as being too hesitant in this campaign, but when he moved north from St. Louis he had no indication that he might become involved in an Indian war. He hoped to end the difficulties by negotiation.

Shortly after the war, President Jackson, Secretary of War Cass, and General Scott all commended Atkinson's leadership in the face of extreme difficulties. These comments must have seemed hollow praise, however, after the biting and continuing criticism he had received during that frustrating summer campaign.

[59] Scott to Cass, July 19, 1832, Jackson Papers, 1st series, Vol. 81.

XI. Jefferson Barracks Days—1832–35

For several years after the Black Hawk War, Henry Atkinson spent much of his time at Jefferson Barracks tending to the administrative duties of the Right Wing. Although frequent Indian alarms frightened the frontier settlers, Atkinson's major task was to keep the Indians from fighting each other and to enforce the federal laws that guaranteed certain rights to the Indians, rather than to protect the white settlers. The period was one of fairly continuous white-Indian friction. There were many incursions on Indian lands and frequent and recurring depredations by the Indians along much of the western frontier.

After the Black Hawk War ended in 1832, Atkinson led his troops from Prairie du Chien south to Jefferson Barracks. Hoping to avoid the cholera which had stricken the troops under General Scott, Atkinson ordered that "No ardent nor vinious liquors shall be vended nor malt liquor to a greater amount than a pint per diem to each." He also ordered the men to report to the surgeon "upon the first appearance of bowel complaint." All troops were to purchase and wear flannel shirts "next to the skin" and to refrain from using fruit and raw vegetables under the assumption that anything that might cause bowel complaints might weaken the system and allow cholera to enter. His medical advisors agreed that fruit and vegetables might, indeed, contain "sources of cholera" and thus should be avoided. In spite of these precautions, cholera struck and ran its course, causing some deaths. By early October the Sixth Regiment was 104 men under the authorized strength of 514, and Atkinson reported his regiment "much reduced."[1]

Although the loss of men was explained partially by cholera, desertion had also reduced the number of troops in the Sixth Regiment and throughout the army. Because of this, Secretary of War Lewis Cass asked the high-ranking officers for suggestions to reduce desertion. Atkinson's reply showed a curious mixture of severity and kindness toward his men. First he wrote that the law for the punishment of deserters was too mild, and he "suggest[ed] most earnestly the necessity of authority by sentence of General Co. Martial of the infliction of stripes for the crime of desertion." On the other hand, he wanted to limit desertions by making military life more pleasant for the enlisted men. He recommended having three-year terms of enlistment rather than the existing five, increased pay for noncommissioned officers, and a 20 per cent increase in the pay of privates at the time of their second enlistment if their conduct had "been uniformly good."[2] None of Atkinson's suggestions was adopted at that time.

Earlier in the fall of 1832, Atkinson had received news of renewed white intrusions on lands of the Foxes at Dubuque's mines in northeastern Iowa. American miners had staked claims on the Indian land along the western bank of the Mississippi before the Sac and Foxes ceded it to the United States government. Even after the Indians ceded the land on September 21, 1832, in a treaty made with General Scott and Governor Reynolds, the miners had to be kept off the land until the treaty was ratified by the Senate. Consequently, Atkinson ordered Colonel Zachary Taylor, then at Fort Crawford, to send a detachment "sufficient to remove from the country all such persons" and leave a guard at the mines to keep the squatters from returning.[3] When the troops arrived, the squatters had fled.

[1] Atkinson to Jones, Oct. 9, 1832, Letters Received, AGO.

[2] Atkinson to Cass, Oct. 29, 1832, Letters Received, unregistered series, SW.

[3] Johnston to Taylor, Sept. 3, 1832, Black Hawk War Papers, ISHL.

In the meantime, continued Indian unrest in central Illinois caused settlers near Peoria to demand that Governor Reynolds remove the Potawatomi and Winnebagos from the state. Reynolds, in turn, relayed these demands and his approval of them to William Clark at St. Louis and to the Secretary of War. When Atkinson learned of this, he wrote to Hiram M. Curry, a Peoria citizen, and commissioned him to "take an interpreter . . . if one can be had" and warn the Indians to stop molesting the whites. Atkinson also wrote Thomas Owen, agent at Chicago, and asked him to investigate reports of horse-stealing and burning of fields and fences by Potawatomi hunting parties near Peoria.[4]

In mid-December Owen traveled south to Peoria. After a short investigation, he reported to Atkinson that it was well understood that the Indians were to retain hunting rights on the ceded territory as long as the land remained under federal control. That month Governor Reynolds received further reports of Indian depredations and again demanded removal of the Indians.[5] Reynolds reported to Henry Dodge, who commanded a company of United States Rangers, that the Indians had indeed committed some depredations and "that the citizens of that part of the State consider themselves insecure . . ." He asked Dodge to move his company of Rangers[6] into the area, but Dodge had to wait for orders from his military superiors or the War Department. Atkinson, meanwhile, remained unconvinced that the Potawatomi presented any danger to the Illinois settlers. In spite of "certain alleged offenses," he wrote to Cass, it was unthinkable that the Potawatomi "will attempt any serious disturbance." To insure safety, however, he decided to move some of the Rangers into the area in the spring of 1833. He also wrote Cass that the Potawatomi were interested in selling their Illinois lands. "I think the whole of the Pottawattomies might be induced to migrate to the west," he added, "[and] such an arrange-

4 Atkinson to Curry, Nov. 16, 1832, Indian Office Files, Box 6, No. 162, SHSW; Atkinson to Owen, Nov. 16, 1832, Indian Office Files, Box 6, No. 163, SHSW.

5 Reynolds to Dodge, Dec. 13, 1832, Governors' Letter Book III, 39–40.

6 This was one of four companies of mounted militia that had been taken into federal service for the year. *U.S. Statutes at Large*, IV, 533.

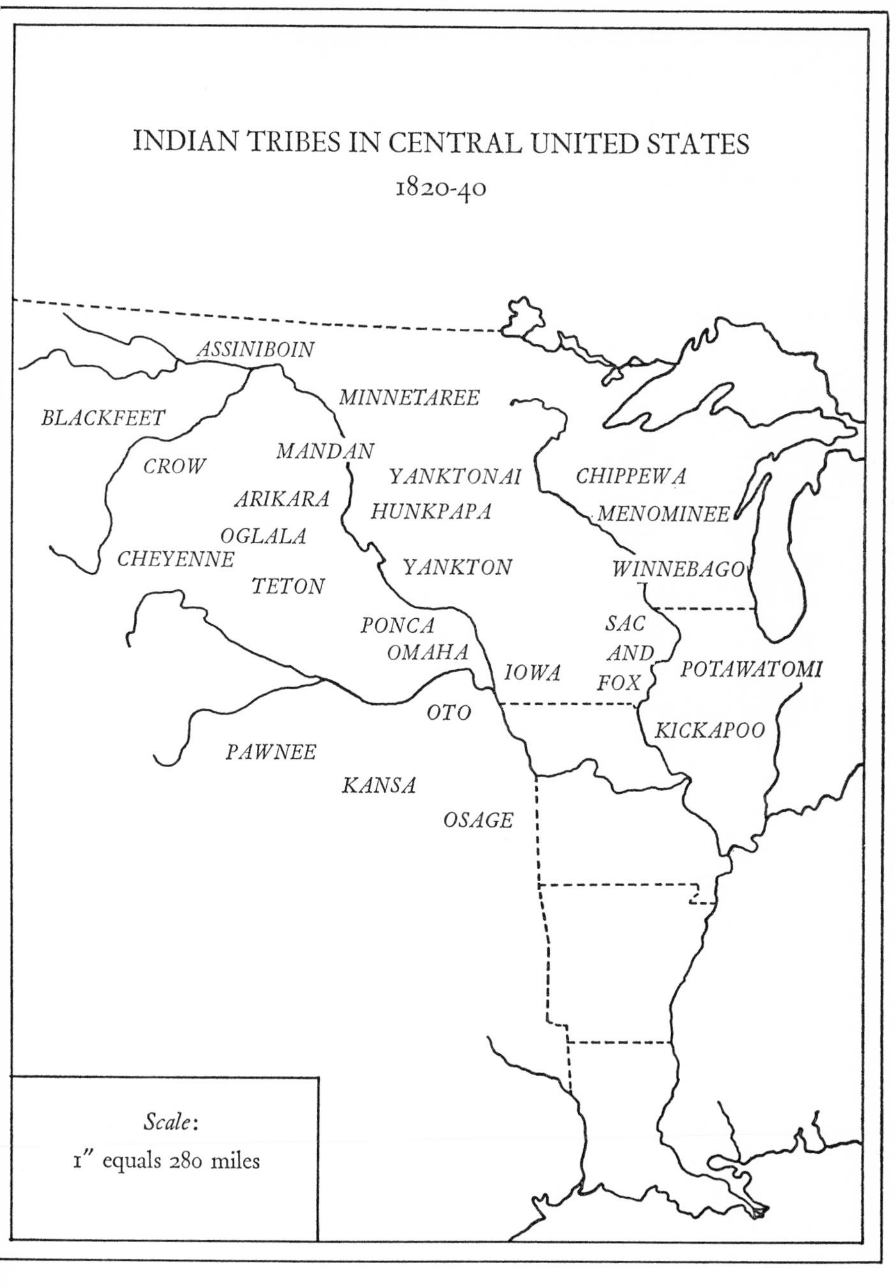
INDIAN TRIBES IN CENTRAL UNITED STATES
1820-40
ASSINIBOIN
MINNETAREE
BLACKFEET
MANDAN
CROW
YANKTONAI
CHIPPEWA
ARIKARA
HUNKPAPA
MENOMINEE
OGLALA
CHEYENNE
YANKTON
WINNEBAGO
TETON
PONCA
SAC
OMAHA
AND
IOWA
FOX
POTAWATOMI
OTO
KICKAPOO
PAWNEE
KANSA
OSAGE
Scale:
1" equals 280 miles

ment is essential to the tranquility of the western frontier of Michigan & Illinois."[7]

Throughout the winter of 1832–33, rumors of Indian unrest spread throughout the West and even reached Washington. Nicholas Boilvin, former Indian subagent at Prairie du Chien, wrote the Secretary of War that Keokuk, leader of one peaceful band within the Sac tribe, was hostile to the white settlers and had sent wampum belts and war clubs to the Indian tribes along both sides of the Mississippi. According to Boilvin, several bands had accepted these invitations, although the Potawatomi had refused to join the conspiracy. Boilvin reported that individual members of that tribe, however, had intimidated settlers in central Illinois and ordered several to leave the country or face death "when the grass would be about six inches high."[8] The War Department also learned that the Winnebagos had threatened settlers. As a result, in January, 1833, Atkinson received orders that "should he apprehend a renewal of hostilities on the part of the Winnebago Indians . . . to order forward the two Companies of Rangers, now in the Eastern Department . . ."[9] By the end of January, Atkinson had reported to General Macomb that the Rangers were ready "for active service at the shortest notice," although he was sure the Indians were not then planning an attack. He preferred to investigate all reports before taking action. Consequently, he intended to keep the Rangers inactive until spring when he would send units to Rock River and the mining district.[10]

In February, Atkinson heard new rumors of Potawatomi depredations near Peoria. The Potawatomi, however, denied their guilt. They accused the settlers of killing each other's hogs and then charging the loss to them. To this, Atkinson had no answer. "But," he observed, "I know there is a determination on the part of the frontier people to prevent the Pottawattomie Indians from hunting

7 Atkinson to Cass, Dec. 28, 1832, Indian Office Files, Box 6, No. 161, SHSW.

8 Boilvin to Secretary of War, Jan. 10, 1833, Indian Office Files, Box 7, No. 1, SHSW.

9 Cooper to Gaines, Jan. 12, 1833, Letters Sent, Vol. 10, AGO.

10 Atkinson to Macomb, Jan. 24, 1833, Letters Received, AGO.

on the ceded lands although they are privileged to do so by the treaty of cession." Once again he sent several persons to investigate.[11]

One group of investigators included Billy Caldwell and Alexander Robinson, who were half-blood Potawatomi chiefs. They submitted a report that cleared the Indians. When asked if Caldwell and Robinson could be trusted to submit a fair report, Atkinson replied affirmatively. "I know them well," he wrote. "They were with me in the recent campaign on the frontier & behaved very satisfactorily." He assumed that their report was generally correct, although he admitted that "under some circumstances a mission of this character would be both unsafe & unadmissable."[12] Early in March another investigator, W. W. Woodbridge, accompanied by Agent Owen, went to the scene of the depredations. Woodbridge reported that he had visited both whites and Indians, and that the latter were probably guilty of having killed some livestock. "The Indians I saw are poor in the extreme," he wrote, "and I presume that hunger caused them to kill the hogs."[13] In spite of these conflicting reports, Atkinson took no further action.

On April 6, 1833, Governor Reynolds received information "that numerous bands of warlike Indians completely armed, are assembled and are assembling at various points through that part of the country which was the theater of the late Sac war." The Winnebagos, Sacs, Foxes, Potawatomi, and Chippewas numbering, according to "the most moderate accounts," at least four thousand warriors and four or five hundred boys, it was rumored, were even then assembled and ready to strike. John Dixon, a trader living along the Rock River, had reportedly visited several Indian villages and found the Indians "sullen and reserved." Dixon had heard from friendly Indians that a coalition was even then "in complete preparation as to arms, ammunition, &c." and that the

11 Atkinson to Macomb, Feb. 17, 1833, Letters Received, AGO.

12 Atkinson to Elbert Herring, Mar. 17, 1833, Indian Office Files, Box 7, No. 28, SHSW.

13 Woodbridge to Atkinson, Mar. 7, 1833, Dept. of the West, Letters Received, USAC.

miners were again in a state of panic.[14] Reynolds forwarded these reports to Atkinson, who replied that the Indian combination was probably the result of a council to discuss removal. Dissatisfied, Reynolds complained to Secretary Cass about Atkinson's lack of action and demanded the Indians be removed.[15] Cass apparently agreed with Atkinson because he took no action on Reynolds' suggestion.

In the spring of 1833, Mr. Elbert Herring, commissioner of Indian affairs, decided to release Black Hawk and the captured Sac and Fox chiefs, but was afraid that they might have a bad influence on tribal affairs. Accordingly, he asked Atkinson for his opinion. Atkinson replied that they could be released, but suggested that they be taken on a tour of major eastern cities first to give them some idea of the size and strength of the United States. Then they could be taken to a western fort where they might later be released to their tribesmen, and thus "be made to feel a dependence on their Chiefs for their release and that the Chiefs may renew their pledge for their future good conduct."[16] The officials in both the Indian Office and the War Department accepted Atkinson's suggestions, and he received orders to send Black Hawk and five other Sac prisoners at Jefferson Barracks to Washington. There they talked with President Jackson and then toured some of the large eastern cities. Then Black Hawk and his companions were returned to their fellow tribesmen during the summer of 1833.

More reports of Indian difficulties reached Washington in the spring of 1833, and Macomb wrote to Atkinson that the Winnebagos displayed "a strong disposition" to remain south of the Wisconsin River on the lands they had ceded the preceding September. The Indians, he claimed, wanted to plant another corn crop, and their presence would cause renewed friction with the mining population. "It is therefore the desire of the Secy of War that these

14 Augustus Langworthy to Reynolds, Apr. 6, 1833, Indian Office Files, Box 7, No. 7, SHSW.

15 Reynolds to Cass, Apr. 13, 1833, Indian Office Files, Box 7, No. 4, SHSW.

16 Atkinson to Herring, May 20, 1833, Indian Office Files, Box 7, No. 97, SHSW.

Indians should be made to fulfill the stipulations of the treaty and remove [north of the Wisconsin River] from the lands which they have ceded to the U. S.," he wrote. If the tribe refused to cooperate, Macomb ordered Atkinson to force them to cross the Wisconsin River.[17] By May 30, Atkinson reported that he was certain the Winnebagos would leave the ceded lands peaceably. He assumed that, since a few of the chiefs had signed a treaty of cession, they would compel their fellow tribesmen to obey the stipulations.[18] In his optimism he overlooked the Indians' attachment for their homes and hunting grounds. In mid-June, Atkinson reported that, according to Colonel Dodge, the Indians might not move voluntarily. Atkinson, however, remained confident that moving them would be but a small matter. Should "the Ranger companies . . . not be sufficient to drive them off," he wrote, "some of the troops at this post will be sent to effect the object."[19]

Some of the Indians moved promptly and without any fuss, but others tried to remain in their old homes, hoping they would be allowed to raise another crop of corn. They soon learned this was not possible, and by mid-July, Dodge had escorted the Winnebagos across the Wisconsin.

Even though the Indians had crossed to the north side of the Wisconsin River, Atkinson assumed that some of them would attempt to return. Dodge, however, hoped to prevent this and stationed the Rangers near the Four Lakes, ordering them to patrol the limits of the cession. In spite of Colonel Dodge and the Rangers, many of the Winnebagos returned south of the Wisconsin to their former homes. Dodge reported this to Atkinson and that he suspected that a Mr. Dougherty and a Mr. Mack, both traders at the Fox-Wisconsin portage, were "secretly advising a part of the Winnebagos to return to the Rock River Country." One of the traders was married to a relative of Whirling Thunder, a leading chief, and, therefore, had some influence. Dodge also suspected the

17 Macomb to Atkinson, May 9, 1833, Letters Sent, Vol. 2, HQA.

18 Atkinson to Macomb, May 30, 1833, Letters Received, AGO.

19 Atkinson to Jones, June 13, 1833, Letters Received, AGO.

Winnebagos and Menominees of planning some resistance together, because they seemed friendly with each other and some Winnebagos were even then hunting on Menominee lands east of the Fox River.[20] When Atkinson received Dodge's report, he wrote, "I am apprehensive that should they be allowed to remain there during the winter it will increase the difficulty of forcing them back across the Wisconsin." He agreed with Dodge that a company or two of Rangers should patrol the Wisconsin River to keep the Indians from returning to the ceded lands.[21] During the fall of 1833, however, more tribesmen returned to their former land, and by mid-November, Atkinson decided that "It will be humane to let those Indians hunt for the winter on their old grounds, otherwise many of them must starve." They had to understand, he added, that this was merely temporary. Atkinson suspected that there might be more difficulties with "these troublesome people" in the future.[22] Their actions during the next seven years proved his prediction more accurate than he imagined.

During the latter stages of the Black Hawk War, four companies of mounted United States Rangers had been organized. After the war, Secretary of War Cass suggested that the Rangers be replaced by a permanent regiment of dragoons or cavalry.[23] In the spring of 1833, President Andrew Jackson signed a bill that authorized the formation of the dragoons. It was hoped this force of cavalry, advocated by many army officers, could meet the challenge of mounted, marauding Indians. The regiment consisted of ten companies of seventy-one men each, and was to be commanded by a colonel. It would receive special training in addition to the regular infantry tactics and would be added to existing units within the military peace establishment.[24] The dragoons, to be equipped and trained at Jefferson Barracks, began arriving there in the late summer and autumn of 1833. Government planners had miscalcu-

20 Dodge to Atkinson, July 14, 1833, Dept. of the West, Letters Received, USAC.

21 Atkinson to Jones, Oct. 15, 1833, Letters Received, AGO.

22 Atkinson to Jones, Nov. 19, 1833, Letters Received, AGO.

23 ASP:MA, V, 18–25.

24 *U.S. Statutes at Large*, IV, 652.

lated, however, and the troops arrived to find that no uniforms, barracks, horses, or stables awaited them. They had to perform all the duties of the infantrymen at the post and build their own barracks and stables as well. Discontent soared and with it desertion. Floggings, placing men in irons, and keeping a heavy guard around their camp had little effect.[25]

In spite of the desertions, the building continued. Work parties dressed in the fatigue uniform of "a blue roundabout trimmed with yellow lace, white pantaloons, and forage caps" marched daily to work, after receiving instruction in dismounted drill, proper dress, and the handling of personal weapons.[26] In September the quartermaster officers began bringing the horses to Jefferson Barracks, and by October 1 some of them were assigned to various companies. By late November, 1833, Colonel Henry Dodge took command of the dragoons and led them southwest to Fort Gibson for the first of several ventures across the plains and into the Indian country of the Southwest.[27]

Meanwhile, army authorities discussed plans for deploying the cavalry. Generals Macomb and Atkinson agreed that the regiment might be successfully divided into three smaller units with the regimental headquarters at Fort Leavenworth. The right wing of the regiment, Atkinson suggested, should be located near the mouth of the Des Moines River and the left wing on the Arkansas. This would "enable either or both wings to act with the center or the center with either wing with great facility and effect." In addition, posts on the Missouri and Des Moines rivers could be maintained with little expense because there was plenty of forage for the horses at both places. If his suggestions were followed, Atkinson would obtain mounted troops to patrol the frontier.[28] Apparently Macomb agreed because the dragoons served in the areas Atkinson had suggested. In mid-June, Atkinson sent Lieutenant Trueman Cross to

25 James Hildreth, *Dragoon Campaigns to the Rocky Mountains*, 45–47.

26 *Ibid.*, 39–42.

27 *Ibid.*, 51, 59.

28 Atkinson to Macomb, May 29, 1834, Letters Received, AGO.

the Des Moines Rapids of the Mississippi (near present Keokuk, Iowa) to choose a site for the dragoon post that he hoped to complete that year.[29] The dragoons would help frontier army commanders to deal more effectively with the Plains Indians, but, at the same time, they would remove much of Atkinson's personal dealings with the tribesmen.

Atkinson spent much of his time trying to keep the Indian tribes along the frontier from warring with each other. According to William Clark, the only way to keep peace among the tribes was to hold the chiefs or headmen responsible for surrendering those who committed depredations or otherwise broke their treaty obligations.[30] Atkinson, however, remained skeptical of this approach. When Keokuk and other Sac chiefs visited Jefferson Barracks in the spring of 1834, they asked why the government would not abrogate their treaty of peace with the Sioux. They claimed that they remained at peace, but "the Sioux are sticking them behind." Atkinson relayed their request to the Indian Office and told the impatient Sacs that he had no power to grant their wish. To one of his subordinates, however, he expressed himself more openly. "I wish I were authorized to grant their request," he wrote. "It would rid us of a great deal of trouble, and no doubt make them more cautious how they would in future get into difficulty."[31] He said that the government was mistaken in trying to maintain peace among tribesmen who could not be controlled. This was a shift in his thinking, because earlier he had advocated this very step. Now he realized that the Indians could not be held liable in the civil courts for their attacks on each other. Even when offenders surrendered, there was no way to punish them; so after a few months they had to be released.

Atkinson also was charged with responsibility to restrain white expansion into areas reserved for the Indians. Under the Treaty of

[29] Atkinson order, June 19, 1834, Jefferson Barracks Orders, Vol. 161, USAC.

[30] Clark to Atkinson, Mar. 21, 1834, Dept. of the West, Letters Received, USAC.

[31] Atkinson to William Davenport, Mar. 29, 1834, Right Wing Letter Book 106, USAC.

Chicago, concluded on September 26, 1833, the Potawatomi had surrendered their land holdings in Illinois. The treaty, however, gave them possession of the country north of that state for another three years. Settlers and speculators, however, had moved into the Indian country even before the Senate ratified the treaty. They simply anticipated ratification and pushed the Potawatomi off the Indians' Illinois lands. North of the state line, Agent Owen reported that "emigrants are constantly exploring the country and some are now actually making locations and improvements." The Indians reacted with predictable anger and appealed to their agent. Owen visited the squatters and reminded them of the Indians' rights, but to no avail. "They seem to pay but little regard either to the common principles of justice or to the authority of the Government itself," he complained. He relayed the Indians' protests and a request for governmental action in their behalf to the Commissioner of Indian Affairs.[32] In reply, Commissioner Herring sent Owen a copy of a Senate resolution asking for yet another change in the Indian boundary. The Potawatomi gave their tentative approval to this, but later refused to make further cessions without appropriate changes in the payments they were to receive.[33]

Besides Indian affairs, Henry Atkinson continued to administer Jefferson Barracks. He planned the training of the troops at the post. He held reviews and inspections, corresponded with superiors, subordinates, and Indian Office personnel, and entertained travelers who stopped to visit the post. He remained busy because of his continuing interest in the detailed operations of the post. For example, General Order 100, dated November 5, 1832, ended the whisky ration in the army. It stopped not only the issue of "ardent spirits" but also their introduction or sale in "any fort, camp, or garrison of the United States . . ." No sutler could legally stock or sell liquor to the troops.[34] In spite of this order, laundry women and wives of enlisted men often brought liquor onto the post. If

32 Owen to Herring, Apr. 29, 1834, Indian Office Files, Box 8, No. 23, SHSW.

33 Owen to Cass, Aug. 22, 1834, Indian Office Files, Box 8, No. 34, SHSW.

34 Quoted in *St. Louis Beacon*, Nov. 29, 1834.

they were apprehended, Atkinson ordered them expelled from the post for a limited time.[35] Civilians near the army posts also made enforcement of this order difficult. They sold liquor to the soldiers and bought their clothing, arms, and military equipment. Liquor peddlers, controlled only slightly or not at all by state law, merely needed a license to "keep a dram shop." Buying military equipment and government property was against federal law. Trying civilians for this offense involved going before a grand jury at Jefferson City. This took so much time that Atkinson could rarely allow charges to be pressed.

Frequently, the conduct of the soldiers brought complaints from the nearby civilians. For example, whenever the supply of fuel ran low at the camp, the soldiers cut timber on the Carondolet town commons. In January, 1833, Atkinson received a notice from the village board of trustees complaining that "soldiers from the Garrison had cut and hauled away large quantities of timber from off our commons." Board Secretary Eugene Leitenschorfer asked Atkinson to "prohibit it in future."[36] On other occasions drunken soldiers shot and mutilated livestock, much to the anger of the townspeople. Atkinson tried to prevent such incidents, but had little success.

Between 1832 and 1835, besides spending much time in the administrative tasks of Jefferson Barracks, Atkinson spent considerable time trying to prevent Indian wars. The Treaty of Prairie du Chien of 1830 had made the army an arbiter of some quarrels between the tribes of the upper Mississippi. This, however, was no permanent solution. Although many of his contemporaries favored trying the Indians in American courts for attacking other Indians, Atkinson thought doing so was a "mere farce." He proposed that the tribesmen should be allowed to settle their own disputes.

[35] Order 5, Dec. 3, 1832, Jefferson Barracks Orders, Vol. 161, USAC.

[36] Leitenschorfer to Atkinson, Jan. 14, 1833, Dept. of the West, Letters Received, USAC.

XII. Wars and Rumors of Wars—1836–37

In late December, 1835, the Seminole War began in Florida. The fighting was caused by the insistence of the federal government that the Seminole Indians remove from Florida to the West. After the war began, the War Department sent most of the troops from Jefferson Barracks and other western posts to Florida or the Gulf Coast. Henry Atkinson and his subordinates who remained in the West had a weakened force to deal with repeated Indian depredations. Atkinson also had some disagreements with the Missouri Militia leaders and the governors because they claimed that he was too hesitant when dealing with the Indians. In addition, he had difficulties with his superiors and associates within the army.

By 1835 the proponents of the Indian removal policy had worked for several years to remove the Seminole Indians from the Southeast. Under the terms of the Treaty of Paynes Landing, concluded in 1832 and ratified two years later, a delegation of five Seminole chiefs had agreed to lead the tribe from Florida to Arkansas Territory.[1] Perhaps the chiefs signed the treaty under duress, or, possibly, the rest of the tribesmen ignored their decision. At any rate, most of the Seminoles refused to leave, and the one chief who openly advocated removal was killed by members of the

[1] Kappler, *Indian Affairs*, II, 249–51.

tribe. In December, 1835, recalcitrant bands of the Seminoles, reinforced by a few Creeks and several hundred Negroes, killed Agent Wiley Thompson and ambushed and killed Major Francis L. Dade and 108 regular soldiers of his command. This began the long and expensive Seminole War.[2] General Gaines, then on an inspection tour in the South, hurried east to Florida, and General Scott was ordered to proceed to the same area. Because of the seriousness of this Indian outbreak, troops were brought in from all parts of the country. On January 25, 1836, the Adjutant General issued orders for the Sixth Infantry to leave Jefferson Barracks for Fort Jesup, Louisiana, "as soon as the season and navigation will permit." Henry Atkinson, however, was to remain at Jefferson Barracks and to remain in charge of the defense of the Northwest.[3] Atkinson, a proud and sensitive man, would surely have objected to the loss of his regiment if he had thought the order was in any way a reflection on his ability or the result of his inept campaign against Black Hawk four years earlier. It is more likely that General Macomb ordered him to remain at Jefferson Barracks so that there would be one general officer who was familiar with the Indians in the West. Macomb may have tried to do Atkinson a personal favor by not sending him to Florida with his regiment, because he knew that Atkinson had been sick from a series of minor ailments during most of the previous year.

By late February the boats were ready to carry the regiment south, and on March 1, Atkinson surrendered command of the regiment that he had commanded since its creation in 1815.[4] Except during the Black Hawk War there had seldom been less than two hundred men at Jefferson Barracks. Now the post was practically deserted. Atkinson was left in command of only three officers and thirty-five enlisted men.[5] For a time the loss of his regiment

[2] John T. Sprague, *The Origin, Process, and Conclusion of the Florida War*, 86–91.

[3] General Order 9, Jan. 25, 1836, quoted in the *Army and Navy Chronicle*, Jan. 28, 1836, p. 64.

[4] Atkinson to Jones, Mar. 1, 1836, Letters Received, AGO.

[5] Post Returns, Jefferson Barracks, 1826–36, AGO.

seems not to have bothered him. By May, however, he petitioned that the Sixth Regiment be returned to the post "as soon as its services are no longer required in the South."[6] He assumed that Jefferson Barracks, the largest, best equipped, and most centrally located post in the West, was essential to frontier defense and that some troops should be stationed there. His plea was ignored, and he remained a general without soldiers.

On March 14, 1836, Colonel George M. Brooke, commander of Fort Howard at Green Bay, reported to the War Department that the Seminoles had sent wampum belts to the northern and western Indians. According to his information, the Menominees and "the Winnebagoes, had recd the same wampum and further that they were purchasing, large stores of powder & lead, in the neighborhood of Galena."[7] The War Department promptly directed Atkinson to "take every precautionary measure" to maintain peace along the frontier. It also authorized him to regroup the dragoons from Forts Leavenworth and Des Moines and to employ the troops then stationed at Forts Snelling, Crawford, Winnebago, Howard, Dearborn, Mackinac, Brady, and Gratiot in "preventing or repelling Indian hostilities."[8]

Atkinson received these orders on April 23 while at Louisville on personal business. He assumed that the rumors were exaggerated and replied, "Notwithstanding the rumors of hostility on the part of the Winnebagoes, I doubt the probability of such an occurrence." He promised to make a quick trip of inspection to the upper Mississippi after his return to Jefferson Barracks to see if there was any danger.[9] When he returned to Jefferson Barracks, however, he changed his mind and ordered several companies of dragoons from Fort Leavenworth to join the dragoons stationed at Des Moines. There, under the command of Colonel Stephen W. Kearny, they regrouped and made a trip through the Indian country east of the

[6] Atkinson to Jones, May 19, 1836, Letters Received, AGO.

[7] Brooke to Jones, Mar. 14, 1836, Letters Received, AGO.

[8] Jones to Atkinson, Apr. 14, 1836, Letters Sent, Vol. 12, AGO.

[9] Atkinson to Jones, Apr. 23, 1836, Letters Received, AGO.

Mississippi. Atkinson hoped their presence would be enough to keep the Winnebagos peaceful.[10]

In the spring of 1836, General Gaines was ordered to go to the border of Texas and maintain the neutrality of the settlers and Indians during the Texas revolution. He ordered the commanders of Forts Towson and Gibson to prevent Texans and Mexicans from crossing the American border. Then he asked the governors of Tennessee, Alabama, and Mississippi for brigades of volunteers. On April 12 he also ordered the dragoons from Fort Leavenworth to the Texas border.[11] These men had been under Atkinson's command and composed nearly half of the defensive force for the northwestern frontier. So in May, when Atkinson received the order from Gaines to send the dragoons south, he wrote to the War Department for advice. He pointed out that the situation in Texas had changed since the order of April 12 and that the troops were no longer necessary. Making them go to Texas would subject them "to a long and fatiguing march with no other result than retracing their steps." On the other hand, if they remained at Fort Leavenworth, they could be moved to the northwest with little difficulty.[12] To Gaines he wrote, "I must beg you to see in this decision of mine nothing that would seem like thwarting your order or an intention to withhold the force in question from the duty assigned it."[13] Then he ordered Captain Matthew Duncan to keep the dragoons at Fort Leavenworth until he received a reply from army headquarters.

This issue remained unsettled, and Atkinson's attention shifted to the Texan war for independence. Indians in the Southwest were threatening nearby whites. When Atkinson learned that Sam Houston had defeated Santa Anna, he relayed the news to Captain Duncan at Fort Leavenworth. Santa Anna's "defeat and capture will open the eyes of the Indians," he assured Duncan, "and disipate the false delusion with which they have been impressed." He

10 Atkinson to Jones, May 5, 1836, Letters Received, AGO.

11 Atkinson to Jones, May 23, 1836, Letters Received, AGO; Silver, *Edmund Pendleton Gaines*, 195.

12 Atkinson to Jones, May 23, 1836, Letters Received, AGO.

13 Atkinson to Gaines, May 23, 1836, Right Wing Letter Book 106, USAC.

suggested that rumors of a Seminole defeat should also be spread among the Indians. Whether these were true or not made little difference because news of twin victories by the Americans, he was sure, would impress the Indians.[14] Atkinson also assured the War Department that "The defeat of the Mexicans will make a favorable impression upon the frontier." In spite of this, he feared that if the Creeks in Alabama went to war the peace on the western frontier would end. The northern and western tribes seemed restless, and he wrote, "They appear to be acquainted with all the occurrences in the south as soon as we are and exult at the success of their red brethren."[15]

Continuing unrest among the frontier tribes worried the War Department officials, and on June 6 the governor of Missouri was asked to call for one thousand volunteers, half to be mounted, to serve for one year during the next two. With this force on call, Atkinson was authorized to ask the governor for whatever troops he thought necessary.[16] The Indian agents and frontier commanders submitted numerous and often conflicting reports to Atkinson. He studied these and occasionally discussed them with William Clark before taking any action. His method of handling Indian difficulties usually kept the War Department satisfied and the Indians reasonably quiet. The Indians demonstrated their trust in his judgment on numberless occasions. For example, in June, 1836, one band of the Missouri Sacs called on their agent for a council. After the meeting they asked that one copy of the proceedings be forwarded to the President and another to "the White Beaver, who has been long acquainted with us."[17]

In mid-June, 1836, Atkinson wrote Colonel Jones, "There would seem to be nothing to be apprehended from the Indians" in Missouri. On June 19, however, a party of five white men exchanged

[14] Atkinson to Duncan, May 26, 1836, Right Wing Letter Book 106, USAC.

[15] Atkinson to Jones, May 29, 1836, Letters Received, AGO; Atkinson to Jones, June 6, 1836, *ibid.*

[16] Macomb to Atkinson, June 6, 1836, Letters Sent, Vol. 12, AGO.

[17] Statement of Council, June 12, 1836, Indian Office Files, Box 11, No. 83, SHSW.

shots with a band of Potawatomi then migrating across western Missouri. The whites were the notorious "Heatherly Gang" of whisky vendors and reputed horse thieves. After an unsuccessful attempt to sell whisky to the Potawatomi, the gang stole eight of their horses. The braves discovered the theft the next morning, and after a brief search they found the stolen horses with the gang. When they demanded that the horses be returned, the Heatherlys opened fire. In the skirmish that followed, the Indians killed two of the whites, drove the rest away, and recovered their horses.[18]

When William Clark told him of this incident, Atkinson ordered Colonel Kearny to investigate. "I presume that the occurrence grew out of a drunken brawl, at some whiskey establishment on the frontier," Atkinson wrote. He was certain the incident would not disrupt peace along the frontier.[19] This time he was wrong. Without asking for assistance or advice, Missouri Governor Daniel Dunklin called out two hundred mounted volunteers to remove all Indians from the state. Atkinson appears to have been angry and bewildered by Dunklin's actions. He had assured the Governor that he would pay close attention to the safety of the frontier settlements but had received no reply. "If the authorities of the state raise troops at [their own] discretion and take the management of Indian difficulties into their own hands," he complained to Macomb, "I cannot be accountable for the results, as my authority is not paramount to the will of the Governor."[20] The Potawatomi who had been involved in the shootings surrendered to Colonel Kearny at Fort Leavenworth, and Atkinson suggested that the Governor arrest the Heatherlys, but the civil authorities took no action.[21] Thus ended the so-called Heatherly War which strained relations

18 Duncan to Kearny, July 21, 1836, enclosed in Atkinson to Jones, August 3, 1836, Letters Received, AGO.

19 Atkinson to Kearny, July 7, 1836, quoted in Willis B. Hughes, "The Heatherly Incident of 1836," *Bulletin of the Missouri Historical Society*, Vol. XIII (Jan., 1957), 168.

20 Atkinson to Jones, July 25, 1836, Letters Received, AGO.

21 *Ibid.* For a more complete discussion of this incident see Hughes, "The Heatherly Incident of 1836," *Bulletin of the Missouri Historical Society*, Vol. XIII (Jan., 1957), 151–80.

FORT CRAWFORD, AT PRAIRIE DU CHIEN

State Historical Society of Wisconsin

After he received Macomb's letter, Atkinson wrote to Gaines and explained his acts since he had received the requisition for the dragoons. He told Gaines that four companies of dragoons were already on detached service and could not be recalled immediately. "Under the force of these instructions I could not divert the services thus required of the Dragoons without first referring the subject to the Dept. of War," he wrote and included a copy of Macomb's letter.[26]

In July, 1836, Congress appropriated $100,000 to build a military road from Fort Snelling in the north to the Red River in the south. This road was to connect existing western military posts and several that were yet to be built. On it troops could be moved easily from one installation to another and could patrol the eastern edge of the permanent Indian frontier. If the Indian tribes consented, the road would pass through Indian territory west of Missouri and Arkansas. If they refused to allow this, it would run within those states. The road was to be built according to the usual military-road specifications; that is, trees were to be cut, marshy places filled with logs and brush, and "cheap bridges" built over small streams that could not be easily forded. Frontier army units were expected to do the work of building roads, whenever it would not interfere with their other duties.[27]

Shortly after Congress authorized the building of the road, Atkinson received orders to appoint commissioners to superintend the survey and construction. He offered the job to Colonel Zachary Taylor, commander of Fort Crawford, but Taylor declined. Major William McNeil, of the Topographical Engineers, was also unable to serve, and Atkinson had to appoint two other officers. This time he chose Colonel Stephen W. Kearny and Captain Nathan Boon, both of the First Dragoons. Then, to avoid further delay, he empowered Kearny to fill any other vacancies that might arise.[28]

Atkinson believed that his responsibilities for the road had

[26] Atkinson to Gaines, Oct. 8, 1836, Right Wing Letter Book 106, USAC.

[27] *U.S. Statutes at Large*, V, 67.

[28] Atkinson Order, Sept. 28, 1836, in 25 Cong., 1 sess., *House Exec. Doc. No. 278*, 12–13.

ended when Kearny accepted the appointment. Kearny, however, reported endless obstacles to the project. First, he needed copies of the correspondence from the Secretary of War that promised the co-operation of the Indian agents along the route. He complained that Major McNeil, the engineer, had been excused from the project, and "there is no one appointed in his place from his department, or who is capable of making the proper surveys as required." Kearny also reported that none of his officers would accept the unwanted and unpaid chore because of the large sums of money that had to be handled. Nobody wanted to assume responsibility for the $100,000. Kearny explained that his officers were afraid that their accounts might not prove acceptable to the treasury department clerks, and that they might have "out of [their] scanty pay, to make it good . . ." Therefore, he concluded, "I cannot expect to fill the appointment."[29] After he received Kearny's letter in late October, Atkinson decided it was too late in the season to get much done because winter made travel on the plains nearly impossible. Therefore, plans for the road were postponed.[30]

Meanwhile, the Florida campaign of Generals Gaines and Scott against the Seminoles earlier in 1836 had failed. As a result, on October 3, 1836, Secretary of War Lewis Cass issued General Order 65 that created a court of inquiry including Major General Alexander Macomb, commanding general of the army, and Brevet Brigadier Generals Henry Atkinson and Hugh Brady. The court was empowered to "inquire and examine into the causes of the failure of the campaigns in Florida against the Seminole Indians, under the command of Major General Gaines and of Major General Scott, in 1836 . . ."[31] On November 4, Henry Atkinson left Jefferson Barracks for Frederick, Maryland. He arrived there on November 21.[32] Frederick, located approximately forty miles

[29] Kearny to Atkinson, Oct. 16, 1836, in 25 Cong., 1 sess., *House Exec. Doc. No. 278*, 13–14.

[30] Atkinson Order, Sept. 28, 1836, in 25 Cong., 1 sess., *House Exec. Doc. No. 278*, 12–13.

[31] *Army and Navy Chronicle*, Oct. 6, 1836, p. 223; ASP:MA, VII, 129.

[32] Atkinson Orders, Nov. 4, 1836, Jefferson Barracks Orders, Vol. 161, USAC.

northwest of Washington, was often used as the site for military courts. It lay far enough from the capital to keep most politicians away, and yet close enough so that newspaper correspondents from Washington could observe.

By early February the court had concluded at least a part of the hearing and submitted their findings in General Scott's case. They decided that he was guilty of "no delay, which it was practicable to have avoided . . ." President Jackson thought otherwise, however, and directed the court to continue the investigation.[33] The court then reopened hearings on both Scott and Gaines. In their final decision the court ruled that General Scott's failure against the Creeks was to be explained by a lack of time, bad climate, the lack of transportation for supplies and ammunition, and Scott's lack of knowledge of the terrain. They ruled that General Gaines had failed because of a lack of subsistence. Both generals, the court decided, could have done little to achieve success. By the end of March, the court adjourned.[34]

After the hearings ended, Atkinson and his family went on to Washington. There he discussed the delay in building the military road with the new secretary of war, Joel R. Poinsett, and General Macomb. Atkinson told his superiors that there were too few troops at the western posts to undertake such a task. "I beg leave to state that, in performing the labor and duty required," he wrote, "the troops cannot, with propriety, do more than afford the necessary escorts, and that the labor should be done by hired assistants . . ." He suggested that the Topographical Bureau furnish trained engineers, funds, and instruments and that approximately $10,000 would be needed to start the project.[35] His suggestions were not adopted at this time.

In July, 1837, Atkinson reopened the subject of the commission

33 Statement of Andrew Jackson, Feb. 14, 1837, in *Army and Navy Chronicle*, Feb. 16, 1837, p. 110.

34 Statement of Joel R. Poinsett, Mar. 21, 1837, in *Army and Navy Chronicle*, April 6, 1837, pp. 209–12.

35 Atkinson to Macomb, Apr. 10, 1837, in 25 Cong., 2 sess., *House Exec. Doc. No. 278*, 16–17.

for work on the "great military road." Colonel Kearny had written him that nothing could be done until some member of the Topographical Engineers reported to him and that Major John L. Smith, the other commissioner, was still at St. Louis. Because of the lack of progress, Atkinson suggested that the commission which was to survey the road be dissolved and that "some officer of rank be instructed to cause the duty to be performed by detail from one or more posts on the Frontier."[36] He had changed his mind about the inadvisibility of using the troops at frontier garrisons to perform the work.

The Secretary of War accepted the suggestion. In July, 1837, he appointed Atkinson to head the road commission and to appoint the other two members.[37] Two engineers were on their way to Jefferson Barracks where they would receive his orders and make the necessary surveys. When Atkinson received these orders, he replied, "It gives me great uneasiness to be compelled to say that I am not able to comply with the Secretary's desire to act as an active member of the Commission." His health was good, he claimed, but he could not spend several months in the saddle, experiencing the "fatigue and exposure of personally attending to the running and marking of a road of several hundred miles through a wilderness country." If, however, the Secretary meant that he was to organize the commission and instruct the members, he was able and willing to do this.[38]

Before he received a clarification of these orders, Atkinson wrote to Colonel Kearny that engineers were on their way to Fort Leavenworth and that, as soon as they arrived, Kearny was to take one of them and an escort on the southern route from his post to the Arkansas River. After he returned, Captain Boon was to take another detachment and an engineer and travel from the junction

[36] Atkinson to———, July 8, 1837, extract in 25 Cong., 2 sess., *House Exec. Doc. No. 278*, 2.

[37] Macomb to Atkinson, July 24, 1837, in 25 Cong., 2 sess., *House Exec. Doc. No. 278*, 2.

[38] Atkinson to Macomb, Aug. 7, 1837, in 25 Cong., 2 sess., *House Exec. Doc. No. 278*, 3.

of the Missouri boundary and the Missouri River north to Fort Snelling. On his return trip to Fort Leavenworth, Boon was to mark the route with the usual blazes on trees or by erecting small earth mounds.[39] Atkinson received a reply from Poinsett in September. The Secretary told him that his appointment to head the commission had been only so that he could issue the necessary orders; he did not have to accompany the surveyors.[40] Atkinson accepted the appointment.

On May 19, 1837, General Macomb announced a reorganization of the army. The Eastern and Western Departments, created in 1821, were to be replaced by Eastern and Western Divisions, that were, in turn, to be subdivided into seven military departments. The Western Division now included all land west of the Mississippi River from its mouth north to Cassville, Wisconsin, and then west of a line from that point north to Canada. It contained only two military departments. The First included the area north of the thirty-seventh parallel, and the Second included the area south of that line.[41] Henry Atkinson was ordered to move south to Fort Jesup located between the Sabine and Red rivers in western Louisiana and to command the Second Military Department.[42] Before Atkinson received this order, however, General Macomb had changed his mind and ordered him to remain at Jefferson Barracks and command the First Department of the Army. This included much of the same area that had been in the Right Wing and, before that, in the Ninth Military Department.

In the meantime, Colonel Kearny wrote Atkinson that the Sioux, Sacs, Potawatomi, Delawares, Shawnees, Otoes, Omahas, Kickapoos, and Iowas had contributed to a string of war wampum then being carried to other tribes by a Sac messenger. "I say again

39 Atkinson to Kearny, Aug. 12, 1837, First Military Dept. Letter Book 106, USAC.

40 Poinsett to Atkinson, Aug. 19, 1837, in 25 Cong., 2 sess., *House Exec. Doc. No. 278*, 4.

41 General Order 32, May 19, 1837, quoted in *Army and Navy Chronicle*, May 25, 1837, p. 334.

42 General Order 31, May 18, 1837, quoted in *Army and Navy Chronicle*, May 18, 1837, p. 319.

it is difficult for me to credit their reports," Kearny wrote, "but I cannot altogether disregard them." Kearny was afraid that the Missouri governor would call out the militia to try to move the Potawatomi and that the Indians would "resist and whip the militia . . ."[43] Atkinson agreed with his subordinate and wrote to Lillburn W. Boggs, new governor of Missouri. He promised Boggs that he would keep "a strict scrutiny upon the actions of the several Tribes . . .," warned the Governor to keep the militia and citizens of the upper counties away from the Potawatomi, and explained that the "General Government" would take what steps were necessary for peace.[44] Then he sent Kearny's report to the War Department and waited for advice.

In June, 1837, Macomb ordered Atkinson to move the Potawatomi north of Missouri. He enclosed a letter from the Secretary of War that explained where the tribe was to move. "Your knowledge of the subject and your acquaintance with the country generally as well as with the Indians inhabiting it," Macomb wrote him, "justifies the belief that you will be enabled to execute the instructions of the Secretary of War in a manner the most satisfactory to the Indians, & to the State of Missouri."[45]

He was allowed to spend up to $10,000 for the expenses of removing and feeding the Indians.[46] The Potawatomi were not on lands allotted to them, but had been left on unoccupied land after being moved west in 1836. Potawatomi agent Edwin James, then in northwestern Missouri, reported that nearly "1600 Pottawattomies and associated Indians" were in his area. These Indians, he wrote, were willing to remove to an area in western Iowa along the eastern bank of the Missouri River between the northern border of Missouri and Boyer River, nine miles south of Council Bluffs.[47]

[43] Kearny to Atkinson, May 19, 1837, Indian Office Files, Box 14, No. 426, SHSW.

[44] Atkinson to Boggs, May 26, 1837, Indian Office Files, Box 14, No. 425, SHSW.

[45] Macomb to Atkinson, June 20, 1837, Indian Office Files, Box 13, No. 287, SHSW.

[46] Harris to E. A. Hitchcock, June 27, 1837, Dept. of the West, Letters Received, USAC.

[47] James to Clark, June 27, 1837, Indian Office Files, Box 13, No. 14, SHSW.

On July 7, Atkinson wrote General Macomb that the Potawatomi, led by two half-blood chiefs, claimed that the government owed them subsistence (food) for one year during and after their removal. They had told their agent that they were willing to emigrate if they received this. "If I should find that they have any good ground to support their representations," Atkinson wrote, "I shall grant it to them." Meanwhile, at Fort Leavenworth, General Gaines had learned of the proximity of whites and Indians in the northwestern corner of Missouri and had decided that he should move the Indians. He hired two steamboats, the *Howard* and the *Kansas*, for this purpose. When Atkinson arrived on July 15, Gaines left him in charge of the removal and he continued his tour of inspection.[48]

Gaines had already met the Indians in council. They had agreed to migrate if the government furnished food and transportation for those of the tribe who were unable to travel overland. This was what Atkinson arranged. On July 22 he met with the tribe, and for the next day and a half he supervised the issuing of rations to the Indians. After the "maimed and blind and such women and children as were not able to move by land" boarded the steamboats that Gaines had hired, Atkinson accompanied them to Boyer River, which emptied into the Missouri a few miles south of the Platte, where they joined their agent, Edwin James. Before returning to Jefferson Barracks, Atkinson ordered James to furnish the Indians with provisions for one year and to begin fulfilling the stipulations of the Treaty of Chicago of 1833. Among the treaty provisions not then being met were those which called for the payment to the tribe of $150,000 for the building of farms, mills, homes for the Indians, agricultural implements, blacksmith shops, and the services of blacksmiths, farmers, teachers, and doctors for the tribe. Another $70,000 was to have been invested in some safe stock and used for a program of education and training in the domestic arts for the women and children.[49] "You are therefore charged with seeing that

[48] Gaines to Harris, July 26, 1837, Indian Office Files, Box 13, No. 39, SHSW.

[49] Kappler, *Indian Affairs*, II, 296–303.

those stipulations are fully complied with," Atkinson directed the agent, "for which purpose you will call on the Superintendent at St. Louis for funds and advice."[50]

His directions to James that he meet the treaty stipulations brought a curt reply from the disbursing agent at St. Louis that there were no funds or instructions for supplying the Potawatomi with the material that Atkinson demanded.[51] The disburser sent Atkinson's directions to Carey Harris, commissioner of Indian affairs in Washington. When Atkinson learned the government had made no provision for meeting its treaty obligations to these Indians, his temper rose. "Now Sir it is impossible for an officer charged with the defence of the frontier to preserve peace," he expostulated to Macomb, "if the agents of the Government do not comply with the terms of the treaties made with the Indians on our border." He enumerated the treaty stipulations and demanded to know why "not one has been complied with?" He had promised the Indians that he would see that they received what had been promised. "I have therefore to request," he wrote, "that you will present the subject to the Honorable Secretary of War that all needful instructions may be given to the officers charged with the direction of that Department."[52]

Carey Harris, commissioner of Indian affairs had asked him to persuade the Potawatomi to remove to the Osage River. Atkinson replied that even if the letter had arrived early enough for him to act on it, the Indians would not consider another move. "The subject has been agitated and they expressed a determination to occupy their lands on the upper Missouri . . ." The tribal leaders realized that their land was more fertile and that the hunting was better there than on the proposed lands along the Osage. If they went to the Osage lands, they would receive nothing for those along the Missouri. On the other hand, if they moved to the Missouri

50 Atkinson to James, July 28, 1837, Indian Office Files, Box 13, No. 23, SHSW.

51 George Maguire to Atkinson, Aug. 7, 1837, Dept. of the West, Letters Received, USAC.

52 Atkinson to Macomb, Aug. 9, 1837, First Military Dept. Letter Book 106, USAC.

River lands, they would eventually be persuaded to move to the Osage, but only after another treaty and further payments from the government.[53]

Colonel Kearny agreed that it was not possible to move the Potawatomi at that time. After he read Harris's letter to Atkinson, he wrote, "I think the credulity of that Man, & his mismanagement of the Indian Dept. should be represented to the Secy of War." He suggested that if the Secretary of War would appoint Atkinson as a commissioner to treat with the Potawatomi, he "could effect it [the move] without much trouble." The Indians, he said, were not as ignorant as Harris seemed to imagine, and to get them to move to the Osage River area would surely cost the government dearly. Chief Billy Caldwell, he pointed out, "is no fool, & understands his interests as well as we do."[54]

On August 26, Harris wrote to Atkinson and thanked him "for the services [he] rendered to the Indian Department, and for the solicitude [he] manifested for the welfare of the red men." After he praised Atkinson's efforts in the Potawatomi removal, however, the Commissioner chided him for his interference in the affairs of the Indian Department. His instructions to Subagent James caused "derangement" and "inconvenience" in the affairs of the department. Although he expressed "great personal respect" for Atkinson, Harris added that instructions to agents or subagents from officials not of the Indian Department caused utter confusion.[55]

When this letter reached Atkinson, he replied, "It would seem from the tenor of your letter that you are under the impression that I have interfered with the details of your duties as general Superintendent of Indian Affairs. In this you are in error." He explained that he had obeyed orders from the Secretary of War to remove the Potawatomi according to the provisions of their treaty. After moving the tribesmen, he had noticed several stipulations of the treaty that the government was obliged to meet. "It became my

[53] Atkinson to Harris, Aug. 9, 1837, First Military Dept. Letter Book 106, USAC.

[54] Kearny to Atkinson, Aug. 19, 1837, Dept. of the West, Letters Received, USAC.

[55] Harris to Atkinson, Aug. 26, 1837, Letters Sent, Vol. 22, OIA.

duty to see the measures were commenced toward fulfilling these . . .," he wrote. In so doing, he had given instructions to the subagent and had reported these instructions to the Secretary of War. He concluded his explanation by writing, "My instructions were full and my authority ample for all I did, in the mere words, remove the Indians agreeably to Treaty." Thus the incident ended. Harris was nettled because he thought Atkinson had interfered, and the General was satisfied that his acts were entirely within his instructions.[56]

By November, 1837, Atkinson heard new rumors of Indian depredations. Colonel Kearny reported that a party of Osage Indians had entered Missouri to hunt and that the militia leaders in the western counties had tried to raise five hundred men to drive them from the state. Kearny had sent a force of ninety-five men to keep the militia and Indians apart and to persuade the militia that the army could keep the Indians under control.[57] By the time Atkinson heard of the incident, Governor Boggs had, too. He demanded that Atkinson furnish a strong military force that could protect the frontier settlements "from the lawless outrages of these savages."[58] In reply Atkinson explained Kearny's actions and assured the Governor that the Indians were still at peace and that he could rely upon Atkinson and his command to "give every facility towards the protection of the frontier inhabitants and their property."[59]

Atkinson's touchiness in his dealings with Commissioner Harris of the Indian Office was merely one incident in a long series of minor personal quarrels in which he became involved. For example, in the fall of 1837 he was criticized by General Gaines because he had tried to retain certain officers at the post after they had been

[56] Atkinson to Harris, Sept. 9, 1837, First Military Dept. Letter Book 106, USAC.

[57] Kearny to Atkinson, Nov. 1, 1837, enclosed in Atkinson to Macomb, Nov. 21, 1837, Letters Received, AGO.

[58] Boggs to Atkinson, Nov. 19, 1837, enclosed in Atkinson to Macomb, Nov. 29, 1837, Letters Received, AGO.

[59] Atkinson to Boggs, Nov. 28, 1837, enclosed in Atkinson to Macomb, Nov. 29, 1837, Letters Received, AGO.

ordered elsewhere. Captain Samuel McRee, an old acquaintance, was ordered to Florida, but Atkinson retained him at the Barracks. When General Gaines learned of this, he ordered Atkinson to send the officer on as ordered and not to interfere with the movements of his subordinates. Atkinson considered the reprimand from Gaines unnecessarily harsh and demanded a court of inquiry to clear his name. General Macomb, however, dismissed this demand. "It would have been, in my opinion, more consistant, with military discipline and duty," he wrote, "if you had not noticed that supposed want of courtesy and confined yourself to an explanation of the causes which led to the detention of the Captain."[60]

By late 1837, Atkinson realized that the Sixth Infantry would probably not be returned to Jefferson Barracks until the Seminole War ended. He saw that that post, once the pride of the western army, was now a neglected and practically deserted installation. His duties had become those of relaying orders and answering letters, rather than directing the defense of the frontier in any real sense. Population had spread into Wisconsin, Iowa, and Arkansas, pushing the Indians farther west ahead of it. The army had kept pace with this move, and the defense of the frontier depended upon younger officers who were stationed nearer to the Indians. Henry Atkinson, often sickly, became obstinate and hard to work with because he sensed his increasing isolation from the frontier and from the direction of army activities in the West.

[60] Macomb to Atkinson, Dec. 5, 1837, Letters Sent, Vol. 3, HQA.

XIII. Twilight Years—1838-42

During the last five years of Henry Atkinson's life the pace of military activity at Jefferson Barracks remained slow. Usually less than a single company of men was stationed there to maintain the post. Atkinson asked repeatedly for the return of the Sixth Infantry but without success. Atkinson himself slowed down, because he suffered from frequent minor sicknesses such as colds, fevers, and stomach disorders. Nevertheless, he continued to operate the post as a center for gathering and equipping recruits and as a staging point from which to discharge Missouri Militia units returning from Florida.

Early in February, 1838, sick and wounded men from the Missouri volunteer units that had been recruited the year before began returning from Florida to Jefferson Barracks. There they were examined, treated, given provisions, and furloughed.[1] In addition, small detachments of recruits arrived periodically. After they received uniforms and equipment, they were moved to other posts. Atkinson asked for permission to assign one subaltern or junior officer to take charge of the recruits and to act as quartermaster and commissary officer for the post. This request brought no response, and he repeated his plea several times throughout the spring and summer.

Minor Indian troubles took some of his time. For example, in

[1] Atkinson to Jones, Feb. 16, 1838, Letters Received, AGO.

February, 1838, some Delawares living near Fort Leavenworth asked Colonel Kearny for permission to tap sugar maple trees on the unsurveyed government land near that post. Kearny consented. When the Indians crossed the state boundary into Missouri, however, Clay County militia leaders called out a force of one hundred volunteers to repel this "Indian invasion." The settlers claimed that the Delawares had killed some of their hogs. When Kearny learned that the militia intended to force the Indians to leave, he complained to Atkinson. He reported that the Indian party included only three men and that the remainder were squaws and children. Besides, the Indians had camped on the "Public Reserve" over a mile from any of the "squatters," so it was unlikely that they had killed the hogs. He further pointed out that "the families belonged to those Delawares who went to Florida at the request of the Secretary of War, to assist in fighting our Battles . . ."[2] Kearny and Atkinson took no action against the Indians.

In May, 1838, Secretary of War Joel Poinsett told Atkinson of plans to abandon Fort Leavenworth and move the troops from that post north to Council Bluffs, the site of Fort Atkinson that had been abandoned in 1827. "I dissent entirely," to any such plan, Atkinson replied, because the troops would be thrown out of position to aid the frontier inhabitants if a war occurred in the south. The proposed move, he claimed, would make it difficult for the commanders on the Arkansas and Red rivers to co-operate with those on the Missouri River. Furthermore, it would expose the defensive line from Leavenworth to the Arkansas, as well as from Leavenworth to the Mississippi. Within that area "reside the most fierce, warlike and dissatisfied Tribes known to us," he wrote, "who could not be checked by a force from the advanced post before the whole frontier would be laid waste."[3] No response to Atkinson's letter has been preserved, but the troops remained at Fort Leavenworth.

On June 12, President Martin Van Buren appointed Henry

[2] Kearny to Atkinson, Mar. 11, 1838, enclosed in Atkinson to Jones, Mar. 25, 1838, Letters Received, AGO.

[3] Atkinson to Poinsett, June 1, 1838, First Military Dept. Letter Book 106, USAC.

Atkinson as the first territorial governor of Iowa. This appointment, along with that of William B. Conway of Pennsylvania as territorial secretary, was confirmed by the Senate the next day.[4] The appointment was, perhaps, given in an effort to remove Atkinson from the army because his health had been poor for two or three years. On the other hand, his experience as an administrator, his familiarity with white-Indian negotiations, and his personal knowledge of the tribes then in Iowa certainly qualified him for the position. Atkinson declined this offer, but left no record of his reasons for doing so. Perhaps he anticipated more active duty in the West. The salary of this position was less than what he received as a brevet general. If he accepted the appointment, he would be unable to enjoy St. Louis society. Whatever his reasons, Atkinson seems to have rejected the position immediately.[5]

In the summer of 1838, Atkinson suggested to the Adjutant General that the hundreds of recruits who were temporarily stationed at Jefferson Barracks be retained there and that the Sixth Infantry be returned to that post. The newly trained troops could be used to strengthen the Sixth. His superiors, however, disapproved, and the post continued to be nearly deserted.[6]

More than eleven years had passed since army units had begun building quarters at Jefferson Barracks. The buildings had remained in good repair while several hundred men had lived at the post, but three years after the Sixth had moved out the Barracks showed signs of neglect. In December of 1838, Atkinson wrote, "The Quarters & Barracks at this post are in such delapitate state that it is indespensable they should be repaired before they are again occupied." Therefore, he ordered Colonel Joshua Brant, the disbursing officer at St. Louis, to hire a carpenter and a bricklayer to visit the Barracks, examine the buildings, and prepare an estimate of the repair costs.[7] A few weeks later he wrote to Quarter-

4 *Journal of the Executive Proceedings of the Senate* . . ., V, 131–32.

5 *Army and Navy Chronicle*, July 12, 1838, p. 25; *Niles Register*, July 14, 1838.

6 Jones to Atkinson, Aug. 8, 1838, Letters Sent, Vol. 14, AGO.

7 Atkinson to Brant, Dec. 18, 1838, First Military Dept. Letter Book 106, USAC.

master General Henry Stanton describing the condition of his own quarters. The hewn-log house which served as the commander's residence had been built in 1827 and needed repair. Accordingly he had ordered that the four-room house be raised and placed on an eight-foot basement and foundation. He then learned that no funds were available and stopped the work. In January, 1839, he reminded the Quartermaster General that the house stood uncompleted. Not only that, but the building material had already been purchased and lay on the ground that winter. He asked for permission to complete the repairs and estimated that the total cost would be $1200.[8] Stanton gave him permission to repair his quarters and to make "those [repairs] recommended for the Barracks and quarters generally at the post—A measure which has been unavoidably delayed in consequence of the entire expenditure of the last annual appropriation."[9] Atkinson ordered the repairs to be made.

While this was being done, Atkinson organized a band for the Sixth Infantry. In mid-February, 1839, he ordered uniforms consisting of army-blue coats faced and trimmed with red cloth.[10] Then he renewed his petition that the Sixth Regiment be returned to Jefferson Barracks. He pleaded that the Sixth deserved to be rotated from Florida because it had been "in the field" for the past three years. "I am confident I could restore it to its former discipline & efficiency," he wrote.[11] This plea, like the earlier ones, received a negative reply.

In fact, Atkinson's recruiting activities caused some displeasure from fellow officers. Lieutenant Colonel William Davenport criticized him when he retained several musicians for his band and a hospital steward to care for the sick recruits and wounded militiamen at the post. Davenport claimed that these men were supposed to serve in Florida. Atkinson explained that the musicians had

8 Atkinson to Stanton, Jan. 6, 1839, First Military Dept. Letter Book 106, USAC.

9 Stanton to Atkinson, Jan. 19, 1839, Letters Sent, Vol. 27, QMG.

10 Atkinson to Whiting, Feb. 16, 1839, First Military Dept. Letter Book 106, USAC.

11 Atkinson to Poinsett, Feb. 23, 1839, Letters Received, AGO.

Jefferson Barracks
From J. C. Wild, *The Valley of the Mississippi* (St. Louis, 1841), pl. 11

Missouri Historical Society

General Henry Atkinson (1832)

Illinois Historical Society

enlisted "in accordance with . . . instructions to Capt. Andrews as to enlisting musicians for our Band," and that they had been placed on the roster with those men enlisted for service in Florida by mistake. He defended detaining a hospital steward because no one at the post could work with the sick and wounded. "One thing you may rely upon," he assured the Adjutant General. "I have never nor will I retain or dispose of soldiers or recruits otherwise than for the public interest notwithstanding the growlings of testy men."[12]

In December, 1839, Henry Atkinson decided that his subordinates should settle minor Indian difficulties rather than waiting for orders from him. He gave discretionary power in dealing with the Indians to Colonel Kearny, who commanded the dragoons at Fort Leavenworth, and to Brevet Brigadier General George M. Brooke, who commanded the Fifth Infantry at Fort Howard.[13] Colonel Kearny had worked with the Indians previously and was able to settle disputes and maintain peace among the tribes near Fort Leavenworth. General Brooke, on the other hand, knew little about the Indians and continued to send reports to Atkinson rather than dealing with the incidents himself. This delayed many necessary decisions rather than increasing the efficiency of the department.

On February 28, 1840, Secretary of War Joel R. Poinsett notified Atkinson that the Winnebago Indians in Wisconsin were to be moved west of the Mississippi and that he was "to take charge of that operation." For several years the Winnebagos had refused to move. When the War Department learned that the Winnebagos were more afraid of the Sac and Foxes than the frontier settlers and the army, it decided to station two companies of dragoons between the Winnebagos and the Sac and Foxes in Iowa. If the Winnebagos still refused to move, Secretary Poinsett ordered Atkinson to move them by force.[14]

On March 18, 1840, Atkinson ordered Colonel Kearny to send one company of dragoons from Fort Leavenworth to Fort Craw-

[12] Atkinson to Jones, Apr. 7, 1839, Letters Received, AGO.

[13] Atkinson to Gaines, Dec. 3, 1839, Letters Received, AGO.

[14] Poinsett to Atkinson, Feb. 28, 1840, Letters Sent, Military Affairs, SW.

ford. He also intended to order three companies of infantry to Prairie du Chien. Then, he wrote to Governor Dodge asking him to have Winnebago subagent, David Lowry, assemble the Indians by April 20, preferably at Prairie du Chien.[15] Dodge replied that the Winnebagos were scattered and that more time was necessary for their agent to gather them for negotiations. He assured Atkinson that the bands along the Mississippi and on the lower Wisconsin River would move. "The only difficulty I apprehend," Dodge continued, "will be in the removal of the Bands residing near the Portage . . ." Dodge advised Atkinson that the best way to get the Portage bands to migrate was to have them gather at Fort Winnebago, where they could be given rations and loaded on boats for removal to Prairie du Chien. Once there, they could be escorted into Iowa by the mounted troops.[16]

In mid-April, 1840, Atkinson ordered Major John Plympton, then commanding Fort Snelling, to send three companies south to Fort Crawford. He also readied the small detachment at Jefferson Barracks, including the Sixth Infantry Band, for the coming campaign.[17] Then on April 14 he wrote his will. "Being about to visit the Indian country and knowing the uncertainty of human life," he left his property to Mary Ann, his wife, and Edward, his ten-year-old son.[18]

On April 16, 1840, Henry Atkinson, with a few officers and a small detachment of troops, boarded the steamboat *Omega* at St. Louis and started up the Mississippi to Fort Crawford.[19] On April 23 he and his companions arrived at the fort. There they learned that about 60 per cent of the Winnebagos had agreed to remove to

15 Atkinson to Dodge, Mar. 19, 1840, First Military Dept. Letter Book 106, USAC.

16 Dodge to Atkinson, Apr. 3, 1840, Letters Received, Prairie du Chien Agency, Emigration, OIA.

17 Atkinson Orders, Apr. 11–13, 1840, First Military Dept. Order Book 107, USAC.

18 Will of General Henry Atkinson, Apr. 14, 1840, Will Book C, St. Louis Probate Court Records.

19 Mary Atkinson to T. L. Alexander, Apr. 19, 1840, Mary Atkinson Letters, B. W. A.; *ibid.*, May 3, 1840.

Turkey River in northeast Iowa. Dodge, Lowry, and Atkinson thought that the move was "the best that can be done at present, particularly as the treaty does not bind them to go further than twenty miles west of the Mississippi." The rest of the bands refused to go. In spite of their refusal, however, several chiefs agreed to meet Atkinson, Dodge, and Lowry for talks, and Atkinson was confident an agreement would be reached.[20]

He realized that one of the main obstacles to a peaceful Winnebago removal was their dread of attacks by the Sac and Foxes. Therefore, he decided to meet with chiefs of the Winnebagos and Sac and Foxes to arrange an armistice between the tribes. He wrote to Governor Robert Lucas and asked him to send a delegation of Sac and Foxes to Fort Crawford.[21] Lucas agreed to send them.

On May 1, Atkinson and Governor Dodge held a council with the recalcitrant leaders of the Winnebagos, and Atkinson explained the treaty stipulations that required the Indians to cross the Mississippi. The Indians begged to remain and claimed that, on their visit to Washington in 1837, the President had told them they would not have to move. Late the next afternoon Atkinson told them he would not allow their agent to give them their promised annuities or provisions until they went to Prairie du Chien. When the chiefs tried to continue the talk, Atkinson stopped them. He promised to send their plea to the President, but told them that his orders were to move them, peaceably if possible but by force if necessary. He dismissed them and told one of the chiefs, "Dandy, I shall expect you to go back and commence moving with yr people in about three weeks." The next morning Atkinson announced that no Indians living near Fort Winnebago would receive food or money as long as they remained east of the Mississippi.[22]

In spite of this threat, the Portage bands led by Yellow Thunder

[20] Atkinson to Jones, Apr. 25, 1840, Letters Received, Prairie du Chien Agency, OIA.

[21] Atkinson to Lucas, Apr. 26, 1840, Indian Office Files, Box 24, No. 172, SHSW.

[22] William J. Peterson, ed., "Moving the Winnebago into Iowa," *Iowa Journal of History*, Vol. LVIII (Oct., 1960), 362–75; Atkinson Orders, May 3, 1840, First Military Dept. Order Book 107, USAC.

and Little Soldier still refused to go. Atkinson was angered by the chiefs' refusal to gather their people at Fort Winnebago and ordered Yellow Thunder and Little Soldier arrested and confined. He claimed that these two chiefs had caused most of the difficulties and wrote, "this arrest may save us a great deal of trouble."[23]

Meanwhile, Colonel William J. Worth, under orders from the War Department, was moving the Eighth Regiment via the lakes and Fox River to Fort Winnebago. This force, strengthened by the three hundred men of the Fifth Infantry, gave Atkinson an army of over one thousand men.[24] He sent a detachment under Lieutenant Joseph Whipple and Agent Lowry to explore the country along Turkey River in Iowa and choose a site for the military post he had promised to build for the protection of the Winnebagos.[25] Then, on May 6 he boarded the steamboat *Chippewa* with three companies of the Fifth Regiment and began the trip up the Wisconsin River to Fort Winnebago.

On May 16 he ordered Captain Isaac Lynde to take one company of infantry from Fort Crawford west to the spot chosen for the new post on Turkey River. He ordered Lynde to build temporary shelters for his command and a temporary building that might later be used as a storehouse for provisions.[26] Three days later he received orders from Secretary Poinsett to stop building along the Red Cedar or Turkey rivers and shift the troops and post south to the forks of the Des Moines River. "Your change of position . . . has thrown me into a great delemma," Atkinson wrote, "as I have pledged . . . that I would establish a garrison on the neutral ground, to protect [the Winnebagos] from the Sauks & Foxes . . ." Without that promise, he said, the Indians would not have gone peaceably, "a promise I feel bound in honor, as an officer of the army, to faithfully preserve . . ." He wrote that the temporary huts

23 Atkinson to Mary Atkinson, May 6, 1840, quoted in Mary Atkinson to Alexander, May 24, 1840, Mary Atkinson Letters, B. W. A.

24 Atkinson to Jones, May 3, 1840, Letters Received, AGO.

25 Atkinson Order, May 5, 1840, First Military Dept. Order Book 107, USAC.

26 Atkinson Order, May 18, 1840, First Military Dept. Order Book 107, USAC.

on Turkey River would cost less than those on the Des Moines proposed by the War Department and that an army unit would protect the Winnebagos. The huts could be abandoned when a permanent post was completed on the Des Moines, and the troops would then move south and west. He suggested that the Turkey River post should have log facilities for one company of infantry and, if possible, one of dragoons, but that the structure be temporary.[27] On June 9 his letter asking for instructions on the location of the new post in Iowa arrived at Washington. Secretary Poinsett replied that the circumstances called for a modification in plans and gave his approval to Atkinson's suggestion that temporary quarters be erected at Turkey River.[28]

On May 19, Atkinson predicted that the tribesmen would be ready to move in another four or five days, but he doubted that he could obtain transportation for such a large party "at this extreme state of water." Therefore, he told the chiefs that the Indians might have three dollars a person if they obtained their own transportation. Quite a few braves made canoes for the coming trip.[29] Atkinson's estimate that four or five days might be sufficient was too optimistic. By May 26, however, most of the large bands had arrived at Fort Winnebago. Guards escorted each band down-river to Prairie du Chien in Durham boats.[30] Indians without their own transportation were taken in boats with the soldiers. On June 3, 1,076 Winnebagos left the post to join their 572 brethren who had gone five days earlier. These were all of the Portage bands except for a few scattered lodges that Atkinson sent the dragoons to find. Atkinson accomplished this movement peacefully in spite of strong and continuing Indian opposition. His major duties concluded, he ordered the Fifth Infantry back to Forts Snelling and Crawford on the Mississippi. He kept the Eighth Infantry at Fort Winnebago

27 Atkinson to Poinsett, May 19, 1840, Letters Received, AGO.

28 Poinsett to Atkinson, June 9, 1840, Letters Sent, Military Affairs, SW.

29 *Ibid.*

30 Atkinson to Jones, May 26, 1840, Letters Received, AGO.

to assist the dragoons in locating the last of the Winnebagos. Then on June 11, Atkinson boarded a steamboat and left Fort Winnebago for Fort Crawford.

There, on June 16, 1840, he held another council with the Winnebago chiefs to discuss the possibilities of peace with the Sac and Foxes. The Winnebagos remained distrustful of their enemies, but agreed to try to live in peace. Atkinson left orders for General Brooke to keep the Winnebagos west of the river, asked him to supervise the meeting between the Sac and Foxes and Winnebagos when these tribes came together for peace talks, and then left for Jefferson Barracks.[31] He and his staff arrived at St. Louis on June 21.[32] In July a Sac and Fox delegation arrived at Fort Crawford, where they met with General Brooke and the leading Winnebago chiefs for several days. Brooke reported that both tribes agreed to terms on July 9, in spite of the breakdown of the talks at one point. He sent a copy of the treaty to Atkinson.[33]

In the summer of 1840, Agent Lowry sent the War Department and the frontier commanders reports that the Winnebagos were returning to Wisconsin. At first Atkinson dismissed these as rumor, but later he was persuaded that they might be true. The Portage and Rock River bands that had given Atkinson and Dodge the most difficulty during the removal decided to remain on the west bank of the Mississippi rather than move twenty miles farther west into closer proximity to the Sac and Foxes. By August both Lowry and Brooke became alarmed because the Indians began to move up the Mississippi. When some bands recrossed to the east side of the river because dysentery and fever broke out among them, Brooke asked Atkinson whether he should ask Governor Dodge for mounted militia units.[34] Atkinson apparently did not consent to calling out the militia.

Meanwhile, the Winnebagos spread out in small bands to get

31 Atkinson Order, June 18, 1840, First Military Dept. Order Book 107, USAC.

32 *Daily Argus*, June 22, 1840.

33 Brooke to Atkinson, July 11, 1840, Indian Office Files, Box 21, No. 508, SHSW.

34 Brooke to Atkinson, Aug. 5, 1840, Letters Received, Prairie du Chien Agency, Emigration, OIA.

fresh food. Atkinson informed the War Department that the Winnebagos had moved back across the Mississippi. He reported that they were scattered and sick, and wrote, "I have not the smallest idea they intend to evade settling themselves on the neutral ground as soon as the summer is over and they receive this fall their annuities . . ." Nevertheless, General Brooke reported that the Indians refused to go back to Iowa.[35] Atkinson was right, however, and the Winnebagos called on General Brooke to explain their actions. They told him that all but a few scattered lodges were again west of the Mississippi.[36]

Even after they returned to Iowa, the Winnebagos continued to cause difficulties for the army. On August 15, Agent Lowry told Brooke that the Winnebagos, in collaboration with several bands of Sioux, were planning to attack the Sac and Foxes. Brooke warned the Winnebagos that he would use troops to prevent such an attack and sent a party of sixty men to patrol the neutral ground. When Atkinson received this report from Brooke and heard that other Winnebago bands had returned east of the Mississippi, he ordered 350 men of the Eighth Regiment, then at Jefferson Barracks for training, to prepare for a return to Fort Crawford.[37] On August 20, before the troops left Jefferson Barracks, Atkinson received Brooke's earlier message that the Indians had returned west of the river peaceably. Atkinson blamed Lowry for the confusion because he spread rumors that convinced Brooke the situation was worse than it really was. He complained about the agent and wrote, "he will not it seems be satisfied till a *Regiment* or two is placed at his disposal."[38] Atkinson canceled the orders to march.[39]

Throughout the autumn months the Winnebagos refused to move farther west, but when the new post neared completion and

35 Atkinson to Jones, Aug. 8, 1840, Letters Received, AGO.

36 Brooke to Atkinson, Aug. 9, 1840, Letters Received, Prairie du Chien Agency, Emigration, OIA.

37 Atkinson to Jones, Aug. 19, 1840, Letters Received, Prairie du Chien Agency, Emigration, OIA.

38 *Ibid.*

39 Atkinson Orders, Aug. 20, 1840, First Military Dept. Order Book 107, USAC.

they realized that some troops might be there to protect them, most of the tribe began to move. General Brooke paid the annuities at the Turkey River post, and Agent Lowry established his residence there. Because of renewed difficulties with the Winnebagos, Governor Dodge asked Atkinson for a mounted force to patrol the eastern bank of the Mississippi. Instead, Atkinson decided to station a troop of dragoons at Black River for the winter, but he was overruled by the War Department. Then in early April, 1841, Atkinson received orders to have a mounted force patrol the neutral ground to restrain the Sacs. Several weeks later General Macomb ordered Atkinson to allow the Winnebagos to remain on either side of the Mississippi "as they choose until further notice."[40] Early in May, Macomb wrote Atkinson that the War Department wanted to renegotiate treaties with all tribes of the upper Mississippi and that any Winnebagos not yet moved west of the Mississippi were not to be "further interfered with, than to prevent them from trespassing or committing depredations upon the settlements . . ."[41]

A month later Atkinson wrote to Adjutant General Jones and suggested the Indians be kept west of the Mississippi. "I am of opinion," he wrote, "that it will be best to detain these Indians in the Country assigned them . . . and I shall advise Gen. Brooke to this effect until the further pleasure of the Sec of War may be known . . ."[42] His unsolicited views brought forth an order to refrain from trying to make policy and to obey orders. On June 16 the acting adjutant general relayed the views of the Secretary of War. Poinsett, began the writer, "directs me to inform you that the expression of your 'opinion' . . . is considered uncalled for by the circumstances."[43] This incident ended Atkinson's dealing with the Winnebagos.

On June 25, 1841, General Alexander Macomb, commanding

[40] Macomb to Atkinson, Apr. 29, 1841, Letters Sent, Vol. 17, AGO.

[41] Macomb to Atkinson, May 8, 1841, Letters Sent, Vol. 17, AGO.

[42] Atkinson to Jones, June 3, 1841, Letters Received, AGO.

[43] L. Thomas to Atkinson, June 16, 1841, Letters Sent, Vol. 17, AGO.

general of the army since 1828, died. This meant that General Edmund P. Gaines or Winfield Scott probably would be appointed to this position. Either appointment would create a vacancy for another brigadier general, and Atkinson hoped to get the position. He was the top-ranking brevet brigadier general in the army, had been exercising his brevet rank for most of the past twenty years, and had formerly been a brigadier general. Immediately after learning of Macomb's death, he wrote to Missouri Senator Thomas H. Benton, his long-time acquaintance, and asked his aid. "I consider myself entitled to fill the vacancy by the rules of the service and every principle of justice," he told Benton.[44] "The General as a matter of course anticipates being promoted," wrote his friend Richard H. Graham. Discussing the rumors and anticipation at Jefferson Barracks, Graham concluded, "General Atkinson, I think, will be much disappointed if he is not promoted . . ."[45] Senator Benton did his part, and Atkinson's North Carolina friends lent their support; but even with this help and the friendship of Winfield Scott, the new commanding general, Atkinson did not win the nomination. President John Tyler nominated Inspector General John E. Wool, a bitter rival of Henry Atkinson, and, after a futile attempt by friends of Atkinson and others in the Senate to block the nomination, the Senate approved Wool by a vote of twenty-five to twenty-four. The opposition claimed that both Hugh Brady and Henry Atkinson were being overlooked, but Wool apparently had more friends and knowledge of Washington politics than the others.[46] Atkinson had done little to increase his chances for promotion since his part in the Black Hawk War nine years before. He had remained in St. Louis while the population had continued to move west. By September, Atkinson learned of Wool's appointment. He said very little, at least publicly, but his wife had

44 Atkinson to Benton, July 8, 1841, enclosed in Benton to John Bell, July 18, 1841, Letters Received, AGO.

45 Graham to Alexander, July 16, 1841, Mary Atkinson Letters, B. W. A.

46 Mary Atkinson to Alexander, Sept. 18, 1841.

much to say. Railing at "the most shameful and outrageous lies" told about her husband's physical and mental condition, she denounced his opposition. Alexander Bullitt, her brother, publicly proclaimed that the letter writers who had attacked Atkinson as a senile incompetent were "vile slanderers and midnight assassins—who set forth lies and then hid themselves in the dark . . ."[47] This was Atkinson's last attempt to receive a promotion.

During the winter of 1841–42, Henry Atkinson corresponded with Governor Lucas of Iowa, with his superiors upon request, and with Colonel Kearny and other subordinates when they asked for instructions or orders. In January, 1842, he commanded the Western Division for a few weeks when General Gaines tended to personal and family matters. Otherwise he was in semi-retirement, with only about one hundred men and officers at the post.[48]

In early 1842 the Sixth Infantry returned to Jefferson Barracks. Atkinson had often asked the War Department to return the unit to the post. Now, with the return of the Sixth, over seven hundred officers and men again were at the post. This reunion proved but a brief interlude, however. On March 26, 1842, the adjutant general issued General Order 18: "The 6th Regiment of Infantry now at Jefferson Barracks will proceed without delay, by the most expeditious route to Fort Towson," on the Red River in southeastern Oklahoma. The Sixth Infantry left Jefferson Barracks early in April, as did nearly all the other troops, and by the end of that month the garrison included only four officers and thirty-one enlisted men.[49]

During April and May, Atkinson continued to work on routine duties, such as ordering an inspection of his division, moving units from post to post, and ordering his unit commanders to confer and co-operate with the Indian agents in their localities. On Sunday, June 12, he became seriously sick. His family called in their medical friends from St. Louis, but Atkinson weakened rapidly, and at

47 *Ibid.*

48 Post Returns, Jefferson Barracks, August–December, 1841, AGO.

49 General Order 18, Mar. 28, 1842, Dept. of the West, Letters Received, USAC.

5:15 P.M. on Tuesday, June 14, General Atkinson died of "billious dysentery" at his home.[50]

Atkinson's death shocked his family and friends who gathered for consolation and prepared for the funeral to be held on June 16. The citizens of St. Louis rented the steamboat *Lebanon* to transport them to Jefferson Barracks to pay their last respects. Because few regular troops remained at the Barracks, the two militia companies of St. Louis volunteered their services and, along with family friends from the city, boarded the *Lebanon* at 9:00 A.M. on Thursday morning. Two hours later the boat docked at the Barracks landing, and the procession climbed the gentle rise to the Atkinson quarters. There, with the St. Louis Greys and the Boon Infantry acting as the military escort, "the procession moved from the late residence of the deceased, to the burial ground in the vicinity of the barracks." At the grave the Reverend Chaplin S. Hedges, former Episcopal chaplain at the post, conducted the ceremony. After the bugler's notes and the noise and smoke of the rifle volley faded, the body was interred. "Thus has closed the earthly career of one well known in our community and much esteemed not only for his military but for his many civic duties," concluded the editor of the *Missouri Republican*.[51]

The North Carolina tobacco farmer had served for thirty-four years as an officer in the United States Army. He started as a captain and climbed to the rank of brigadier general. Now his career was over. A few fading notes from a bugle and the echo of a rifle volley, fired not by his beloved regulars but by the much despised volunteers, echoed across the Mississippi from Jefferson Barracks in fleeting tribute.

During Henry Atkinson's career in the West, many changes occurred. When he arrived in St. Louis in 1819, there was only one state west of the Mississippi River. At his death in 1842, Missouri

[50] *New Era*, June 15, 1842; *Missouri Republican*, June 15, 1842; Graham to Jones, June 14, 1842, Letters Received, AGO.

[51] June 17, 1842; *Daily Evening Gazette*, June 17, 1842.

had also become a state, and Arkansas and Iowa were territories. The Indians, who had been as far east as Indiana in the Old Northwest in 1819, were nearly all west of the Mississippi in 1842. During the 1830's the federal government had tried to establish a permanent Indian frontier west of Arkansas and Missouri, and had moved eastern tribes onto the plains. The Santa Fe trade, the Oregon Trail, and opportunities to get land in Texas had led Americans beyond this line into the Far West. Between 1819 and 1842 the population of the United States had nearly doubled, increasing from nine and six-tenths million to eighteen and three-tenths million by the latter date. What had been wilderness when Atkinson arrived at St. Louis now contained farms, roads, and towns. Steamboats, that had proved ineffective when employed on the Missouri Expedition of 1819, plied the Missouri with little difficulty by 1842.

During these years, Atkinson had likewise experienced changes in his status within the army. He had led the Missouri and Yellowstone Expeditions, had risen to the rank of brigadier general and then been reduced to colonel with brevet rank as general, had moved troops north into Wisconsin to prevent a war with the Winnebagos and to fight one with the Sac and Foxes. After the latter he had returned to Jefferson Barracks and had continued to direct army operations in the north and west. His duties and responsibilities after the Black Hawk War of 1832, however, were of less importance than those before it had been. During the last decade of his life he had to remain at St. Louis, often hundreds of miles from the scene of army activity, as an administrator. Atkinson's lack of aggressiveness in the Black Hawk War and his failing health were probably responsible for his being pushed aside during the 1830's. Earlier he had led in the move west, but after 1832 he was merely a policeman, far from the frontier.

Atkinson had spent considerable time and energy trying to maintain peace between frontiersmen and Indians in the West. Usually he was successful, but in the Black Hawk War his efforts to avoid fighting failed. He had hoped that the whites and Indians could live near each other in peace, but found this was impossible.

Atkinson's career was important, not because of battles won or discoveries made, but because he was conscientious in facing the routine duties of policing the frontier and because he managed to keep peace throughout most of the twenty-three years he served in the West.

Atkinson's part in the westward movement is difficult to judge. By commanding the troops that offered some protection to settlers and legal traders and by building military roads near the frontier, he may have aided Americans as they moved west. On the other hand, by trying to enforce the laws which regulated Indian trade and by using troops to enforce treaties and keep American squatters off of Indian lands, Atkinson may have delayed the spread of population into certain small areas of the West. His career shows that to a large extent the army acted more often as an agency to maintain peace and enforce laws than it did as a fighting machine.

Bibliography

This bibliography is what might be called a "use bibliography." That is, it includes chiefly those sources which have been cited in the footnotes throughout the study. Certain other items, particularly well-known secondary materials which discuss the army or the lives of Atkinson's contemporaries, have also been included. Anyone who is interested in the complete bibliography may examine the original manuscript which is available at the Memorial Library of the University of Wisconsin, Madison.

I. *Primary Sources—Unpublished*

A. Manuscript Sources

William B. Archer–Jacob Harlan Letters, Illinois State Historical Library, Springfield.

Army Papers, Missouri Historical Society, St. Louis.

Henry Atkinson Papers, Missouri Historical Society, St. Louis.

Henry Atkinson Papers, Chicago Historical Society, Chicago.

Mary Atkinson Letters, Private collection, Gen. B. W. Atkinson, San Diego, California.

Black Hawk War Papers, Illinois State Historical Library, Springfield.

Nicholas Boilvin Letters, State Historical Society of Wisconsin, Madison.

Jacob Brown Letter Books, Library of Congress, Washington.

Choteau Collections, Missouri Historical Society, St. Louis.

Clark Papers, Missouri Historical Society, St. Louis.

William Clark Papers, Draper Collection, State Historical Society of Wisconsin, Madison.

Pascal P. Enos Papers, Illinois State Historical Library, Springfield.

Forsyth Papers, Missouri Historical Society, St. Louis.

Thomas Forsyth Papers, Draper Collection, State Historical Society of Wisconsin, Madison.

Charles K. Gardner Papers, New York State Library, Albany.

Thomas Hempstead Letter Book, Yale University Library, New Haven, Connecticut.

William Henry Papers, State Historical Society of Wisconsin, Madison.

Indian Papers, Missouri Historical Society, St. Louis.

Andrew Jackson Papers (microfilm), State Historical Society of Wisconsin, Madison.

Thomas S. Jesup Papers, Library of Congress, Washington.

Thomas Kavanaugh Journal, Coe Collection, Yale University Library, New Haven, Connecticut.

Stephen W. Kearny Papers, Missouri Historical Society, St. Louis.

Kennerly Papers, Missouri Historical Society, St. Louis.

Letters of Officers of the War of 1812, Dreer Collection, Historical Society of Pennsylvania, Philadelphia.

Minutes of an Examination of Indian Prisoners taken by order of Major General Scott, 1832, Illinois State Historical Library, Springfield.

John O'Fallon Papers, Missouri Historical Society, St. Louis.

Thomas A. Smith Papers, State Historical Society of Missouri, Columbia.

Frank E. Stevens Papers, Illinois State Historical Library, Springfield.

Joseph M. Street Papers, State Historical Society of Wisconsin, Madison.

Zachary Taylor Papers (microfilm), State Historical Society of Wisconsin, Madison.

United States Indian Office Files, 1803–42, State Historical Society of Wisconsin, Madison.

Bartlett Yancy Papers, Southern Historical Collection, University of North Carolina Library, Chapel Hill.

B. Archival Material

1. *Illinois State Archives, Springfield.*

Illinois Governors' Correspondence, Letter Books 2–3.

2. *National Archives, Washington, D. C.*

Records of the Adjutant General's Office, Record Group 94

Early Regimental Records, 1808–21.
General Orders, 1834–42.
Letters Received, 1812–42.
Letters Sent, 1808–42.
Post Revolutionary Commands, 1808–21.
Post Revolutionary Papers, 1808–21.
Register of Letters Received, 1812–42.
Returns of Military Posts, 1820–42.

Records of the Headquarters of the Army, Record Group 108

Letters Received, 1828–42.
Letters Sent by the Commanding General, 1828–42.
Letters Sent by General Macomb, 1837–41.

Records of the Office of Indian Affairs, Record Group 75

Journal of the Treaty Commission, 1825.
Letters Received, 1824–42.
Letters Sent, 1824–42.
Prairie du Chien Agency, Letters Received, 1824–42.
St. Louis Superintendency, Letters Received, 1824–42.
St. Peter's Agency, Letters Received, 1826–41.

Records of the Office of the Quartermaster General
Record Group 92

Consolidated Correspondence File, 1808–42.

Letters Received, 1818–42.

Letters Sent, 1818–42.

Records of the Office of the Secretary of War
Record Group 107

Letters Received, Registered Series, 1808–42.

Letters Received, Unregistered Series, 1808–42.

Letters Sent, Military Affairs, 1800–42.

Register of Letters Received, 1808–42.

Records of United States Army Commands, Record Group 98

Department of the West, Letters Received, 1825–42.

Department of the West, Letters Sent, 1821–36.

First Military Department, Letters Sent, 1837–42.

First Military Department, Orders, 1840.

Jefferson Barracks, Orders, 1828–37.

Ninth Military Department, Orders and Letters, 1819–26.

Right Wing, Letters Sent, 1834–37.

Sixth Infantry, Orders and Letters, 1817–26.

United States Census

Caswell County, North Carolina, 1800–10.

Person County, North Carolina, 1800–10.

3. *North Carolina Department of History and Archives, Raleigh*

Caswell County Records

Tax Lists, 1777–91, 1800–17.

North Carolina Gravestone Index

Person County Records

Estates Papers, 1795–1830.

Land Papers, 1775–1808.

Marriage Contracts, Index, 1790–1835.

Tax Records, 1792–1808.

Wills, Inventories, Sales of Estates and Taxables, 1792–1830.

4. *St. Louis, Missouri, Civil Records*

Records of the St. Louis Probate Court, 1842–50.

II. *Primary Sources—Printed*

A. U.S. Government Publications

American State Papers: *Indian Affairs*. 2 vols. Washington, 1832–34.

American State Papers: *Military Affairs*. 7 vols. Washington, 1832–61.

Annals of the Congress of the United States. Washington, 1808–24.

"Annual Report of the Secretary of War," 1813–42, in *Senate Documents*. Washington, 1814–43.

Carter, Clarence E., ed. *The Territorial Papers of the United States*. 26 vols. Washington, 1934–62.

Heitman, Francis B., comp. *Historical Register and Dictionary of the United States Army, From Its Organization, September 29, 1789, to March 2, 1903*. 2 vols. Washington, 1903.

United States Congress, House of Representatives. *House Executive Documents*

"Documents Accompanying the President's Message to Congress . . . Document from the War Department." *No. 2*, 20 Cong., 1 sess. Serial 169.

"Documents in Relation to the Claim of James Johnson . . ." March 1, 1821, *No. 110*, 16 Cong., 2 sess. Serial 55.

"Hostile Disposition of Indian Tribes on the Northwestern Frontier." May 21, 1828, *No. 277*, 20 Cong., 1 sess. Serial 175.

"Military Road, Western Frontier." March 24, 1838, *No. 278*, 25 Cong., 2 sess. Serial 328.

"Movements of the Expedition which lately Ascended the Missouri River." November 23, 1825, *No. 117*, 19 Cong., 1 sess. Serial 136.

"Papers relating to the disturbances in . . . Illinois, by . . . Black Hawk." November 19, 1831, *No. 2*, 22 Cong., 1 sess. Serial 216.

Journal of the Executive Proceedings of the Senate of the United States of America, 1805–1845. 6 vols. Washington, 1828–87.

Kappler, Charles J., comp., *Indian Affairs: Laws and Treaties.* 2 vols., Washington, 1903–1904.

Official Army Register, 1815–1842. Washington, 1816–43.

The Public Statutes at Large of the United States of America, 1789–1845. 5 vols. Boston, 1848.

United States Congress, Senate. *Senate Documents*

"Message of the President . . . to the Senate . . ." *No. 1,* 20 Cong., 1 sess. Serial 163.

"Report . . . in Relation to the . . . Removal of the Winnebago Indians." March 20, 1840, *No. 297,* 26 Cong., 1 sess. Serial 359.

Thian, Raphael P. *Notes Illustrating the Military Geography of the United States, 1813–1880.* Washington, 1881.

Treaties Between the United States of America and the Several Indian Tribes, From 1778–1837. Washington, 1837.

B. Newspapers

Army and Navy Chronicle (Washington, D.C.).

Buffalo Gazette (New York).

Connecticut Gazette (New London).

Daily Argus (St. Louis).

Daily Evening Gazette (St. Louis).

Daily National Intelligencer (Washington, D.C.).

Globe (Washington, D.C.).

Military and Naval Magazine (Washington, D.C.).

Missouri Gazette and Public Advertizer (St. Louis).

Missouri Intelligencer (Franklin and Columbia).

Missouri Republican (St. Louis).

New Era (St. Louis).

New York Herald.

Niles Register (Baltimore, Maryland, and Washington, D.C.).

St. Louis Beacon.

St. Louis Enquirer.

The War (New York).

C. Other Printed Materials

1. *Books*

Beckwourth, James P. *The Life and Adventures of James P. Beckwourth, Mountaineer, Scout, Pioneer, and Chief of the Crow Nation of Indians*. Ed. by T. D. Bonner, New York, 1858.

Black Hawk. *Ma-Ka-Tai-Me-She-Kia-Kiak: Black Hawk, an Autobiography*. Ed. by Donald Jackson. Urbana, Illinois, 1955.

Bonneville, Captain B. L. E. *The Rocky Mountains: or scenes, incidents, and adventures in the Far West*. Ed. by Washington Irving. Philadelphia, 1837.

Calhoun, John C. *Correspondence of John C. Calhoun*. Ed. by J. F. Jameson. American Historical Association, *Annual Report, 1899*. Washington, 1900.

Clark, Walter, and William L. Saunders, eds. *The Colonial and State Records of North Carolina*. 26 vols. Goldsboro, North Carolina, 1876–1907.

Cooke, Philip St. George. *Scenes and Adventures in the Army: or Romance of Military Life*. Philadelphia, 1857.

Coon, Charles L., ed. *North Carolina Schools and Academies, 1790–1840: A Documentary History*. Publication of the North Carolina Historical Commission. Raleigh, 1915.

Edwards, Ninian. *The Edwards Papers*. Ed. by E. B. Washburne. *Chicago Historical Society Collections*, III. Chicago, 1884.

Forry, Samuel, comp. *Statistical Report on the Sickness and Mortality of the Army of the United States*. Washington, D.C., 1840.

Hildreth, James. *Dragoon Campaigns to the Rocky Mountains*. New York, 1836.

Hitchcock, Ethan A. *Fifty Years in Camp & Field, Diary of Major General Ethan Allen Hitchcock, U. S. A.* Ed. by William A. Croffit. New York, 1909.

Jackson, Andrew. *Correspondence of Andrew Jackson*. Ed. by John S. Bassett. 7 vols. Washington, 1926–35.

Kennerly, William C. *Persimmon Hill: A Narrative of Old St. Louis and the Far West*. As told to Elizabeth Russell. Norman, 1948.

Keys, Erasmus Darwin. *Fifty Years' Observation of Men and Events, Civil and Military*. New York, 1884.

Kinzie, Mrs. John H. *Wau-Bun, the "Early Day" in the North-West*. Ed. by Milo M. Quaife. Chicago, 1932.

McCall, George A. *Letters from the Frontiers Written During a Period of Thirty Years' Service in the Army of the United States*. Philadelphia, 1868.

McKenney, Thomas L. *Memoirs, Official and Personal*. New York, 1846.

Reynolds, John. *Reynolds' History of Illinois, My Own Times: Embracing also the History of My Life*. Chicago, 1879.

Riley, Bennet, and Philip St. George Cooke. *The First Military Escort on the Santa Fe Trail, 1829*. Ed. by Otis R. Young. Glendale, California, 1952.

Scott, Winfield. *Memoirs of Lieut.-General Scott*. 2 vols. New York, 1864.

Thwaites, Reuben G. ed. *Early Western Travels, 1748–1846*. 32 vols. Cleveland, 1904–1907.

Wheeler, John M. *Reminiscences of North Carolina: Historical Sketches of North Carolina from 1584–1851*. Columbus, Ohio, 1884.

Wilkinson, James. *Memoirs of My Own Times*. 3 vols. Philadelphia, 1816.

2. *Articles and Published Documents*

Atkinson, Henry, and Benjamin O'Fallon. "Journal of the Atkinson-O'Fallon Expedition, 1825," Russel Reid and Clell G. Gannon, eds., *North Dakota Historical Quarterly,* Vol. IV (October, 1929).

Atkinson, Henry. "Report of the Yellowstone Expedition of 1825," Roger L. Nichols, ed., *Nebraska History,* Vol. XLIV (June, 1963).

Beckwith, Hiram M. "The Winnebago Scare", in J. Y. Scammon, comp., *Addresses . . . at the Annual Meeting of the Chicago Historical Society*. Fergus Historical Series, No. 10 (1887).

Cass, Lewis. "Cass Letters," *Michigan Pioneer and Historical Collections*, Vol. XXVI (1908).

Clark, William. "William Clark's Diary," Louise Barry, ed., *Kansas Historical Quarterly*, Vol. XVI (February, 1948); Vol. XVI (May, 1948); Vol. XVI (August, 1948); Vol. XVI (November, 1948).

Gratiot, Henry. "Journals and Reports of the Black Hawk War," Milo M. Quaife, ed., *Mississippi Valley Historical Review*, Vol. XII (December, 1929).

Hickling, William and Gurdon S. Hubbard. "Sketches of Billy Caldwell and Shabonne," in J. Y. Scammon, comp., *Addresses . . . at the Annual Meeting of the Chicago Historical Society*. Fergus Historical Series, No. 10 (1887).

Hubbard, Gurdon S. "Narrative," in J. Y. Scammon, comp., *Addresses . . . at the Annual Meeting of the Chicago Historical Society*. Fergus Historical Series, No. 10 (1887).

Hubbell, William D. "The First Steamboats on the Missouri; Reminiscences of Captain W. D. Hubbell," Vivian K. McLarty, ed., *Missouri Historical Review*, Vol. LI (July, 1957).

Hughes, Willis B. "The Heatherly Incident of 1836," *Bulletin of the Missouri Historical Society*, Vol. XIII (January, 1957).

Johnson, James. "The Life and Letters of James Johnson of Kentucky," James A. Padgett, ed., *Register of Kentucky State Historical Society*, Vol. XXXV (October, 1937).

Kennerly, James. "Diary of James Kennerly, 1823–1826," Edgar B. Wesley, ed., *Missouri Historical Society Collections*, Vol. VI (October, 1928).

"Letters of Joseph M. Street to Governor Ninian Edwards, of Illinois, 1827," *Wisconsin Historical Society Collections*, Vol. XI (1888).

Lockwood, James H. "Early Times and Events in Wisconsin," *Wisconsin Historical Society Collections*, Vol. II (1903).

McKenney, Thomas L. "The Winnebago War of 1827," *Wisconsin Historical Society Collections*, Vol. V (1907).

Nichols, Roger L., ed. "The Black Hawk War: Another View," *Annals of Iowa*, Vol. XXXIV (Winter, 1963).

Peterson, William J., ed. "Moving the Winnebago into Iowa," *Iowa Journal of History*, Vol. LVIII (October, 1960).

Robinson, Doane, ed. "Official Correspondence of the Leavenworth Expedition of 1823 into South Dakota for the Conquest of the Ree Indians," *South Dakota Historical Collections*, Vol. I (August, 1902).

Saunders, Romulus M. "Letters of Romulus M. Saunders to Bartlett Yancy, 1821–1828," A. R. Newsome, ed., *The North Carolina Historical Review*, Vol. VIII (October, 1931).

Smith, Henry. "Indian Campaign of 1832," *Military and Naval Magazine*, Vol. I (August, 1833).

Snelling, William J. "Early Days at Prairie du Chien and Winnebago Outbreak of 1827," *Wisconsin Historical Society Collections*, Vol. V (1907).

Whittlesey, Charles, "Recollections of a Tour Through Wisconsin in 1832," *Wisconsin Historical Society Collections*, Vol. I (1903).

Wilson, Peter. "The Letters of Peter Wilson, First Resident Agent Among the Teton Sioux," Harry H. Anderson, ed., *Nebraska History*, Vol. XLII (December, 1961).

III. *Secondary Materials*

A. Books

Barge, William D. *Early Lee County, being some Chapters in the history of the early days in Lee County, Illinois*. Chicago, 1918.

Beers, Henry P. *The Western Military Frontier, 1815–1846*. Philadelphia, 1935.

Clarke, Dwight L. *Stephen Watts Kearny: Soldier of the West*. Norman, 1961.

Cox, Isaac J. *The West Florida Controversy, 1798–1813*. Baltimore, 1918.

Edwards, Ninian W. *History of Illinois from 1788 to 1833: and Life and Times of Ninian Edwards.* Springfield, Illinois, 1870.

Elliott, Charles W. *Winfield Scott: The Soldier and the Man.* New York, 1937.

Goetzmann, William H. *Army Exploration in the American West, 1803–1865.* New Haven, Connecticut, 1959.

Hagan, William T. *The Sac and Fox Indians.* Norman, 1958.

Hamilton, Holman. *Zachary Taylor, Soldier of the Republic.* Indianapolis, 1941.

Hamilton, Peter J. *Colonial Mobile.* New York, 1897.

Jacobs, James R. *Tarnished Warrior: Major General James Wilkinson.* New York, 1938.

Kendall, John S. *History of New Orleans.* 3 vols. Chicago, 1922.

Lossing, Benson J. *The Pictorial Field Book of the War of 1812.* New York, 1869.

Mahan, Bruce E. *Old Fort Crawford and the Frontier.* Iowa City, 1926.

Prucha, Francis P. *American Indian Policy in the Formative Years: The Indian Trade and Intercourse Acts, 1780–1834.* Cambridge, Massachusetts, 1962.

———. *Broadax and Bayonet: The Role of the United States Army in the Development of the Northwest, 1815–1860.* Madison, 1953.

Scanlan, Peter L. *Prairie du Chien: French, British, American.* Menasha, Wisconsin, 1937.

Silver, James W. *Edmund Pendleton Gaines, Frontier General.* Baton Rouge, 1949.

Sprague, John T. *The Origin, Process, and Conclusion of the Florida War . . . .* New York, 1848.

Stevens, Frank E. *The Black Hawk War*, Chicago, 1903.

Wesley, Edgar B. *Guarding the Frontier: A Study in Frontier Defense from 1815–1825.* Minneapolis, 1935.

Wheeler, John H. *Historical Sketches of North Carolina from 1584 to 1851.* Philadelphia, 1851.

B. Articles and Other Printed Material

Atkinson, Benjamin W. "The Founder of Fort Atkinson," *Nebraska History and Record of Pioneer Days*, Vol. III (April-June, 1920).

Dick, Helen D. "A Newly Discovered Diary of Colonel Josiah Snelling," *Minnesota History*, Vol. XVIII (December, 1937).

Foreman, Grant. "River Navigation in the Early Southwest," *Mississippi Valley Historical Review*, Vol. XV (June, 1928).

"Fort Atkinson, Iowa," *Annals of Iowa* (3rd series), Vol. IV (July, 1900).

Hagan, William T. "General Henry Atkinson and the Militia," *Military Affairs*, Vol. XXIII (Winter, 1959–60).

McKee, Howard L. "The Platte Purchase," *Missouri Historical Review*, Vol. XXXII (January, 1938).

Mattison, Ray H. "The Indian Frontier on the Upper Missouri to 1865," *Nebraska History*, Vol. XXXIX (September, 1958).

Ryan, Howard W. "Daniel Bissell—His Story," *Bulletin of the Missouri Historical Society*, Vol. XII (October, 1955).

———. "Daniel Bissell—'Late General.'" *Bulletin of the Missouri Historical Society*, Vol. XV (October, 1958).

Watson, Richard L., Jr. "Congressional Attitudes Toward Military Preparedness, 1829–1835," *Mississippi Valley Historical Review*, Vol. XXXIV (March, 1948).

Webb, Henry B. "Sketch of Jefferson Barracks," *New Mexico Historical Review*, Vol. XXI (July, 1946).

Wesley, Edgar B. "A Still Larger View of the So-Called Yellowstone Expedition," *North Dakota Historical Quarterly*, Vol. V (July, 1931).

C. Unpublished Theses

Barron, Alice E. "In Defense of the Frontier: The Work of General Henry Atkinson, 1819–1842." Unpublished Master's Thesis, Loyola University, Chicago, 1937.

Crowe, Fletcher S. "National Policy of Frontier Defense, 1815–

1825." Unpublished Master's Thesis, Washington University, St. Louis, 1922.

Hagan, William T. "The Black Hawk War." Unpublished Ph.D. Dissertation, University of Wisconsin, Madison, 1950.

Hughes, Willis B. "The Army and Stephen Watts Kearny in the West." Unpublished Ph.D. Dissertation, University of Minnesota, Minneapolis, 1955.

Neal, Annie. "Policing the Frontier, 1816–1827." Unpublished Master's Thesis, University of Wisconsin, Madison, 1923.

Robbins, Roy M. "The Defense of the Western Frontier, 1825–1840." Unpublished Master's Thesis, University of Wisconsin, Madison, 1926.

Smith, Eudora. "Stephen Watts Kearny as a Factor in the Westward Movement, 1812–1834." Unpublished Master's Thesis, Washington University, St. Louis, 1925.

Index